MW01293945

EZEKIEL

God's Prophet
and
His Puzzling Book

(Dry Bones Will Live Again)

Preston A. Taylor

PRESS

Dedication Page

—⟋⟍—

This book on Ezekiel is dedicated with profound gratitude and fond memories of three men (along with their families) who have invested their lives teaching young men and young ladies how to share the Holy Scriptures more effectively.

Dr. Marvin E. Tate. He taught in the Bible Department in Wayland Baptist Univeristy of Plainview, Texas, following his Ph. D. degree in Old Testament. Also he served as visiting professor at the Singapore Baptist Seminary, and has been pastor and interim pastor of various churches. Dr. Tate is presently (2006) Senior professor of Old Testament at Southern Baptist Theological Seminary, Louisville, Kentucky.

Dr. F.B. Huey, Jr. Former missionary to Brazil. Emeritus Professor of Old Testament and Associate Dean for the Ph.D. Degree, Southwestern Baptist Theological Seminary, Fort Worth, Texas. He has led Bible conferences and other church engagements far beyond his native State of Texas. Dr. Huey was one of the team translators for the NIV and NASB Bibles.

Dr. Wayne E. Ward. Pilot of air-rescue and hospital planes in the Pacific during WWII. His planes crashed two times into the sea, and he states that God miraculously saved him both times. Dr. Ward is a multiple author, has served as pastor and interim pastor of various churches, and he is Emeritus Professor of Biblical Languages and New Testament, Southern Baptist Theological Seminary, Louisville, Kentucky.

Table of Contents

—◊◊◊—

Author's Introduction

—ᗩᗩ—

For one year, the members of Trinity Baptist Church of Mirando City, Texas, participated with me in the study of Ezekiel. I am profoundly grateful to this group of wonderful friends for being a "laboratory" as we did these studies together.

In this bilingual church, the Hispanics have been most supportive during the Sunday morning walk through Ezekiel. The Sunday night group of Anglos also participated wholeheartedly in the studies.

I have a twofold aim in this writing. One reason has been personal and selfish. Since I had never studied Ezekiel, I wanted to delve into the book for my own benefit. My life on planet earth will come to an end one day. Upon my arrival in heaven, I don't want Ezekiel to be a total stranger to me. In the second place, the Bible is for all of God's people. My desire has been to share with this congregation, as well as any beyond us, everything that we could discover about Ezekiel and his book. The attempt has been to present this material in simple, non-technical language that anyone can understand.

As we read the book of Ezekiel, we discover God saying sixty-five times that He is LORD. In the sixth-century B.C., as well as in the twenty-first century, God's sovereignty needs to be understood. In our mixed-up world of religion, work, play, and academics, we need to hear the words, "Then shall they know that I am God (Yahweh)."

God's mission objective is that all the world may know Him through redemption — to acknowledge and accept the LORD through love, trust, and obedience. Jesus stated in John 3:16 that God's redemption is universal; His message is for "all nations." The

ix

only way to have life is to have a personal relationship with the Giver and Sustainer of life.

As we struggle to understand the difficult book of Ezekiel, we can find help by seeing the writing in broad outline. Chapters 1-24 of Ezekiel are messages (oracles) of warning to Israel about a soon-to-be judgment because of their rebellion against God. If we had been in "their shoes," we would probably have sinned just as they did. The first three chapters include the vision of the "chariot throne" and God's commission to Ezekiel. In chapters 25-32, the prophet gives messages of judgment against seven nations that surrounded Israel.

A Bible map will help the reader visualize Ammon, Moab, Edom, Philistia, Tyre, Sidon, and Egypt. Chapters 33-39 describe God's restoration of the Israelites. In 539 B.C., Cyrus of Persia allowed the exiles in Babylon to return to Jerusalem, if they wanted to do so. The Persian Empire replaced the Babylonian kingdom.

Chapters 40-48 give a vision of God's "ideal temple." Those final nine chapters along with chapters 37-39 relating to the Valley of Dry Bones and Gog and Magog have produced more theological debates (bitter and sweet) than all other chapters in the book.

We need to keep in mind that much of Ezekiel is written in symbolic or figurative, rather than literal language. In particular, remember the visions in this writing. In the first chapter, the "throne-chariot" appeared to Ezekiel in a vision. While the prophet was in Babylon, he witnessed, in vision, the departure of God's glory from Jerusalem (chapters 8-11). The vision of the valley of dry bones appears in chapter 37. The temple vision and the return of God's glory occupy the last nine chapters.

Theological words are prominent throughout this book. The "Son of man" title occurs ninety-three times. God said, "You will know that I am the Lord," sixty-five times. The expression "the glory of the Lord" occurs eleven times in the first eleven chapters of Ezekiel. Idols and idolatry are mentioned forty times. Sin, transgressions, evil, wicked, abominations, and iniquity appear more than one hundred fifty times. The word "Israel" is given one hundred seventy-seven times. The expression "Lord God" is found more than two hundred times. Sin offering is listed fourteen times. The theological words along with references to Ezekiel's being "in the midst of" the exiles shows him to be a preeminent theologian and pastor who lived with his people.

Although we may have different interpretations of the book of Ezekiel, we recognize it as God's Word. We believe the Scriptures are God's eternal, authoritative Word, even though our interpretations may vary.

Two additional statements are made about this writing. One: Dr. Marvin E. Tate, senior Old Testament professor of the Southern Baptist Theological Seminary in Louisville, Kentucky, has labored long hours over this manuscript, making valuable changes on it. He has placed us in his debt with his scholarly revisions, although all his suggestions may not have been followed. Thank you, Dr. Tate, for being a mentor, friend, and more! A second note is that the Scripture citations come from the New King James Version of the Bible, unless otherwise indicated. My prayer is that this writing on Ezekiel will enrich your life, despite all its shortcomings for which I am responsible. Tell a few of your friends about this book, will you?

Preston A. Taylor
(Close to the Rio Grande,
near Laredo, Texas)

Chapter 1

Ezekiel the Prophet

—ɯ—

Someone asked a man the secret of his life. He answered, "I have friends." All of us have friends. Some have been with us for a long time. Others may have moved into our friendship circle in recent months. Anyone can find friends in church, at entertainment events, at work, in school, on airplanes, and many other places. We can also meet friends through books. Hopefully, through this book you will feel that Ezekiel has become your friend as you read more about that Old Testament prophet.

Ezekiel's name means "God strengthens." Ezekiel's book has forty-eight chapters and nearly 1300 verses. This much about the prophet is common knowledge. To understand the book, we need to learn three major truths that relate to Ezekiel. First, we need to know something of the prophet's background. Second, we should review the influences that made an impact upon his life. Third, we need to see the contributions he made. Let's look at these three areas of Ezekiel's life.

I

In order for us to understand Ezekiel in a better way, let's consider the identity and formation of the prophets in ancient Israel. Questions like who were the prophets, when did they live, what nations were prominent in their times, and other related questions need to be considered.

The word "prophet" may be defined as a person who speaks God's message. The true prophet "bubbled forth" his message. The prophet had mental perception as a "seer," that is, one who could see spiritually. The Bible gives various descriptive titles for prophets such as "servant of the Lord," "messenger of the Lord," "watchman," "man of God," "friend of God," and others.

Many Israelite evil or false prophets lived among the true prophets of God. They spoke "out of their own hearts" (13:2, 17, etc). They had personal interests, even as they declared false hopes of Israel's escape from judgment (Jeremiah 14:14; 23:26; Ezekiel 13:2-3, 17, etc.). Pagan religions had hundreds of prophets, too. Many of those served Baal and other pagan deities. One familiar story relates to Elijah who challenged the prophets of Baal on Mount Carmel (1 Kings 18). About twenty-five false gods are mentioned in the Old Testament, promoted by pagan prophets.

The time-line of God's Old Testament prophets is extensive. God called Abraham a prophet (Genesis 20:7). Aaron was assigned to be a "prophet" for Moses (Exodus 7:1), and Moses is referred to as a prophet in Deuteronomy 34:10. Miriam, the sister of Aaron and Moses, had the title of prophetess (Exodus 15:20). Deborah, Huldah, Hannah, Anna, and four daughters of Philip are listed in the prophetic line (Judges 2:1; 4:4; 2 Kings 22:13; 1 Samuel 2:1; Luke 2:36; Acts 21:8-9). However, the majority of prophets were men.

Samuel is among the first of the "official prophets," and he may have been the first to have started schools for prophets (1 Samuel 3:20). Later on, Elisha had "schools of prophets" in several places, such as Ramah, Bethel, Jericho, and Gilgal (2 Kings 3:3, 5; 4:38). Two groups of God's prophets are listed. The first group includes the prophets such as Elijah, Elisha, and other non-literary or non-writing prophets (1 Kings 19:18). The second group includes the writing prophets.

The prophets who wrote their messages are defined as major and minor. This definition is given because of their longer or shorter writings. The major prophets were Isaiah, Jeremiah, Ezekiel, and Daniel. The minor group includes those from Hosea to Malachi. The approximate dates for both groups go from about 850 to 400 B.C. (or BCE, Before the Common Era). In the Hebrew Scriptures, the books of Joshua, Judges, Samuel, and Kings are treated as the "former prophets," while Isaiah, Jeremiah, Ezekiel, and the Book of the Twelve are the "latter prophets."

The messages of God's prophets were dual in nature. They spoke about the moral failure or corruption of priests, politicians, princes, kings, false prophets, and common people. Their major thrust was ethical, calling God's people back to God and warning that judgment would come unless they repented.

The prophets also had strong predictive messages. They told of events that would take place quite soon, such as Jeremiah's prophesy that Hananiah would die that year (28:17). Of course, many predictions concerned events that would take place years and centuries ahead of their time. The central prophetic word for the future related to God's kingdom and the coming Messiah whom they identified with several terms, such as: the Branch, One like Moses, Holy One, Son of David, My servant David, Shepherd, the Everlasting Father, Root out of a dry ground, etc. (Genesis 3:15; Deuteronomy 18:18; Psalm 16:10; Jeremiah 23:5; Ezekiel 37:24; Isaiah 7:14; 9:6; 53:1ff; Daniel 4:3, etc.).

The prophets also wrote about God's judgment of His people and their restoration. The LORD would give them a "new heart, a new spirit" (Jeremiah 24:7; Ezekiel 36:26). The LORD would initiate a New Covenant (Jeremiah 31). The message of the prophets showed that God was and is "The LORD of all nations" (Psalms 24:1; Jeremiah 1:5; Ezekiel 18:4; Malachi 3:12, etc.).

God called Abram from Babylon around 2000 B.C. (some say about 1800). An important foundation of Hebrew history is linked to Abraham, as well as to Isaac, Jacob, and Joseph. Briefly, it might be noted that Egypt held the "sons of Jacob" in captivity from about 1700 until about 1300 B.C. (dates vary). God led the Israelites out of Egypt through Moses. They lived in the Promised Land under the Judges from 1250 until 1050 (circa). The nation then became a kingdom under Saul, "maturing" during the reigns of David and Solomon. At Solomon's death in 928 B.C. (931?), the kingdom divided into the ten northern tribes called Israel, and the two southern tribes called Judah.

In 722 B.C. the Assyrians captured the Northern Kingdom of Israel. In 612 B.C., Babylon conquered Assyria (Nineveh, the capital) and rose to world supremacy. In 597 B.C., Nebuchadnezzar carried about ten thousand of the best people of Jerusalem captive — artisans, soldiers, politicians, and religious leaders. (2 Kings 24:14; 2 Chronicles 36:6; Jeremiah 52:30 lists the number as four thousand six hundred). Ezekiel was among them.

Babylon continued as a world empire from 605 B.C. when Nebuchadnezzar became king until 539 B.C. when Persia replaced Babylon as the leading world empire. The Greeks rose to supremacy over Palestine by 323 B.C., ten years after the death of Alexander the Great. The Romans replaced the Greeks in 63 B.C. , and the Roman Empire lasted until nearly 500 A.D. Interestingly, Israel lived under the dominating power of Egypt, Assyria, Babylon, Persia, Greece, and Rome. This perspective of Israel's subjugation and exile helps in our understanding of the Hebrew nation.

Ezekiel lived in the midst of political and religious upheavals. When he was taken captive to Babylon, he had his eyes opened to God's rule over history. The journey from Jerusalem to Babylon of about seven hundred miles undoubtedly toughened Ezekiel for his years in captivity. The Israelites walked that distance with their families and a few possessions. They must have heard whips popping over their heads and shouts of the Babylonian soldiers giving them orders as they marched day after day. They had to prepare their own food through those months of slow travel. They slept on the ground and walked during the heat and cold of the day during the four or more months' journey.

Ezekiel came to understand sufferings as he and his fellow Israelites struggled through seven hundred miles from their homeland to the country between the Tigris and Euphrates rivers. God used that time-line of history to shape the "son of man," into the person He wanted him to be. The "son of man" title in Ezekiel means "man" or "human being."

II

To understand and know Ezekiel, we need to give consideration to some major influences that helped shape his life.

Ezekiel's family made a great impact upon his career. The first chapter of Ezekiel states that he was the son of Buzi. His father may have been a priest from Zadok's line, and probably influenced his son. Ezekiel mentions the Zadok line of priests in chapter 43:19. Zadok remained faithful to David during the upheaval of his kingdom, and the shift in priesthood moved from Abiathar to Zadok (1 Kings 2:35; 1 Chronicles 29:22).

Ezekiel's wife, without doubt, had an important role in his life. At the time of the fall of Jerusalem, she died suddenly (24:18). Even though the LORD for symbolic reasons told Ezekiel not to be sad over her death, he felt that loss deeply. We could wish that more insight into the prophet's companion had been given, but Ezekiel 24:15-18 gets to the point in describing her as "the desire of his eyes."

Another influence in the life of Ezekiel was his preparation for the priesthood. Aaron, the brother of Moses, became Israel's first high priest. Exodus 29:20-21 lists the consecration ceremonies of the priesthood. Blood was placed on the right ear, the thumb on the right hand, and the big toe on the right foot of the priests. That ritual symbolized that everything the priests would hear and do and every place they would go would be consecrated to the Lord. The priests ministered in sacred things in the tabernacle and later in the temple. Regulations about their purity and ministry run throughout the book of Leviticus.

Priestly training was intensive in order that priests would serve well in the tabernacle and later in the temple. Their work included studying, instructing the people, taking care of their families, making animal sacrifices, disposing of sacrificial left overs, cleaning and guarding the temple, etc. Their job was to facilitate worship. The Levitical line furnished all the priests for Israel. The Levites served as teachers, musicians, officers, and judges (Deuteronomy 10:8; 1 Chronicles 33; 2 Chronicles 34:12-13; 35:3).

Priests never worshiped for the people. They assisted or mediated by expediting the worship of the people in various ways. For instance, today pastors and other staff people, including lay people, lead in prayer, read the Scripture, direct the music, etc. Anyone may help facilitate the service of worship, but each person worships the Lord for himself or herself. No person worships for another. Priests in ancient Israel served by leading the people as they performed various rites. Jesus ended the Levitical-Aaronic system and became the believer's Great High Priest, and He is the only Mediator between God and man (1 Timothy 2:5; Hebrews: chapters 8-10). All believers are a part of God's priesthood, meaning that each goes to God for himself or herself through Christ (1 Peter 2:9; Revelation 1:6; 5:10; 20:6). Ezekiel trained for the priesthood, but God called him to be a prophet, a calling not hereditary as the priestly order had been. The prophets received their messages from God and spoke to the people for God.

A third influence in Ezekiel's life was the reformation under King Josiah in 621 B.C. Josiah became king at eight years of age when his father Amon died (2 Chronicles 33:25). Both Amon and Manasseh, the father and grandfather of Josiah, had failed the LORD. These two were evil rulers as nearly all Hebrew kings. Josiah, however, proved to be an exceptionally able spiritual leader. He served as King of Judah from 639 until his unfortunate death in 609 B.C.

In the eighteenth year of Josiah's reign, when repair work was being done in the temple, Hilkiah (the High Priest) found a scroll. He said to Shaphan the scribe, "I have found the Book of the Law in the house of the Lord" (2 Kings 22:3, 8). Shaphan read the book to King Josiah. Upon hearing the words, Josiah tore his robe in shock and grief at how the people of Judah had disregarded God's command- ments. When he asked Hilkiah and Shaphan to inquire about the writing, they took the scroll to the prophetess Huldah, who declared that it was God's word. Josiah ordered an end to idol worship that Israelites had been practicing all around Jerusalem (2 Kings 23:24; 2 Chronicles 34:33). Terrible stories of idol worship and corrupt moral lives may be found in 2 Chronicles 35 and 2 Kings 22 and 23. The reformation began in 621 B.C. when King Josiah was twenty- six years of age. The reformation began about the time of Ezekiel's birth, and people must have been talking about it during his youth.

Another influence in the life of Ezekiel came from the writ- ings of Moses in the Pentateuch, and some of the Psalms of David. We assume that Ezekiel knew the writings of the major and minor prophets before his time as well as the messages of his contempo- raries. About the time of Ezekiel's birth (circa 623 B.C.), Jeremiah began his preaching ministry. Even though Ezekiel never mentions Jeremiah, the younger prophet probably heard Jeremiah preach a number of times as well as read the earlier part of his book. Many of the ideas in the book of Jeremiah appear in Ezekiel. They both lived in Jerusalem, both trained for the priesthood, and their lives overlapped for a few years.

Daniel also had an impact upon Ezekiel. Daniel was taken captive to Babylon in 606 B.C. (Daniel 1:1, 6 give the date as the third year of Jehoiakim's reign). At that time Ezekiel was about sixteen years of age, and would have been an apprentice priest. Nine years later in 597 B.C., Babylonian forces carried him into captivity. Since both Daniel and Ezekiel lived as exiles in Babylon, they possibly had contact with one another either by letter or personal visits. Ezekiel 14:14, 18 states that even if Noah, Daniel, and Job were praying for Jerusalem, God would not save the place. Ezekiel possibly knew the story of Daniel's disciplined life as well as other experiences about him.

The Israelites were not captives in the sense of war-time prisoners or prison inmates today. Those who had been located along the Chebar canal in Mesopotamia lived in their own houses, farmed, and did other work (Jeremiah 29:5; Ezekiel 3:24). In the king's court in Babylon, Daniel had a high office and probably had freedom to move about. It is possible that those two men of God could have been in communication and talked about God's purposes in history. However, accounts of such visits are never mentioned.

The divine influence upon the life of Ezekiel cannot be overlooked. God called Ezekiel to be a prophet after he had been in Babylon five years. Three times in his book, the words appear about God's hand being upon him (Ezekiel 1:3; 8:1; 40:1). The expression carries with it the idea of God's direct intervention in the life of this prophet.

The LORD equipped and gave strength to Ezekiel so that He could do God's will in the midst of Israelite exiles who were compared to "scorpions, briars, and thorns" (Ezekiel 2:6). Like Jeremiah, Ezekiel seemed to have been a "reluctant prophet." He would have preferred life in Jerusalem, not in Babylon! Ezekiel states forty times that "the word of the Lord came to him." Above every other influence, God's hand upon Ezekiel certainly ranks as the most important.

III

The third way we come to know Ezekiel is to consider his contributions. Those contributions to his nation and the world continue to be far-reaching.

One contribution of Ezekiel was his service as prophet, teacher, pastor, and critic. He gave an appraisal, evaluation, and perspective of the "whole house of Israel." The elders (leaders) who were among the captives visited Ezekiel on at least three occasions (Ezekiel 8:1; 14:1; 20:1). They lived near the prophet as colonists by the River Chebar. Actually, the so-called river was an irrigation canal that diverted water from the Euphrates River to the farmland. Ezekiel's home was in that area (3:24; 8:1).

Ezekiel wrote about the elders who visited him. Those men may have asked Ezekiel questions about what was happening in Jerusalem, how long the captivity would last, what the future held for them; however the words that he spoke never won their sympathy or support. That inquiring time lasted from 593, when God called Ezekiel to be a prophet, until the destruction of Jerusalem in 586. Ezekiel's messages of condemnation and inevitable judgment continue in the book until chapter 33:22 when news of Jerusalem's fall comes to those in Babylon. The first half of Ezekiel's ministry provoked anger and bitterness among the exiles because of his messages of judgment. After Jerusalem's fall, Ezekiel began a ministry of hope and restoration until his last message dated 572 B.C.

Another contribution of Ezekiel was his preaching. We do not know the extent of his preaching and prophesying, but his recorded messages give something of an insight into this phase of his ministry. Some of the dramatic acts of Ezekiel reflect the ways in which he proclaimed God's Word. Once he drew a diagram of Jerusalem on a large brick, depicting an assault on the city to demonstrate that the Babylonians would attack and destroy it (4:1-3). At other times he lay on his left side for three hundred ninety days, and on the right side forty days (4:4-6). His verbal and sign preaching impacted his hearers, whether they accepted or rejected his messages.

Perhaps the greatest contribution of Ezekiel was the book for which he is responsible. His book continued to be a warning for the rebellious people as well as to give a message of hope following the destruction of Jerusalem. This book of forty eight chapters is one in which he shows God's judgment upon Israel, upon foreign nations, and the eventual rescue and restoration of Israel so they would become united and enter into a renewed covenant relationship with God, under the new King David (34:23; 37:25).

The book of Ezekiel closes with a vision of God's temple. From that temple a symbolic river would flow and give hope to a desolate world. We give thanks to the Lord for Ezekiel. He held out hope in those captivity years when God's people needed his message about God's judgment as well as His abounding grace. He assured his fellow exiles in Babylon as well as those in Jerusalem that God would restore His people. Let's explore together this fascinating book that had a message for the people of Ezekiel's time and also has a message for the twenty-first century.

Chapter 2

Visions of a Prophet
Ezekiel 1:1-28

—⁓—

The best book that has ever been written is the Bible. However, the book of Ezekiel is not the most popular book of the sixty-six books in God's Word. Most people back away from this writing because it seems too complicated to read or understand. And yet, Ezekiel's document makes sense when we understand that the central idea is that God is on His throne above the storms of life, and He can bring His people through all their troubles with hope for the future.

Ezekiel was taken into Babylonian captivity in 597 B.C. along with a large number of fellow Israelites. Five years after his deportation, God called him to be a prophet (1:1). At that time the prophet was probably thirty years of age, assuming that the unexplained thirty in 1:1 refers to his age. One day while Ezekiel sat "among the captives" near the Chebar canal, heaven opened and he had "visions of God" (1:1). God's word came to Ezekiel, and the Lord placed His hand upon the newly-called prophet (1:3). God moved in the life of Ezekiel in a profound way and endowed him for his prophetic role.

Even though the captive Israelites in Babylon did not suffer extreme physical punishment, most sat down and wept as they remembered Jerusalem. As their captors led them away from their homeland, they gazed upon the ruins of their beloved city and temple — much of it still smoldering, leaving a picture of desolation, loneliness and despair in their minds that would never be erased. The suffering and death of multitudes of their fellow citizens had been blazoned upon their minds. They awakened to the shock of being in a strange land as they tried to begin a new life along the banks of the Chebar river. Psalm 137 states that they hung their harps on the willow trees beside the river as their captors taunted them with the words, "Sing us one of the songs of Zion." The echo from their hearts rang out, "How shall we sing the Lord's song in a strange land?" (vs. 2-4). Seventy long years faced them before the youngest among them would be free to return home. The story of the Israelites in Babylon has unforgettable episodes. Let's look at the first fast-moving chapter in Ezekiel.

I
The Storm Cloud: God's Whirlwind of Judgment
(1:4)

Ezekiel saw a storm cloud coming out of the north. He experienced something like a vision/trance as he was by the Chebar canal (1:1; 10:15). The more recent enemies of Israel normally came from the east, but they moved around desert areas and came down upon Jerusalem from the north. Hence, the vision had the cloud coming from that direction. All of us have seen storm clouds, but no one has witnessed a sight like Ezekiel saw. Within that storm cloud, there appeared the likeness of a great fire. The fire made circular motions, as though it chased itself. The roaring, rolling fire "enfolded" itself. The fire seemed to chase itself, maybe a movement similar to that of a dog that goes round and round in an attempt to get hold of his tail.

The fire had a brightness, a glow, an expression that Ezekiel had not seen before, and it continued to circulate within the storm cloud as though it were chasing itself. God's judgment was about to fall upon Jerusalem as judgment had come against the Northern Kingdom more than a century before. The armies of Nebuchadnezzar would ravage Jerusalem for eighteen months in the 587-86 B.C. Babylon had become the "rod in God's hand" to punish His people. Payday was coming to Jerusalem.

II
The Four Living Creatures: The Cherubim
(1:5-14)

As we fast forward to chapter 10 of Ezekiel, we discover that the prophet called the four living creatures "cherubim," a special order of heavenly beings. Cherub is singular; the word "cherubim" is plural for any number of cherubs. One function of the cherubim was to block anything unholy from God's presence (Genesis 3:24). Other references to cherubim are given in Exodus 25:18-20, 26:31, 1 Kings 23, Revelation 4:6-7.

Several words are used in describing these heavenly beings in the vision. The word "likeness" in Ezekiel chapter 1 is used fourteen times to give an idea of what he saw, and "like" is used six times, and the word "appearance" is used twenty eight times. The words "lightning" and "lamps" are used one time each (1:13). The prophet uses poetic language and word pictures to describe what he saw. What he saw was a vision, but there was reality behind the image. The Bible says, "No man can see God and live" (Exodus 33:20). Thus the revelation of God comes in a semblance, likeness, or appearance. We're on a better road to understanding Ezekiel when we don't take him too literally. The truth is there, but the truth is in symbols.

Take an example of an image or likeness of something. The term "ice cream" brings a lot of ideas to one's mind. Some may see an ice cream freezer, a big bowl of ice cream, or an ice cream cone. Ezekiel saw something "like a lamp" that was darting back and forth within the fire and cloud. Visions. Hmm!

The living creatures have four faces, four wings, two legs with feet like calves' feet, and two hands. Each cherub has hands under its wings and the outstretched wings touched one another. The hands and wings symbolize readiness for service. The straight legs give the idea of going forward without deviation from God's will. The "cloven feet" like those of a calf seem to indicate solid firmness.

Each heavenly being had four faces, symbolizing their seeing in all directions without having to turn. An acrostic or set of letters that makes a word may help us remember the faces of the living creatures. The word "mole" may help us remember the faces: man, ox, lion, and eagle.

Man: He represents the highest of all creation, the most intelligent of all. Did you ever know of monkeys or ants to build computers, airplanes, or microwave ovens?

Ox: This animal is known for his strength as a domesticated creature. Oxen are known for their patience, too.

Lion: This animal is "the king of the forest." He can take care of himself. God is not defenseless. He's the King of the universe. Whatever opinion one may have of the LORD, everyone needs to know that the Lord is God.

Eagle: That's the grandest bird of all. The eagle soars high and has great vision; a symbol that helps us understand God and His creatures a little better.

The cherubim are dependent on God. Verse 12 states that wherever the Spirit wanted to go, the heavenly beings went. They moved as God indicated, allowing the Lord to control their movements, going in any direction without turning. Their four faces looked in all directions. The Spirit animated all the living creatures, giving them unity in their service for God. What about our movements? Can it be that people work out their plans and then ask God to bless them in what they decide?

The appearance of the living creatures "was like burning coals of fire, like the appearance of torches" (v. 13 ASV). The cherubim ran and returned as the "appearance of a flash of lighting" (v. 14 ASV). How fast can lightning zigzag across the sky? God's movement is pictured here. But not one cherub moved out of control. All moved "as the Spirit" moved them. What a lesson for us. Are we under God's control? What about denominations, churches, and individuals?

III
The Wheels
(1:15-21)

Chapter 1 gives an impressive, unforgettable picture of wheels. No one has seen wheels like the wheels that Ezekiel saw as he sat by the Chebar Canal.

Each cherub had a wheel by its side. Ezekiel saw "wheels in the middle of wheels," criss-crossing each other (1:16). That arrangement represents freedom to go in any direction without having to turn. The wheel by the side of each cherub comes down to the earth, perhaps picturing God's engagement in the affairs of mankind where nothing can stop the Sovereign Lord. The wheels shine, possibly indicating that there is brightness in God's kingdom work! Where did we get the idea that to be spiritual one has to be dull? The wheels were all alike. That is, they had a similar work to do.

The wheels had rims. Old farm wagons had rims around the spokes that had their connection with the hub. A bicycle wheel can give the idea. Countless eyes appeared around the rims of the "wheels within wheels." The rims on all the wheels "were full of eyes" (v. 18), symbolizing that God sees everything. He's omniscient, and He is ready to judge. He knows about everything that goes on in His universe. God says, "My eyes are on all their ways; they are not hidden from My face, nor is their iniquity hidden from My eyes" (Jeremiah 16:17). If nations or individuals think they can get by without God knowing about them, they've overlooked God's omniscience.

God knew about the predicament of Israel centuries before the coming of Jesus. God also knows about everything that goes on in our contemporary world. He's not running around in heaven, shaking His head and wringing his hands, wondering what is going to happen next. God gives the world freedom to obey or disobey Him, but He controls the currents of history. The Lord will bring everything in personal and international life to its consummation in His time because He is omniscient.

Those wheels are under the control of God's Spirit. When the Spirit wanted them to move, they did. When the Spirit wanted the wheels to touch the ground, they descended. Verses 20-21 are clear. Wherever the Spirit wanted the cherubim or the wheels to go, they responded.

IV
The Firmament or Crystal-like Platform in the Sky
(1:22-25)

Our heads may spin because of the details of Ezekiel's vision. Maybe we need to stop and think about what has been seen up to this point in Ezekiel's vision. We sometimes don't see the forest for the trees. Let's keep in mind that this unique prophet had "visions of God." That dramatic vision or unveiling is to help us "see" God.

A quick glance at Ezekiel 1:22-25 gives us a view of what was above the cherubim and their wheels. We can see what's happening above the storm. If we take a look at a shimmering sea at sunset or sunrise, we may get something of the picture that's given near the end of chapter one in Ezekiel. Or, perhaps a picture of a field covered with ice might help explain what Ezekiel saw.

Ezekiel wrote that the likeness or appearance of the firmament (dome, platform, solid vault) above the heads of the living creatures was something like a crystal. The idea is of a brilliance that's reflected, a sight more glorious than words can describe. Let's have a quick "flash back." Think about the wings that are a part of the cherubim vision. The two sets of wings in flight made unusual sounds: like ocean waves, the voice of God, or the noise of an army marching. If you listen to the sound of ocean waves or pick up a sea shell and listen to the roar inside the shell, then magnify that sound a hundred times, you might have an idea of the *sound* of Ezekiel's Chariot scene.

The voice that spoke above the firmament caused the living creatures to "let down their wings" (1:24). They stopped in awe of the presence of God and were ready to hear what the LORD had to say. Are we?

V
God's Throne
(1:25-27)

The "Chariot Throne" is possibly related to the Ark of the Covenant that Moses placed in the Holy of Holies. The gold cherubim attached to the ark are identified as God's chariot in 1 Chronicles 28:18. Two giant-sized cherubim with their wingspan of thirty feet had been carved on the walls of the Holy of Holies in the temple (2 Chronicles 3:7, 10, 13;

1 Kings 8:6-9). The small box measured three feet long, two feet wide, and was two feet tall (Exodus 25:10). That box or ark was about the size of a communion table.

The ark was the house or container for the Ten Commandments. The mercy seat of pure gold was the covering on the Ark of the Covenant. The covenant was the agreement that God made with Abraham and reaffirmed with Moses, that God would be the Lord of Israel and they would be His people. At the end of the ark were gold cherubim with wings outstretched as their faces looked down upon the mercy seat (Exodus 25:19-21; 37:9; Hebrews 9:5). God revealed His glory between the cherubim on the Ark of the Covenant (Exodus 25:22, Numbers 7:89, 1 Samuel 4:4, 2 Samuel 6:2, 2 Kings 19:15, Psalm 80:1, 99:1). The Ark of the Covenant had two poles placed in two gold rings on each side so it could be carried (Exodus 25:12).

Let's move from the Ark of the Covenant scene in the Holy of Holies to the storm scene in Ezekiel chapter 1. The "Throne Chariot" may be visualized in Ezekiel's "visions of God" (Ezekiel 10:19). The four cherubim within the Holy of Holies appear in the vision scene. In place of the four golden rings and two poles for transportation, wheels appear by the side of the cherubim. Ezekiel 1:26-27 describes something that "looked like" God's throne as being above the "platform" or what appeared to be a firmament of crystal. The same word, "firmament," appears in Genesis 1:6. The beauty, splendor, glory, and awe of that throne could not be fully described because of its dazzling majesty. Ezekiel wrote that the entire presentation appeared like sapphire or a transparent blue-purple gem. But we must not gaze too long at the throne, or we might miss what the vision is all about.

The throne is occupied. As Ezekiel gazed upon the scene, he saw the appearance of the likeness of a man upon the throne. God, in His breathtaking splendor and glory, is above the Ark of the Covenant, between the cherubim. Daniel wrote about that throne and the figure upon it (7:9). He called that person "the Ancient of Days." The apostle John had a vision of Jesus on the Isle of Patmos, with some of the features of Ezekiel's vision (Revelation 1:13). Ezekiel saw a vision of "the appearance of the likeness of the glory of the Lord" (1:25-28). Judgment was about to be unleashed against God's people, and He is above everything and oversees world events. He has not left His place as Sovereign of the Universe. God never abdicates. James Russell Lowell wrote about this truth in one of his poems, slightly revised.

Truth forever on the scaffold? Wrong forever on the throne?

Yet that scaffold sways the future, and behind the dim unknown,

God stands within the shadow, keeping watch above His own.

Come what may, the LORD is on His Throne. Nations rise and fall…rulers come and go. History tells this lesson again and again, but humans stay in the cradle-roll department and fail to learn the lesson that God reigns eternally — He is on His throne.

Ezekiel 1:27 gives a quick glimpse of the One on the Throne. He is ablaze with glory. From His waist up, and from His waist down, the One on the throne has the appearance of fire (1:28). A brightness encircles Him. The color of amber or gold seems to go through all that is there. The glory of the Lord defies explanation.

VI
The Rainbow of Hope
(1:28)

Judgment would soon be turned loose with all its fury against Jerusalem. Ezekiel told about the onslaughts from the enemy before those events happened. The forces of Nebuchadnezzar would leave the city and the temple in total ruin — complete devastation. The people who escaped languished in miserable conditions. Thousands died from famine, pestilence, and sword within the city walls. Thousands more suffered untold misery on the march of seven hundred miles to Babylon. The story is bleak, and sadness reigns supreme. But in the midst of the destructive storm and holocaust, hope appeared. Ezekiel saw a rainbow.

Consider the lesson of Genesis 9:13. The Flood destroyed the earth because of man's evil ways. But when the storm ended and Noah left the Ark, God told Noah that He had placed a rainbow in the cloud. That bow or rainbow was a ray of hope, a covenant that God made with man. A new beginning came.

The appearance of the brightness of the rainbow around the throne gave a message of hope to Ezekiel. In the midst of that storm when death and destruction ravaged the land, God spoke through a symbol of a new beginning. Another day can dawn for anyone. The rainbow is a symbol and picture of God's grace, goodness, and love. What a spectacular sight — colorful and meaningful! The One on the Throne offers hope in the midst of life's conflicts and defeats. This is God's word for today.

As we think about some entanglements of life, we need to know that the Lord is greater than anything that overwhelms us. God is not limited to the temple in Jerusalem because He is the Lord of all creation. Ezekiel's vision shows that God is "here," and He is holy, powerful, and majestic. No matter how monumental our problems, God loves His own. Look above the storm clouds and you will see God's beautiful rainbow.

Ezekiel's Response
(1:28)

When Ezekiel saw in vision the likeness of the throne and the likeness of One on the throne, he fell upon his face (1:28). He was overwhelmed. God is awesome, all glorious, all knowing, all-powerful. He is the Eternal One before whom Ezekiel fell prostrate upon the ground. God spoke to Ezekiel and gave His word to him.

We need to have a vision of "the heavens opened." We then can understand that in good times as well as when the worst happens that God stays active in the midst of everything and has control. The

LORD of history and eternity wants us to respond to Him and do His will. What's our response going to be?

Chapter 3

Non-Stop Witnessing
Ezekiel 2:1-3:27

—⟰—

The name of Bill Bright is a household word among evangelicals. He launched the international organization called "Campus Crusade for Christ" in 1951. That small beginning has mushroomed into a worldwide witnessing team for the gospel of Jesus Christ. After the death of their leader in July of 2003, those people kept going. Campus Crusade now numbers more than twenty thousand full-time staff members with about one-half million volunteers in one hundred eighty-six countries of the world. Half the world's population in nearly six hundred languages has seen their film <u>JESUS</u>. We can praise the Lord for those dedicated servants of Christ who do non-stop witnessing.

God called Ezekiel to be a faithful witness. He said, "Son of man, I have made you a watchman for the house of Israel" (3:17). Even as the Babylonians soon would set battering rams around the walls of Jerusalem, so God set or placed Ezekiel to give words of warning to the Israelites. He was to "hedge about," shepherd, and give God's messages to His people. Ezekiel 2:9-3:4 pictures God's outstretched hand, giving the prophet a scroll to eat, a symbolic consuming of God's entire message. The scroll was about eighteen inches wide and perhaps twenty feet long, containing the messages of judgment and warning for all of God's people (2:10). Even though the message from God was "bitter" for the Israelites, in the prophet's mouth it was "like honey in sweetness" because he was doing God's will (Ezekiel 3:3; 21:6).

Even though Ezekiel had been taken away from his own country as a captive and lived in a colony by the River Chebar, he carried on a ministry for at least twenty-two years. During those long, hard years from 593 B.C. when God called him to be a prophet, until 573 B.C., he continued preaching and writing (40:1). The exiles knew that God's man lived among them (33:33). God's people from those ancient years to the present time have read, been refreshed, and often perplexed by Ezekiel's book.

Whoever we may be, we need to be faithful in our witness. We need an awakening in the area of talking about God and His redemptive work. We need to get outside the walls of worship centers, knock on doors, and meet people in the marketplace with the old, old story of salvation. Pastors need to lead people on witnessing crusades. Music leaders need to know that their principal business should be to witness. Youth leaders, Sunday School teachers, Bible teachers, business executives, employees from all ranges of work, students, children, husbands, wives, grandparents, and the list goes on of God's people who need to tell the story of redeeming grace. Witnessing is not circumscribed by the word "talk." Ezekiel demonstrated his witnessing in various ways. Let's explore chapters two and three of Ezekiel that challenge us to share God's message.

I
A Spiritual Witness
(2:2; 3:12, etc.)

We need to witness in the Spirit (2:2; 3:12). The word "Spirit" is ruach in the Hebrew language. The word means "breath," "spirit," or "wind." In the book of Ezekiel the word "spirit" is given almost every time in reference to the Spirit of God.

The Spirit is mentioned fifty-two times by Ezekiel in his document. One-seventh of all the references to the Spirit in the Old Testament are found in the book of Ezekiel. This fact means that the prophet was truly a "man of God." He had God's anointing upon his life. He knew when the Spirit of God "lifted him up" (3:14; 8:3, 5).

He was aware that "the hand of the Lord was upon him" (1:3; 3:14, 22; 8:1; 37:1). Those kinds of experiences in which God empowers, revitalizes, and equips His people need to be duplicated in the lives of believers in every place. Every Christian needs to be "filled with the Spirit" (Ephesians 5:18). Whatever the work we do in home, business, or elsewhere, we need to do it under the control of the Spirit of God. God's hand needs to be upon us today.

As we witness in the Spirit, our witness will be fresh. On the small farm where I grew up, we had a fresh-flowing spring of water. Water has been flowing from that spring for years. The water from that spring forms the headwaters of the Buckalew Creek that flows down to the Ouachita River. Interestingly, the water is always fresh and invigorating. I drank and quenched my thirst from that spring time and time again as we came from nearby fields.

When we get connected to the perennial flow of the Holy Spirit, we'll be refreshed. Jesus declared that out of the believer's heart will flow rivers of water. He said, "...If anyone thirsts, let him come to Me and drink. He who believes in Me, as the Scripture has said, out of his heart will flow rivers of living water (John 7:37-38). The refreshing presence of the Spirit will keep us from becoming dull and stagnated.

As we witness in the Spirit, we become fearless witnesses. The prophet Ezekiel didn't have an easy call. His fellow exiles never liked his condemnatory messages. God told the prophet that he was going to live among thorns, briars, and scorpions (2:6). They would not be complimentary and supportive. They were going to hector, heckle, and hound him until he would want a "new church field!" But God said to the prophet, "You stay where I want you to be." The LORD's message continued to echo in the ears of God's prophet, "Son of man, I am sending you to the children of Israel, to a rebellious nation that has rebelled against Me to this very day...And you, son of man, do not be afraid of them" (Ezekiel 2:3, 8; 3:4). In other words, "Stay put, Ezekiel!" He did, but he did not covet that work. He wrote, "So the Spirit lifted me up, and took me away, and I went in bitterness, in the heat of my spirit" (3:14). Missionaries, teachers, Sunday School workers, people on the farm, executives, and everyone may learn lessons from God's demands upon Ezekiel — do the job where God places you.

Furthermore, the LORD let Ezekiel know that the reason for his being among the Hebrew captives in that faraway land was to let them know that God's people were suffering because of their idolatry and immorality. Later, this prophet would give them hope for the future. God wanted Ezekiel to keep going with his fearless witnessing. We can learn this truth, can't we?

II
A Sympathetic Witness
(3:17, etc.)

We need to witness with sympathy. When Ezekiel had a vision of God's glory, he fell upon his face. The revelation that God gave was more than the prophet could look upon. When Ezekiel fell to the ground, he heard a voice saying, "Son of man, stand on your feet, and I will speak to you" (2:1). The Spirit of God lifted Ezekiel from the ground and gave him instructions to go to those by the Chebar and begin his ministry.

The text calls for an understanding of the predicament of God's people. Ezekiel 3:15 reads, "Then I came to the captives at Tel Abib, who dwelt by the River Chebar; and I sat where they sat, and remained there astonished among them seven days." The word "astonished" in this text means "overcome, devastated, appalled." We may say that Ezekiel had empathy, sympathy, heartfelt sorrow, or other similar expressions. He sat among the people and felt their pain, shame, sorrow, despair, and defeat. If we witness in the right way, it must be with true and profound empathy.

Few among those whom Ezekiel visited seemed joyful. Even though they had begun to settle down, farm, and pursue their own trades, they felt overwhelmed with despair. They had been yanked away from their homes, their city, and the temple in Jerusalem, and in a few years they would hear about the destruction of all they had called sacred in their homeland. They faced pagan religions and uncertain days, and the dangers they faced staggered even a strong man like Ezekiel.

36

False prophets said something like the following, "Everything is going to be all right. God takes care of his own" (Jeremiah 28; 29:15-23; 37:19; Ezekiel 13:1-3, 8). Ezekiel said, "Yes, God is in control, but suffering, heartbreak, loneliness, and tribulation stand before you. Don't build your hopes upon false premises."

We live in a world of turmoil. Life is flipping topsy-turvy in virtually every nation. Most denominations face bewilderment, or worse. Governments buckle and fall. The known and the unknown suffer doubts and fears. And yet, those in the midst of deepest need can find a new day when they get right with God.

The USA has become a mission field. Statistics in 2003 state that thirty-three million people in the USA are foreign-born. Ninety-five percent of the taxicab drivers in New York are immigrants, most of whom are ignorant of the Bible and the Christian faith. Young people from our churches and families move out into a pagan atmosphere. We need to witness with heartfelt concern for people everywhere who live in the midst of spiritual darkness.

III
Witness about the Cost of Sin
(3:17-21)

We are to witness about the dangers of sin. God told Ezekiel, "Give them warning from me" (3:17-21; 33:4-5). The Lord's message is understandable, even though God's people may reject it (3:5-6, 11). Sin wreaks havoc and brings destruction. Sin is a reality. The word "sin" appears hundreds of times in the Bible. The synonyms for sin in Ezekiel include words such as "transgressions, iniquities, rebellion," and "evil." We need to wake up to the ruin that sin brings. We need to be bold and declare the truth about the devastation of sin. Our message cannot be always, "You're Okay; I'm Okay." Doctors don't tell their patients that they are all right when cancer cells appear throughout the body or when the arteries going into the heart are ninety-five percent clogged. Teachers, parents, evangelists, pastors, and all Christians must be honest about sin's awful results.

Sin is deceptive. The Israelites in Jerusalem and in Babylon had an illusion that they could get by with idolatry. They thought they could emulate their pagan neighbors and replace God, or make Him a little god among all the others. They discovered the tragedy of their wrong doings. Drugs, alcohol, immorality, greed, unforgiveness, and demon-infested music harm those who go these routes. Since sin blinds the eyes of the sinner, we should warn others about the horrible consequences of wrong doing. Anyone can take what he or she wants, but that one has to pay for the transgression.

When I was a child, I sometimes "set" bird traps in the wintertime. When snow was upon the ground, birds did not always find as much food as they wanted. Near the traps I would place bread crumbs, and toss a few crumbs on the inside of the see-through trap. The birds that hopped around eating the crumbs would also hop beneath the elevated side of the trap. As they hopped upon a little lever, the cage would fall down around them. The redbirds would squawk and try to defend themselves as one or another was gently lifted from the cage. Later, I would let them go, but they perhaps told their friends, "Watch out for that kid's bird traps!" Sin lures us into its web and won't let us go until we get under the shelter of God's mercy.

Sin is destructive. If what Ezekiel wrote earlier about sin had been missed, he repeats the message in understandable language, "The soul that sins shall die" (18:4). Sin's penalty is horrific. Achan thought he could get by when he stole a Babylonian garment. Also, he looked upon a stack of gold and silver that had been salvaged from Jericho and he grabbed some of those items (Joshua 7:21). However, he paid a big price for his wrongdoing. The Israelite army lost the first battle against Ai because of Achan's sin, and he and his family were executed because of his transgressions (Joshua 7:25). Sin has a deadly venom. The Bible states, "The wages of sin is death" (Rom. 3:23). Everyone needs to learn this truth and avoid the Achan tragedy.

IV
Witness whether Successful or Unsuccessful
(3:11, etc.)

We are to witness with or without success. God told Ezekiel to witness "whether they hear or whether they refuse " (3:11). Most of those who heard Ezekiel looked upon him as one "out of step." Some of the captives along the Chebar canal returned home saying to one another in today's language: "We've got a crazy preacher... The guy has a beautiful voice, but he keeps pounding away about our wrongdoing. Why doesn't he tell us how wonderful we are?" (Ezekiel 33:32). Someone said to Evangelist Billy Sunday of a previous generation, "You are rubbing the cat's fur the wrong way." The evangelist answered, "Then tell the cat to turn around." The message of Ezekiel didn't need to be changed, but the people did.

Ezekiel was never voted Citizen of the Year among the Hebrews in Babylon. They didn't send an announcement back to the "Jerusalem Journal" about the gifted and applauded evangelist by the name of Ezekiel. God, however, told him to declare the message with or without success (3:11).

We witness to those who receive God's message. For several years, Ray Summers taught at Southwestern Baptist Seminary in Fort Worth, Texas. Once he served as interim pastor of a church in Texarkana, Texas. While on the way home on the train known as the "Texas Eagle" early one Monday morning, he had a headache. As Dr. Summers walked through the coach to get water, he saw the porter, a black man. Speaking to him, he asked the man if he were a Christian. The porter answered, "No sir, but several years ago the president of your seminary talked to me about being a Christian." When the man said that he had never asked Jesus to be his Savior, Ray Summers said, "Let's pray now and ask the Lord to save you." The porter agreed and was wonderfully saved. A few weeks later a black man stopped the seminary professor on a street in Ft. Worth, saying, "Sir, do you know me?" Since the man didn't have on his porter's uniform, the seminary professor didn't recognize him. Then the man said, "I am the porter who was on the train that you led to faith in Jesus. And I want you to know that I've joined a church here in Ft. Worth and am happy in the Lord." Some people will make a ready response to the invitation to become a disciple of Jesus.

We need to witness to those who reject God's message. Many say "no" to God's message. Ezekiel did not have a responsive, sympathetic audience. Yes, he lived among people who symbolically were like thorns, briars, and scorpions (2:6). And yet, God gave His prophet instructions to speak to "the house of Israel" (3:4).

Jesus sent out seventy disciples to witness across the Holy Land. He said if they were not received in one town that they should shake the dust off their feet and keep going (Luke 10:11). When Paul and Barnabas made their first missionary journey to Asia Minor, they soon faced a "ton of trouble." Paul and his companion obediently shook the dust off their feet, and moved on to another town (Acts 13:50-51).

Our duty is to keep telling the story of God's judgment and grace to everyone. We witness to those who receive as well as those who reject God's message. God said to Ezekiel, "Whether they hear, or whether they refuse" (3:11). God gave Ezekiel the task of being "a watchman for the house of Israel," with or without success (3:17; 33:7). He faithfully completed his ministry. God wants all His people to join the ranks of those who witness for Him. Will we start today?

Chapter 4

A Drama of God's Judgment
Ezekiel 4:1-5:17

—ɷ—

Many people have read or heard of the book entitled <u>Through Gates of Splendor</u> by Elizabeth Elliott. The book tells the story of five American missionaries who died at the hands of Auca Indians of Ecuador in the 1950s. One of the missionaries was Nate Saint. One of Mr. Saint's brothers also served as a missionary in Argentina. Phil Saint, the brother, was a Spirit-filled evangelist, leading thousands of people to personal faith in Jesus Christ. Phil Saint was also an artist. As he preached he would draw symbols of his messages on a chalkboard. He would, for instance, speak about the storms of life. During the message, he would paint a storm scene in magnificent colors. The scene might be one of Jesus and His apostles on the Sea of Galilee, and he would take his audience step by step through the drama of a storm, showing how Christ helps those who face all kinds of problems.

Ezekiel preached like an artist. He demonstrated his messages in "live pictures." We like this kind of teaching. A child learns more easily when he or she is able to see as well as hear the message. God led Ezekiel to preach by demonstrating his messages for at least two reasons. One, the message would be understood by the people. Another reason Ezekiel demonstrated his messages was that everyone would remember what he said. They could not forget what he had drawn before their eyes. Neither can we forget those

messages that we hear and see. Ezekiel's messages were those of
hope beyond judgment. And yet, a warning of God's judgment had
to be given by the prophet, if he remained true to God.

In chapters four and five we have a revelation of God's judgment that soon would take place. The messages of Ezekiel remind
us that God judges sin. We must face the reality that sin has consequences. The drama of judgment is enacted through signs that come
from Ezekiel. Let's look at four signs of judgment in chapters four
and five.

I

A Clay Chalkboard and an Iron Plate
(4:1-3)

Everyone knows about chalkboards. Who hasn't stood with chalk in
hand in front of a thing like that? Teachers may ask students to go
to a chalkboard and write some chemical formula or multiply some
numbers.

Ezekiel made something like a chalkboard to describe his
message. He had a tile or large board of clay. Before the clay hardened, he was able to make a diagram of the city of Jerusalem upon
the tile. We may think that he drew every line carefully as he outlined
the city. Perhaps the likeness of the Temple of Jerusalem glowed
in bright sunshine as he sketched it. Residential and business areas
might have been added. As the exiles saw that picture on the clay
tablet, they may have wept as they remembered their homeland.
They had walked for months from Jerusalem to their settlements
along the Chebar canal, just off the Euphrates River. They remembered with deep emotion their homes, the work they had done, and
that which had been their sacred city.

Jerusalem impressed everyone. The impregnable walls of that
city were about thirty feet in height and fifteen feet in thickness. On
top of the walls, carpenters had built watchtowers. Those towers
stood about thirty feet in height. The people felt that their defenses
would keep out all would-be invaders, and a real sense of security
filled their lives because of the walls. Guards stayed at their posts day
and night as they watched for any movements outside the city. Who

could harm them with such fortifications? Through his portrayals Ezekiel said, "Let me show you!"

When they besieged Jerusalem, the Babylonians piled tall mounds of dirt outside the high walls that encircled the city. All around it, the Babylonian soldiers put up their tents. The army had battering rams in place to batter away at the walls (Jeremiah 1:15; 52:4, 13-14). Ezekiel let his pictorial sermon tell the story. The exiles in Babylon looked and listened as the prophet gave the idea of troop movements, and as soldiers began to look over the walls and down into the city. Arrows rained down upon the terrified Israelites inside the city of Jerusalem. They suffered from shock and helpless feelings as they heard the shouts of thousands of enemy soldiers. The pounding from the battering rams sent the people into a frenzy, and they shook with fear.

The soldiers outside the city felt jubilant. They had plenty of food supplies. Nebuchadnezzar had a well-planned battle strategy. A few years previously in 606 and 597 B.C., Babylon had taken thousands of the best of the Israelites into captivity. They had no reason to doubt that they could conquer Jerusalem.

Ezekiel's message on the clay tablet should have been enough to convince anyone that God's people could not hold out against the enemy. And yet, prophets told the people that Jeremiah's message about Jerusalem and Ezekiel's words of warning from Babylon would not come to pass (Jeremiah 14:13-14; 28; Ezekiel 13:2). Didn't the people in Jerusalem have God's temple and covenants to keep them safe? Why should they fear? Ezekiel wanted to make them afraid, and soon panic would take over like rigor mortis.

Ezekiel continued his drama. He placed a big sheet of iron, perhaps something like an iron pan, between himself and the city. Greenberg states that the iron griddle was "an impenetrable barrier, representing the total severance of relations between the city and God" (Ezekiel, p. 104). He also states that some see this symbol as sin that separates God's people from Him. Thus, God would no longer hear their prayers because of their sins (Isaiah 59:1-2). Additionally, the sheet of iron also may have symbolized the irresistible force of Nebuchadnezzar's army that soon would invade and destroy them. One sign of judgment closes, and another is soon to begin.

II
The Prophet's Prone Position
(4:4-6, 8)

We may feel astounded and step back in unbelief when God said that Ezekiel had to lie on his left side three hundred ninety days and on his right side forty days. And yet, we need to look closely at an interpretation of these words.

The prophet's prone position may be explained this way. You may ask barbers or beauticians how long they have been in business. The beautician may say, "I have been cutting hair for fifteen years." A statement like that does not present a problem. We know that a beautician may stay in her shop four or five days a week. She goes home on the weekends, she goes home at night, she leaves her shop for lunch, or maybe she takes several coffee breaks. Interruptions come at any time. We don't expect such a person to be glued to a place of business all the time.

Look at another illustration of this case. W.A. Criswell served as pastor of the First Baptist church of Dallas for a little more than fifty years. Some say the pastor preached in his church for half a century. Not really. Dr. Criswell served the church during that time, but he did not preach non-stop for fifty years! Pastors go on vacations two or three weeks each year, have crusades and conferences outside their church, and have other activities. A pastor preaches two or three times a week for one half-hour in each message. And yet we say, "The pastor has been preaching in his church for fifty years." (Some sermons may sound that long!). In truth, many sermons are *too* long!

During his three hundred ninety day assignment, Ezekiel carried out several activities. He visited with his wife, perhaps helped her cook food and wash clothes, talked and debated with those who came his way, and had other jobs to do. Possibly two or three times a week, Ezekiel would give a dramatic message by placing himself on the ground in order that people could see his message demonstrated, as well as hear it. In other words, during that extended time when people came to see Ezekiel, he would preach his message while lying on the ground.

The time allotted for the prophet to be on his left side, representing Israel's time of rebellion against God, added up to three hundred ninety days — one day for each year of rebellion. Their transgressions brought about their captivity.

From the time of the divided kingdom after the death of Solomon in 931 (possibly 928 B.C.), the Northern Kingdom had nineteen kings. All lived and governed in evil ways and helped lead the Israelites down the slippery slope of immorality and idolatry. Ezekiel possibly became a representative of "the sin bearer," as he demonstrated the sinful years of those who fell into Assyrian hands in 722 B.C. Ezekiel stayed on his right side for forty days to symbolize the forty years' iniquity of the two southern tribes (Judah and Benjamin). He did not remain in that prone position all during that month and ten days as chapters four and five might seem to imply. As noted already, he carried out other assignments such as cooking his food, cutting his hair, etc.

III
The Prophet's Arm
(4:7-8)

Ezekiel's pictorial sermon shows him with his arm uncovered (v. 7). The "bare arm" may signify the powerful arm of the Lord. Isaiah 52:10 mentions that God "made bare his holy arm." Isaiah 5:25 states that the Lord "stretched out His hand against" His people. Also, the act of rolling up his sleeves or taking off his shirt could have been to let those who saw and heard him get a glimpse of his muscles and remind the people that the enemy had strong muscles which they would use in their attack on Jerusalem. God's instrument for punishing His sinful people was the Babylonian army that encircled Jerusalem.

The prophet lay "paralyzed" upon the ground (4:4, 8). That statement may be interpreted as meaning that Ezekiel did not move back and forth from one side to the other. He would be on his left side until those days had been fulfilled for Israel's sins, meaning the Northern Kingdom. The same position on the right side symbolized Judah's rebellion. Whether or not the people in Jerusalem heard the story of Ezekiel's dramatic actions, the people in Babylon heard that those in Jerusalem had passed the point of no return. Ezekiel 14:14 and 14:18 state that even if Noah, Job, and Daniel were to pray for them that judgment would not be averted. God's people faced payday for their sins.

IV
A Diet to Demonstrate Danger-Filled Days
(4:9-17)

None of us would welcome a bread and water diet. Not for eigheen months, anyway! And yet, Ezekiel told the exiles in Babylon that the people in Jerusalem would soon be facing death by a long famine.

Ezekiel rationed out for himself a paltry amount of grain for bread (4:9f). He would never gain a pound from the eight or ten ounces of food that he prepared for himself each day. The food was a mixture of wheat, millet, lentils, and barley. He mixed the grain with beans and vetches. Ezekiel ate coarse, non-appetizing meals to remind his fellow countrymen of the starvation problem that soon would strike in Jerusalem.

The use of repulsive fuel signified even more a departure from all that was "kosher" in their meals (4:12, 15). The food and its preparation was a warning about the days of death that Jerusalem would face. The fuel from animal dung, used to cook the food, placed more emphasis upon the repulsive nature of the bread. God's prophet would not die of thirst, but neither would he find extra drops of water in his glass. He would drink one-sixth of a "hin" of water a day, a little more than one pint.

The expression "Watch your p's and q's" came from the taverns of England. One who overindulged at the bar was told to watch his "pints and quarts." Hence, the term "p's" and "q's." Ezekiel didn't have a problem of drinking too much water nor of eating too much bread. He did not search through diet books for weight loss secrets during the ordeal of four hundred thirty days (three hundred ninety plus forty). He had less than one-half pound of bread per day, barely a survival diet.

God's prophet didn't have meals from a well-known restaurant. His menu didn't call for T-bone steak. He never had the luxury of a tossed salad with Thousand Island dressing. No one brought him butternut ice cream and chocolate cake. He had ordinary food that the poorest people struggled to get. For Ezekiel, his meal came once a day, leaving him weak and hungry until the next meal. His bread and water diet was prophetic of the famine that soon would strike the people in Jerusalem. They faced difficulties which they never imagined, and he wanted the exiles in Babylon to hear the message.

V
The Sign of the Sword
(5:1-12)

Ezekiel did not cultivate the habit of going to a barbershop. In those long-ago centuries, some prophets and priests seldom had a haircut. The Nazarites lived under a vow never to let a razor come upon their hair or beard. Interestingly, Paul wrote that nature teaches that long hair is the glory of a woman, but a disgrace for man (1 Corinthians 11:14-15).

Ezekiel had a reminder again from God that he was a mere man, that he didn't need to do any strutting, or make any pretenses. He simply had a connection with the human race. Hence, God called Ezekiel "son of man" again. In Hebrew, "son of..." means the category or class to which someone or something belongs" (Marvin Tate). Ninety-three times in Ezekiel his name appears this way. That kind of address ought to keep any person humble!

God told the prophet to take a sword and use it as a razor (5:1). Ezekiel gave himself a shave and a haircut with his sword. We can't help but wonder if his wife watched the prophet with surprise and perhaps a tinge of humor as he botched up his hair and beard! God gave Ezekiel instructions to cut his hair and beard, weigh the hair, and place it in three stacks. The symbol of dividing the hair is stated in Ezekiel 5:1-4. One-third of the people in Jerusalem would die of starvation, and one-third would die from slaughter by the sword. The final third would be scattered in the wind.

Starvation would claim one-third of the city. The Babylonian army camped around Jerusalem for about eighteen months. During that time in 587-86, the food supply within the city quickly began to diminish. Who has enough groceries in the house to last a year and a half? What grocery chain has a supply of products that could be distributed to stores for a long time? We are not usually ready for that kind of an emergency.

Starvation became rampant within the city of Jerusalem. In fact, hunger became such a problem that cannibalism soon began (5:10). Parents began roasting their children, and children began cooking and eating their parents. The event of starvation within city walls had happened once before to Israel. During the days of Elisha, the Syrians encamped around Samaria and closed the people off from the outside world. The Hebrews on the inside of the city began to die from starvation until God alleviated the problem by causing the Syrian army to flee in panic (2 Kings 7).

In the case of Jerusalem in 587 B.C., God did not remove the enemy. Babylonian forces remained camped around the city as one-third of the people on the inside died because their water and food supply ran out. Slaughter by the sword claimed one-third of the people. 2 Kings 25:21 and 2 Chronicles 36:20 give something of that terrible story of suffering and death as Babylonian swords claimed their lives.

The scattering of one-third of Jerusalem's population was demonstrated by Ezekiel as he cut his hair, picked up one stack of it, and tossed the mangled-tangled hair into the air to let the wind blow it in all directions, symbolizing the scattering of God's people. However, not all of the scattered ones died. Ezekiel placed a few strands of hair in the fold of his clothes as God had instructed him. That hair represented the remnant that would be saved. Ezekiel took a few strands of hair that represented the remnant and threw that into the fire, indicating that some who seemingly had found safety would die (5:4).

Some of this story is related in the book of Jeremiah (chapter 52). We read about King Zedekiah who escaped at night through a hole in the city wall. As the king along with his family and soldiers ran from the city, Babylonian soldiers caught them, killed the king's sons, and gouged out the eyes of Zedekiah. Then soldiers put chains on the king and took him to Babylon, where he lived in prison until his death (Jeremiah 39:1-7).

VI
Motives for Judgment
(5:13-17)

The people of Jerusalem suffered punishment that might seem cruel to a modern mind, but God had reasons for chastening His people. The basic reason the Israelites faced judgment was God's own honor and their salvation. 2 Chronicles 36:15-17 gives specific insights into why God punished the Hebrews.

1. They refused to listen to God's Word, delivered by His messengers.
2. The Israelites, despite their spiritual enlightenment, failed to live up to the higher standard to which God had called them.
3. They had defiled God's temple. Their evil sacrifices within the temple and the idols they carried into God's house brought God's wrath down upon them.
4. God had chosen His people to be "a light to the nations," but they failed to be a good witness in the countries where they had been.
5. God taught the Gentile nations that if they rejected the revelation through creation of God and His judgment, they also would be punished.
6. The LORD punished His people to show that He is Sovereign. If God judged His ancient people who failed to obey Him, what happens if we disobey?

Chapter 5

Judgment on the Mountains
Ezekiel 6:1-14

—◊◊◊—

God does not want us to miss any of the basic truths that He has for everyone, and therefore, they are emphasized several times.

Ezekiel sometimes let people hear what he said three or four times. The prophet's audience had no reason to misunderstand what he had presented. In Ezekiel chapter 6, he grabs the attention of anyone who hears or reads his message. The prophet states at least sixteen times in the book that what he is saying comes from God (1:3; 3:16; 6:1; 7:1; 11:14; 12:1, 8, 17, 21, 26; 20:2; 23:1; 33:1; 34:1; 36:16; 37:15; 38:1). Ezekiel 6:1 reads, "Now the word of the Lord came to me." We need to know that God speaks and we need to obey His words.

God told Ezekiel to set his face against the mountains of Israel and to preach against them, to give words of condemnation and judgment against Israel, wherever they might be. The immediate audience for Ezekiel's message was for the exiles in Babylon who still had too much confidence in Jerusalem. However, the message related to the entire land of Palestine. That is, the mountains, valleys, streams, and hills came under the scrutiny of God's eyes. The exiles needed to know what God was going to do.

I
Woe to the Mountains
(6:1-7)

The sacred can become scarred and tainted with sin. The beautiful can lose its luster. The holy can become vile, raw, and unholy. God's mountains that formerly reflected His sanctity became defiled by His chosen people. Three ugly human elements brought contamination to God's holy mountains. The idols, images, and incense altars took away the glory and wonder of God's creation.

Idolatry lifts its ugly head. In the book of Ezekiel, idols are mentioned about forty times (6:4; 14:6; 18:6; 20:18; 22:4; 23:49; 37:23, etc). The prophet repeatedly admonishes the people to turn from and reject idolatry. The word "idolatry" means that which is a "dung pellet" or dirty thing. "Idolatry originally meant the worship of idols, or the worship of false gods by means of idols, but came to mean among the Old Testament Hebrews any worship of false gods, whether by images or otherwise, and finally the worship of Jeh (God) through visible symbols" (ISBE, v. 3, p. 1448). Paul makes idolatry the fundamental sin in Romans chapter 1. Idolatry contaminates life, causing God to reject the idolater. Back in the time of Solomon when he married heathen wives, they turned his heart from God to idolatry (1 Kings 11:4-8). In the time of Ezekiel, all of God's people suffered untold agony because they disobeyed the command to stay away from idol worship.

The idolatry problem still hangs around and haunts us. We've made something of a "god" out of sports, income, retirement, houses, and education. And what about the idolatry problem related to the economy, military force, sexual prowess, or success at "climbing the corporate ladder?" Of course, God does not condemn people for having possessions or being successful. If that were so, then Abraham, Job, and a few other biblical people would have been in deep trouble. God does not condemn those who have houses or obtain education. The problem comes when we let anything stand between God and us. That "anything" can become an idol that replaces God.

Idolatry had already entrenched itself in the time of Ezekiel. When God gave the Ten Commandments, He spoke clearly about not having "other gods" and graven images (Exodus 20:3-4). His words rang out, "Don't make unto you any graven image...Don't bow down to them...Don't serve them." In the tabernacle and temple services, priests offered their incense to God as a "sweet-smelling savor," indicating that the lives of God's people were being given to Him. However, God's people burned incense to pagan deities, which were nothing but physical works of human hands. Perhaps some thought they would appease the false gods just in case they were wrong about the true God.

Idolatry had its roots deep in Israelite history a long time before Ezekiel. When God gave the Ten Commandments to Moses, the Hebrews at the foot of that holy mountain took their gold and silver and made an image like one of the bulls of the Canaanites (Exodus 32). Aaron offered a puny excuse when confronted by Moses, saying he didn't know what had happened. He said they threw their jewelry and gold into the fire and "out came this calf!" Who could imagine such an accident? Moses broke the calf into pieces, ground it into powder, threw it into the water, and commanded Aaron and those around him to drink it (Exodus 32:20)! Idolatry brings on cata-strophic judgment.

2 Chronicles 22 records the awful fifty-five year reign of King Manasseh in Israel (696-641 B.C.). He had the longest reign of any king, and was the most wicked of all. Judah's king led the nation in worship of idols, and child-sacrifice to pagan deities, and polluted the tribe through which the Messiah-Redeemer would come.

The people in Jerusalem took the gold and silver they had used to beautify God's house. They made images to heathen deities from those priceless treasures. They converted the mountains surrounding Jerusalem into places of idol worship in its most degraded forms. God said that He would bring a sword against the people and destroy their high places. He would make their altars desolate, break down their incense altars, cast down slain men, and scatter their corpses before their idols, leaving their bones all around the altars (6:3-5).

The exiles in Babylon needed to hear from Ezekiel that those in Jerusalem had a wholesale disregard for God and His word to them. Therefore God's prophet never "soft pedals" the judgment that the people face because of their idolatry and immoral living. Ezekiel speaks in chapter 6 what the exiles needed to hear about those in Jerusalem who had an abhorrent disregard of God's commands. They practiced their idolatry, disregarding all warnings about disaster that would come to them. Even though they hear that their dwelling places and cities are going to be made desolate and lie in ruins, they never seem to have a letup in their treks to pagan altars. God said that He would cut down the incense altars to pagan deities and abolish their work as the slain would fall in their midst. The purpose in such judgment, Ezekiel says, is that the people might know that the LORD is God. In fact, four times in chapter 6, this expression about the LORD as Sovereign is given (6:7, 10, 13, 14).

God told His people when they began life in Palestine not to touch the idolatrous stuff all around them. We need to hear that same message again. First John 5:21 states, "Little children, keep yourselves from idols. A-men." If we fail to obey that commandment, we desecrate God's sacred property.

II
A Remnant Remembered in the Midst of Judgment
(6:8-12)

Even when God's swift hand of judgment is about to fall upon Jerusalem as Ezekiel continues to declare, God gives a flicker of hope for the salvation of His people. God speaks through His prophet that in the midst of the time when the sword falls in judgment, He is going to save a remnant. The Lord says, "Yet I will leave a remnant, so that you may have some who escape the sword among the nations, when you are scattered through the countries" (6:8). God said He would spare some from among the scattered. Out of the midst of those who perished from being slashed with the sword, famished for lack of food, and died from disease and pestilence, God reached out to a remnant who would be purged and purified through the fires of judgment and made "pure gold." God would not and could not be defeated, and He would begin again.

The scattered remnant would remember the Lord (6:8). Even as Ezekiel and other exiles could not forget God, even so the ones who are going to miraculously escape death during the fall of Jerusalem, would become a part of the remnant. They would be taken into strange lands, but there they would remember God. Deuteronomy 30 prophetically states that God's people would worship pagan gods and because of their unfaithfulness God would "scatter-banish" them among the nations, but then the remnant would return to the Lord, and He would bring them back from captivity, showing compassion for them (Deuteronomy 30:1-6). In Deuteronomy 4:30-31 Moses spoke to the Israelites who soon would enter the Promised Land. He said to them that in "latter days" after they had been scattered because of their transgressions that they would turn to God in their distress and God would not forget His covenant with them. Indeed, the remnant would remember God. They would recall His judgment, but they would know His incredible grace.

Yes, the remnant would also remember that they broke the heart of God through their unfaithfulness (6:9). Ezekiel's word to the exiles may have been a surprise to them. They as well as the people back in Jerusalem may have realized at times that they hurt themselves and hurt one another by their wrong doing. But most probably never realized before that God had felt pain, agony, and "crushing" by His people. His people whom He had created, called, protected, and saved from awful enemies – they needed to know that their sin was bringing deep wounds to the LORD. He says, "I had a broken heart because of their adulterous heart which was faithless to Me" (v. 9). Does God still feel pain when His people wander away and become unfaithful to Him? If so, His times of grief must be enough to awaken every serious-minded believer that it's time for all of us to love Him with all our being, and rip out any part of an adulterous heart from ourselves.

Jesus talked to Scribes, Pharisees, and Sadduccees in Jerusalem one day. He wept, saying that He would have gathered the people together as a hen does her chicks when danger comes, but His people refused to respond (Matthew 23:37). Their house was left desolate because they rejected Him. We need to remember that sin brings grief to God.

The Israelites see themselves as they've never imagined before. The text reads, "And they shall loathe themselves for the evils which they have committed in all their abominations" (Ezekiel 6:9). Two words should be noted: "evils" and "abominations." God's diagnosis of one's wrong runs like a research team's analysis. God's people commit evils. They're guilty of abominations. If repentance takes place, the guilty "loathe themselves." They hate themselves for their evil deeds. They change and go in a new direction when they repent. The person who repents charts a new course through God's help. Should a lot of self-loathing take place among God's people today?

We ought to loathe ourselves because our hearts do not stay fixed on God. The first and greatest commandment is to love the LORD with all your heart, mind, soul, and strength (Deuteronomy 6:5). Where is our first love? If it's not God, then we need to put on "sackcloth and ashes." We need repentance, revival, and a return to God.

We ought to loathe ourselves because of lustful eyes. God said that with their eyes they played the harlot after their idols (6:9). We once had a dog named Ted. He was a super rabbit-dog. When Ted chased a rabbit that ran into a hollow log, the furry animal would be out of the dog's reach. Ted would run around the fallen tree, scratch in the dirt, and chew on the log, trying to reach his prey.

Ezekiel wrote of God's people who had an insatiable lust for the forbidden. But now those scattered among the countries would "loathe themselves for the evils they committed in all their abominations" (6:9). They let idols take the place of the living God, but now the story changes. They put away their idolatrous and abominable deeds and followed the LORD.

Today we need automobiles and airplanes for transportation. We need jobs in order to sustain our families and ourselves. Nothing is wrong with material goods. God says, however, that when we let "things" replace Him that we are becoming idol permeated people. God wants our allegiance. Are we giving Him first place in life? If not, calamity may fall upon us as it did God's ancient people (6:10).

III
The Mountains Hear a Declaration
(6:11-14)

A threefold distress call sounds again: sword, famine, and pestilence. The Israelites could not miss the message of Ezekiel 6:11. God tells Ezekiel to smite with his hand and stamp (stomp) with his feet. We can almost see the prophet as he slaps his hands together and pounds the ground with his feet, shouting, "Listen! Destruction knocks at your door! See what is happening. God is stretching out His hand against all who are guilty. Your abominations cannot be tolerated anymore" (6:11).

Again Ezekiel declared that the sword, the famine, and the pestilence will come upon the sinful people (6:11-12). God says, "Thus will I spend My fury upon them" (v. 12). The holy anger and intense punishment would land upon His people because of their transgressions. When God turns His fury loose on His people, they will realize that He is the LORD (v. 13). The idolaters are going to be dead among their idols, and their carcasses will pollute their false gods. On top of the mountains and on every high hill the slain will be scattered. Beneath the green trees and under the once-beautiful oaks where incense floated up to dead idols, the bones of the dead worshipers will be scattered (6:13). Judgment will come from one end of the land to the other (v. 13). The day of judgment will come to all who put God out of life. God's well-inscribed phrase that flashes across the Book of Ezekiel ninety-three times appears again, "You shall know that I am the LORD" (Ezekiel 6:7). What response are we making to God's words of warning?

Chapter 6

Doomsday Has Dawned
Ezekiel 7:1-27

—⟋ⱳ⟍—

In bygone years men in small rowboats traveled up and down the Niagara River. Some who loved to go on sightseeing trips would row downstream and get as close as possible to the Niagara Falls. A few have gone over the Falls because they could not turn their boats around. Someone placed a sign along the banks of the river that read, "Beyond the Point of No Return." The men in rowboats who passed that point had little chance of avoiding disaster.

Warning after warning had been given to the Israelites about a day of reckoning. In the country of Babylon, Ezekiel told the exiles that God's people had failed to heed the warning of repentance. Finally, the Hebrews by-passed the "point of no return." The Babylonian army stormed into their holy city and would not be denied victory. Doomsday dawned for the stubborn sinners. Chapter 7 is largely a poetic account of impending disaster. God's people faced divine judgment.

I
No Hiding Place
(7:1-2)

God's message about the end of all things for Jerusalem flashed loud and clear across the ancient Hebrew sky. God declared, "The end has come" (v. 2). These simple words speak of the present time, meaning that the end time has started. It had not culminated as Ezekiel wrote, but the process had begun. Three times in Ezekiel 7:6 the message rings out, "An end has come. The end has come…Behold, it has come." Ezekiel gives that message thirteen times in the seventh chapter. Time has run out.

A compass has four cardinal points — north, east, south, and west. The word from God in verse two reads, "The end has come upon the four corners of the land." No one could find a hiding place from danger. Death lurked in every direction.

A few centuries before the time of Ezekiel, Moses had written, "The eternal God is your refuge, and underneath are the everlasting arms" (Deuteronomy 33:27). The "sons of Jacob experienced God's protection as they left Egypt after centuries of slavery. The desert air turned cold as they camped out at night. God's "pillar of fire" overshadowed them after sundown each day and that fiery pillar provided warmth and light for their wellbeing. When the heat would have started beating upon them during the day, God stepped in with His "glory cloud" and did not allow the sunrays to scorch or suffocate them. God was their certain refuge.

When the Hebrews settled in the "Promised Land," God gave them six cities of refuge to which a sinner might flee to save his life (Numbers 35, 1 Chronicles 6:57, 67). David wrote in Psalms 46:1 that "God is our refuge and strength, a very present help in trouble." Psalm 104:18 states that God provides the high hills for wild goats. Some time later Isaiah wrote that God is our refuge when storms beat upon us (25:4). We, like the ancient exiles, have found God to be our eternal refuge.

The Israelites in Ezekiel's day knew about those past times when God had been goodness to them. The story then took a quick turn, because they did not find God as their refuge as in former times. Isaiah had written about those who "made lies their refuge" (28:15). He said the hail had swept away their refuge of falsehood (v. 27).

God had pleaded with His people to let Him be their refuge. He sent His prophets who faithfully proclaimed His message. The rebellious, "stiff necked" people continued to go their own way. Finally, the death knell sounded and doomsday came, or would come. No one had a place to hide. The "four corners" of the country had been marked for destruction, and no one could find shelter from God's fury. The end had come. They could not find a place to hide from the Babylonians.

II
Bad Conduct Medals
(7:3-10)

Let's take a ride on the wings of poetic imagination, as we consider the degenerated lifestyle of the people addressed by Ezekiel. God declared that He would judge them according to their ways and reward them for their abominations (v. 3). The word "abomination" appears forty-eight times in the book of Ezekiel, clearly describing the Israelite lifestyle at that time as detestable to God (5:9; 33:29).

Webster's dictionary defines abomination as that which is disgusting, disagreeable, and unpleasant. The way the Israelites lived and treated one another caused God to say that they had become an abomination. Their conduct became reprehensible. None that fell under condemnation wore medals of honor; rather, their lives had become smeared, scarred, and tarnished because they turned from God to idolatry and immorality.

When our daughter was eight years of age, she said to her mother one day, "Mom, why is it that the more I pray for you and dad, the worse you two become!" The Israelites became worse, no matter how much the true prophets preached to them, and they deserved "bad conduct medals." They defiled God's sanctuary with their idols and images (5:11). Solomon's temple became defiled with raw paganism and despicable acts. Despite all the praying for the ancient people of God, they became worse.

Elijah faced four hundred fifty prophets of Baal on Mount Carmel (1 Kings 18). Those false prophets had a chance to have Baal answer their prayers. They prayed for hours. They screamed and cut themselves and made all kinds of contortions to persuade their pagan god to answer. No luck. Baal never answered their prayers, and Elijah mocked them for serving a god who could not respond. Elijah took his turn to prove that Yahweh was and is the true and living God.

That prophet built an altar and dug a trench around it. After he placed a sacrifice upon the altar, he called for several barrels of water to be poured upon the sacrifice. Water filled the encircling trenches after the sacrifice and altar became soaked. Elijah knelt before that altar and called upon God to consume the sacrifice that he had placed there, and God answered by fire. The sacrifice, water, and altar disappeared under the awesome power of God. The Baal worshipers met their doom as Elijah prayed and proved that the Lord is God (See: Isaiah 44; 46; Jeremiah 10).

Soon after Elijah's ministry came to a close, the Israelites returned to their heathen gods. Two centuries after Elijah, worship of Baal started again along with the god Ashtoreth (2 Kings 23:13). Then a new pagan deity named Tammuz crept into their perverted worship (Ezekiel 8:14). They could not keep their hands off pagan idols and images. Incense burning to those deities increased like mesquite trees in Mexico. The Hebrews became addicted to a life of immorality. Jump ahead in the writing of Ezekiel to chapter 16 of his book. The prophet said that God's people had increased and multiplied their acts of fornication, even unto pagan lands (16:28-31). More than a century before, the sins of Israel brought God's wrath upon their heads, and He let Assyria take them captive. In that pagan country, the northern tribes joined those of Nineveh in their sins. Judah sinned in Babylon, just as Israel did in Assyria.

Look at today's world. Walk into grocery stores and service stations and one sees ugly, sexually explicit magazines. Television and radio have become corrupt with scene after scene of that which is reprehensible. Immorality is not an innovation of our times. It's as old as the forbidden fruit on the tree in the Garden of Eden. People of every age deserve "bad conduct medals" because of immorality and idolatry.

The book of Numbers has frightful scenes of sin. In chapter 25:1-9 a story appears about idolatrous and immoral acts of the people during their wilderness wanderings. God sent a plague among them because of their sin. God's fury came down, causing twenty four thousand to die. Moses never had a long line of Hebrews waiting for "Good Conduct Medals" as he led them toward the Promised

Land. Ezekiel never celebrated high spiritual hours by presenting good conduct medals to God's people.

God declared a Day of Doom for His rebellious people. He said that He would judge and recompense them according to their ways and abominations. Some exiles surely must have trembled as they heard Ezekiel tell about God's judgment. God's word reminded them that doomsday was at hand to teach them the unchanging lesson: "You shall know that I am the Lord who smites" (7:4, 9).

III
The Flea Market Fiasco
(7:12-13)

Practically everyone knows about flea markets. That business got its name when a few people first started a market for old sofas and chairs. Dogs and cats had been sleeping on them and, consequently, buyers took home flea-infested furniture. The largest flea market in the USA is located in Canton, Texas (near Dallas). Hundreds of vendors stalk around that place on the first Monday of every month, selling everything from rusty nails to antique furniture. That "trades day" has been expanded to include five days during the first week of the month.

Let's make a "poetic prance" and imagine that Jerusalem had the original flea market. The sound of soldiers at the city walls gave the Jerusalemites a new fervor for sales. Everyone wanted to get rid of everything old and new. Invasion was about to happen and they had to leave everything behind. Sellers held up any stuff that would sell fast. The first bidder would get the product. The owner had no time to waste. Take it and run! And yet, everyone faced two problems at that "flea market."

The ones who sold their goods didn't have any place to stash away the cash. If they sold their furniture, they didn't know what to do with the money. If they sold their land, they would not be able to return and reclaim the property in "the year of jubilee." The stock market had crashed, and banks had closed. Safety boxes were not secure, and money was worthless. The seller stewed in his self-made dilemma.

The ones who bought goods did not have a place to put them. Their houses would soon be occupied by foreign troops, and all goods left behind would go to the invaders. They could not put their purchases on wagons and get out of town because soldiers blocked all highways leading out of the city. The buyer could not rejoice because of a bargain he had found, and it was too late for the seller to cry (7:12). Divine wrath fell upon the whole multitude. The flea market became a failure. When doomsday arrives, all selling and buying stops.

IV
Military Reserves Refuse to Respond
(7:14-17)

Who wants to fight a superpower when one has to meet the enemy with his bare hands? Who would face an enemy with their military might when God says they are His weapons to chasten His people? The exiles heard the message from Ezekiel that "the end has come." If those in Jerusalem heard any part of Ezekiel's final warning about the day of doom, why would they want to fight? The reaction of "we can't fight" permeated panic-stricken Jerusalem as pestilence and famine devoured those within and the sword dealt death to those who dared leave the city (Jeremiah 39).

Ezekiel 7:14-16 tells of those who refuse to heed the sound of the trumpet and go to war. An army can never call itself an army if it has troops that refuse to gather and refuse to fight. Countless Israelites died within the city of Jerusalem from the sword, pestilence, and famine. Those who escaped death languished on the mountains and in the valleys. Their very existence reminded one of doves with their lonely, mournful sounds. The escapees mourned over their own iniquities (7:16). They didn't have strength to defend anyone against the enemy.

Mark Eckhardt played the trumpet in a church where I served, and he's terrific with that instrument, too. The people in Jerusalem needed Mr. Eckhardt in the days of Ezekiel. They didn't have anyone who had enough pulmonary power to get the sound waves moving out of their houses and across town. No wonder the reservists didn't rush into Jerusalem's "induction centers." They didn't hear the bugle sounds, and if they had, they would not have responded.

Weak hands can't handle battle weapons. Ezekiel 7:17 states that all hands will grow feeble. Why weak hands? The men had been working in fields, carpenter shops, and on top of mountains as they made their idols and images from gold and silver taken from the temple. Could women help defend the city? Most likely they had strong hands from having worked in their houses and from having assisted their husbands in their work. But the scene would drastically change as enemies would surround their city. Food supplies would vanish as fast as snow melts on a hot, summer day. The one-time strong hands would tremble as the "cry to arms" is sounded. No one can go to battle when hands can't hold a bow and arrow, or lift a sword from a scabbard.

A group of soldiers can never be counted on as a fighting force if their knees buckle under fear and their feet refuse to march. When "knees are as weak as water," the military possibilities are depleted (7:17). Soldiers who are filled with fear and are shaking in their boots are not in military-preparedness units. The trumpet may sound, but for those with weak knees, it's time for flight, not fight. Not one soldier answered the muster call. If any response to the bugle sound was made, it was to quickly put their hands to their ears and not hear.

V

Too Late for Sackcloth and Ashes
(7:18-22)

God's people remembered in earlier years that He had saved Nineveh, the capital city of Assyria. Jonah did not want to go to there, but God forced him to go. That prophet didn't want to see God showing mercy to the enemies of his own nation. Jonah preached in the streets of Nineveh for forty days and nights. He had one "walk-athon sermon" that he delivered over and over again. Without any love in his heart, he shouted to the people that within forty days God would destroy them. But everyone from the king to the beggar put on sackcloth and ashes and repented, and God spared them. The people knew that "a prophet had been among them." Never before had an entire city turned its face to God, and everyone experienced reformation and put themselves at the mercy of God..

In one desperate move, Jerusalem put on a "show of repentance," but they would not give the Lord the opportunity to turn away from judgment. They dressed in sackcloth as the Ninevites had done, but with unchanged attitudes toward God and His prophets. The citizens of Judah's capital girded themselves with rough clothes and perhaps cast ashes upon their heads, but sackcloth would not help. They had trifled with God too long without any evidence of repentance, and only had regrets over their personal losses. They had cast God aside and let idols, images, and incense to pagan deities become their first love. Doomsday had come and a detour around that danger could not be found. They had become spiritually bankrupt, and hope had gone.

Perhaps they remembered Jeremiah. Oh yes, that prophet had said that a day would come when Babylon would trample to pieces the city of Jerusalem. They remembered how some had mocked that prophet. King Jehoiakim had allowed Jeremiah to be thrown into a cistern filled with mud and water. Ebed-Melech plea-bargained with the king to let him pull the prophet out of the place of certain death. The king sat before a warm fire in his palace as Jeremiah huddled in a cold corner of a jail after his rescue from the muddy cistern. Since no one would hear Jeremiah preach, Baruch wrote the prophet's sermons (36:4, 27, 32; 51:60). Someone found Jeremiah's scroll and took it to the king. After Jehoiakim read a few lines from the long scroll, he cut it into shreds. As the king sat before a roaring fire on that winter day, he threw the shredded document into the fire. With frenzied glee, the wicked king sat and watched the writing burn (36:29).

Ezekiel had lived among the people in Jerusalem until 597 when Nebuchadnezzar took him and the best people of Jerusalem into captivity. When Ezekiel preached in Babylon, his fellow exiles didn't like his messages. They looked upon him as something of a clown. After all, who wants a preacher around who warns of judgment and the wrath of God? They said "No" to Ezekiel as they had said "No" to Jeremiah.

"Spiritually bankrupt"— those two words describe God's people in Jerusalem and in Babylon during the days of Ezekiel, Jeremiah, and Daniel. God had poured out upon His people countless blessings, but they had turned their backs upon God. They had plenty of material possessions, but their spiritual treasures had long since been depleted. A frightening time came. The enemy camped around Jerusalem, and the sword, pestilence, and famine ravaged the people inside the walls (7:15). Everyone wanted to run. What could they do with their gold and silver and other treasures, except fling them into the streets (7:7-9)?

Ride down the trail of years to modern history. A display in a museum in Deadwood, South Dakota, includes an inscription scrawled many years ago by a horrified gold prospector. The inscription reads, "I lost my gun. I lost my horse. I am out of food. The Indians are after me. But I've got all the gold I can carry."

In 1847 the steamship Washington was the pride and joy of her manufacturers. Soon it would be in a race with Britain's Britannia, but would lose. One day as the steamship was moving down the Potomac, the fire alarm sounded about a fire that had started in the engine room. One man ran to his cabin, quickly opened a trunk and loaded his pockets with gold and other coins that he had stored for safekeeping. He jumped overboard to escape from what he thought was going to be a burning ship. The weight from the coins that he had crammed in his pockets carried him to the bottom of the river and he lost his life. When the end comes, what will we do with the stuff we have grabbed for ourselves?

When the Israelites in Jerusalem with all their cache of gold and silver saw the dawning of doom, panic and pandemonium broke out in every place. They had "all the gold they could carry," but had no place to run. They cast their silver and gold in the streets and kissed it all good-bye (7:19). Material wealth would not do any good when death stared them in the face.

VI
An Endless Chain Gang
(7:23)

The Israelites would soon learn about a chain being prepared for their enslavement (Ezekiel 7:23). Sooner than they could realize, the Babylonians would have thousands of them in chains on a march of seven hundred miles back to the country between the Tigris and Euphrates rivers. The foreign army would take with them "their silver and their gold" (7:19). The beauty of their ornaments would be tarnished by the Babylonians (v. 20). All the treasures of Jerusalem would become as "prey and spoil" for the strangers who had descended upon their land. God said that He would bring "the worst of the heathen" who would occupy their houses, burst their bubbles of pride, and defile the holy places (v. 24).

The price of sin is a chain gang. God's people had become guilty of bloody crimes and violence (v. 24). The prophets for years had warned the people over and over again about judgment for their robberies, pillage, murder, and rape. From north to south, the waves of evil continued to roll. God's chosen people had cast out God's commandments and built a hedonistic society. They lived in a post prophets-of-God climate. They built for themselves bigger and better barns so that they might say, "Soul, you have much goods laid up for you. Eat, drink, and be merry." They refused to believe that "whatever a man sows, that shall he also reap" (Galatians 6:7). They had sowed the wind and now reaped the whirlwind (Hosea 8:7). Doomsday would not be denied.

King Zedekiah rebelled and Nebuchadnezzar caught him and his sons as they tried to escape one night through a hole in the walls of Jerusalem. The Babylonians killed Zedekiah's sons in his presence, and then put out the eyes of the king (Jeremiah 39:7). For weeks he would hear the rattle of the chains on his arms as the foreign forces shuttled him across hundreds of miles to Babylon.

The price of sin is "no peace" (7:25). God had said earlier, through His prophet Isaiah, "there is no peace to the wicked" (48:22). The Hebrews had heard those words in the temple and from the tops of tall mountains and in the deepest valleys. Prophet after prophet had reminded them of a false peace and false security. They had "ears to hear, and did not hear." They would not accept God's message. They had their own philosophies, their own standards. They reenacted the scene of their own history's "Dark Ages" when "everyone did that which was right in his own eyes" (Judges 21:25). Yes, "the end is come." Ezekiel stated those words thirteen times in this chapter!

VII
Don't Gamble on an Empty Religion
(7:24-26)

Noah, Moses, Abraham, David, Isaiah, Daniel, Jeremiah, and Ezekiel had shown God's people "the real thing." The Hebrews knew about "pure religion that is undefiled before God and the Father" (James 1:27), but they did not practice it. They walked their own way.

They wanted to receive encouraging words from Israel's fake or false prophets who had told them that Jerusalem would not be destroyed, but those prophets had no "vision" to give them. Any message they might give would be only a repetition of the vain, useless words expressed before (7:26). When the Israelites rejected God's word and His true messengers, they had a religion that was as lifeless as the mummified kings in Egypt's pyramids.

Let the powerless priests step forward and give counsel to the people. They had failed to be true to God, and most of them undoubtedly failed to have an effective teaching ministry. Ezekiel 7:26 states, "The law shall perish from the priest." The priests had not pointed to the Ten Commandments (Exodus 20). They didn't teach children to honor their parents nor the parents to teach their children. The truths about honesty and integrity had been overshadowed with theft, murder, and pillage. Jeremiah wrote that the priests practiced deceit and became greedy for gain (6:13; 8:10). Priests with their empty religion couldn't help anyone.

Let the elders who had been counseling people during heartbreak times be a spiritual resource in the day of calamity. But counsel from those older ones had failed, because they had been unfaithful for decades. The Israelites had been counting on an empty, dead religion, but it failed them.

If we take another scenario and look at faithful prophets, priests, and elders, we learn that God would not give those like Jeremiah and Ezekiel fresh visions and encouraging messages for the Israelites who had trifled with God too long. God's people had "sinned away their day of grace." They had waited too long to call upon God. Doomsday had dawned!

VIII
Politicians Become Paralyzed
(7:27)

If the enemy surrounds Jerusalem with its destructive power, the people want to call on the politicians who make promises of a utopian future. God says, "Go ahead and call on them. They are going to fail you too!"

Call up the king (7:27). After all, he is the one chosen by God, and the people bow before him. He has a retinue of servants. He has banquet tables laden with food. He has connections with other nations. Let's shout, "God save the king!" But look at poor King Zedekiah a short time later. His sons have been slain before him and the soldiers gouged out the king's eyes. The thirty-two year-old king weeps as he stumbles and falls on his way to Babylon. That chief of politicians can't help.

Call up the princes. Can those who pranced and danced in the court of the king help? History provides the names of a few of them, but they're as desolate and powerless as the king who staggers and stumbles in a long chain gang.

Call up the people who have been subservient to the wishes of the king and princes. All of "the hands of the people of the land" are troubled (v. 27). They have no security. The "whole multitude" is helpless because the enemy has come. God has put an end to His wayward, abominable people. Doomsday has dawned!

As the Israelites faced doom, they must have asked themselves over and over again, "What's wrong with the LORD?" Quickly and nervously as the thunderous thuds of the enemy's battering rams continue pounding away on the walls of Jerusalem, someone could have read from a scroll written by Moses that states that God is merciful, gracious, and long-suffering (Exodus 34:6-7). Another could have shouted, "Micah 7:18 says that God delights in mercy." Others then might have thought, "Yes, but Micah 3:12 declares that 'Jerusalem shall become heaps'."

Israel knew that unfaithfulness to God would bring on punishment, but they kept on with their transgressions despite all warnings. In essence Ezekiel said, "Let's get to the point: Doomsday is here so that everyone might know that He is the Lord (7:27). This message about God's sovereignty is sounded sixty-five times in Ezekiel's book. God's ancient people learned the lesson of judgment too late. What about us?

Chapter 7

Abominable Portraits
Ezekiel 8:1-9:11

—⟋⟋—

S ome people suffer "shell shock" when they shop at grocery stores. The price of goods does not cause as much perplexity as the display of reading material at the checkout counters. Unfortunately, a lot of magazines have become sordid and pornographic. You may feel that you need a spiritual bath or a confessional booth after you've waited in line for a few minutes to pay a bill. We have to look in other directions or close our eyes to avoid seeing things which should make any person blush.

The Israelites kept splashing around in pools of iniquity during the time of the prophets. Six hundred years before Christ, Jeremiah and Ezekiel tried to persuade them to turn from their abominations, but without success. In 591 B.C. some elders visited Ezekiel in his home (8:1). As the group sat before the prophet, God's "hand" came upon him. At that time in "visions of God," he saw the likeness of a man who had the appearance of fire. The heavenly visitor had a fiery glow from his waist down. From the loins or waist upward, the appearance seemed to be bright brass or the color of amber.

The special agent of God put forth his hand and symbolically took Ezekiel by the hair of the head, lifted him up between heaven and earth, and carried him to Jerusalem. In his vision Ezekiel saw the bad behavior of those in Jerusalem. He used the words "abomination" and "abominable" at least fifty times in describing the conduct of the people (examples: Ezekiel 4:14; 5:9; 8:10; 33:29). The Hebrew root for abomination means "to be filthy, to loathe, to abhor." Again, "abomination is used to describe specific forms of idolatrous worship that were specially abhorrent" (ISBE, v. 1, p. 16). Thus, that which is abominable is repulsive and detestable. It is an evil thing of such character that it needs to be totally rejected. Ezekiel described the behavior of Israel and Judah as "abominable." Look at some portraits of abominations practiced by some Israelites.

I
The Portrayal of the "Image of Jealousy"
(8:1-6)

The text in 8:3 refers to "an image of jealousy" in the inner court of the temple. The image or idol possibly was one of the Canaanite goddesses, Ashtoreth. Soon after the death of Joshua, the Israelites began to follow Ashtoreth and her male counterpart, Baal. (ISBE, v. 1, p. 271).

King Manasseh of Judah (697-642 B.C.) imported foreign gods, idols, wizards, and sun worship. (See 2 Chronicles 33:7; 1 Kings 11:5, 33; 2 Kings 21:7; 23:13, etc.). Josiah (639-609 B.C.) had a religious reformation, and during his reign he destroyed all the graven images, idols, groves, and cast out many of the false prophets. However, soon after his death, God's people started their idolatrous practices again.

When God gave Ezekiel a vision of the "image of jealousy," he saw false religion in full bloom. Ashtoreth had the name "the image of jealousy" because its presence in God's house caused the Lord to be jealous. Several reasons may be given for God's righteous jealousy.

One, God redeemed His own people and had blessed them across the centuries from the call of Abraham to that moment. Two, the Israelites robbed God of the worship due Him as they worshiped the pagan idol. Three, the idol was placed in the entrance to God's House where everyone could see it as they entered and left the temple area. Four, the people worshipped the idol without shame and looked upon it as their own god. It may be true that a few Israelites identified Ashtoreth with the Lord, probably as His consort. Five, Ashtoreth was not far from the altar of sacrifice that should have reminded the Israelites that God made forgiveness of sins possible. Six, God refuses to reveal His glory if an idol takes His place.

Ezekiel suffered shell shock like a soldier might experience during a battle. He could hardly believe what he was seeing in the vision. God said to the prophet, "Son of man, wait a minute! I want to show you greater abominations than the one you have just looked upon" (8:6). The drama continues. But first, what can we say about that kind of deviate worship? Let's give ourselves a test.

Consider the idol of pleasure. What replaces God from His central place in our lives? Do we love pleasure more than we love God? What about sports? Which comes first, God or the number one sport or diversion in our lives?

Look at the idol of possessions. We need houses, food, and clothes. However, if things push God out of life, idolatry takes place. Jesus told the story of a man who had a big harvest. He said that he would build bigger barns and enjoy all the things he had. But he left God out of his life and the man's death came soon (Luke 12). Think about the idols of projects. God is in the center of what we do, or we exclude Him from life. The Bible states, "Little children, keep yourselves from idols. A-men" (1 John 5:21). Do we have an "image of jealousy" in our lives?

II
The Portrayal of Animal Worship
(8:7-13)

As Ezekiel symbolically stood in the temple's courtyard, he saw a hole in the wall and was told to dig into the wall and make the hole larger (v. 8). Then he moved through the hole into a room where he saw other "wicked abominations."

The walls were covered with portraits of ugly beasts and repulsive creeping creatures. The gods of Egypt had been taken into the secret chambers by the leaders of Judah. Every form of creeping thing may have included bugs, lizards, rats, and snakes. Israel had made an Egyptian or Caananite calf idol while God was giving Moses the Ten Commandments (Exodus 32). Seventy elders or leaders had gone to the foot of Mount Sinai when Moses met God on top of the mountain (Exodus 24:1). They saw the mountain blazing with the glory of God. However, Ezekiel saw seventy elders standing in God's house and worshiping before creeping things and abominable animals.

When the Tabernacle in the wilderness was built, twelve golden spoons or saucers full of incense were used during its dedication (Numbers 7:86). The spoons filled with incense represented the twelve tribes of Israel. The priests in the Holy Place offered up incense to God. The elders were not priests and they did not have the right to be performing priestly duties. In the worship rituals, God's priests from the tribe of Levi had censers filled with incense or sweet smelling perfume. They put the perfume into a shovel-like instrument and placed the incense on coals of fire on a golden altar. The smell of the incense rose up to God as a sweet-smelling odor, representing the prayers of God's people (Exodus 25:6; 31; Numbers 7: 16; Revelation 8:3-4). David wrote in Psalm 141:2, "Let my prayer before you be as incense; and the lifting up of my hands as the evening sacrifice." God had joy as His people worshiped and talked to Him in prayer. However, the elders had diverted the prayers away from the Creator to abominable creatures. They had gone "a whoring after other gods" (Ezekiel 6:9; 23:30).

Shaphan, the scribe, was with Josiah when he destroyed the idols in Israel. He celebrated when the worship of Jehovah was being purified. In his vision Ezekiel saw Shaphan's son, Jaazaniah, among those who worshiped the detestable creatures from a pagan world (8:11). Instead of incense being offered to God, the elders took on the role of priests and offered incense to the "abominable creeping things." A "thick cloud" from the sweet-smelling incense trickled up to the noses of the abominable creeping things that became gods for the seventy who secretly worshiped in their dark chambers (8:11).

The sinful Hebrews found excuses for their wrongdoing. They worshiped the abominable creatures in private chambers, where they thought God would not see them (8:12). In the first place, they forgot that God sees everything. We can't make enough secret chambers to keep God from seeing us (Psalm 139). Hebrews 4:13 states that everything is open to the eyes of God. He sees everything that takes place on planet earth and across His universe. We can't hide anything from God, no matter how hard we try.

In the second place, the elders said, "The Lord does not see us, the Lord has forsaken the land" (8:12). They had forsaken God, but God had not left His creation. His revealed glory would depart, but He still would be present, invisible to human eyes. We need to put the word "omnipresence" in our vocabulary. We can't escape the presence of God. The seventy elders could not hide from God by getting in a dark chamber; neither can we escape His presence (Psalm 139). Any philosophy is false that says, "Let's do what we want to do because God doesn't see and He does not know." Scene three opens.

III
A Portrayal of Women Weeping for Tammuz
(8:14-15)

God's special agent took Ezekiel in the vision to the north gate of the temple. At that place, the prophet saw women as they sat in grief and mourning. They may have been screaming, lifting their hands in despair, and expressing agony in other ways. Death had come to their god Tammuz, and they wept in desperation for one week as they "funeralized" the deceased god.

The Bible's only reference to Tammuz is in Ezekiel 8:14. Originally, he was the Babylonian sun god who warmed the earth and gave fertility. Tammuz was the husband of Ishtar (Aphrodite of the Greeks). He supposedly caused everything to be productive from plants and animals to human beings. However, during the hot days of summer when vegetation started to wilt, Tammuz lost his vigor and died, too. He departed to the nether world until the end of the winter season and returned in the spring. Tammuz left for six months, and the women wept because of his departure. Then the spring of each year became a time of celebration with the return of Tammuz. All kinds of orgies took place among the Babylonians and Phoenicians. The Israelites who had adopted this god also celebrated with wild parties. With unlicensed conduct, immorality flourished as they followed the pagan deity.

Another shocking truth about God's people is that they worshipped Tammuz in the temple. God's house became a house of religious prostitution for the Israelites. God called their way of life abominable because that's how they treated the place where His glory dwelled. Stop and ponder the wicked behavior of God's people in His house! The word "abomination" appears six times in chapter 8 of Ezekiel to highlight the deplorable conduct of God's own people. One more scene appears.

IV
A Portrayal of Sun-Worshiping Priests (8:16-18)

The angel gave Ezekiel more tour-time through God's house. After what he saw, perhaps God's prophet wanted to spend the rest of his life in Babylon. However, another scene of the unfolding drama of degradation awaited him. Ezekiel must have wondered if anything worse could be seen when a voice said that he would see "greater abominations" (v. 15). More words sounded in the prophet's ears, "Yes, Ezekiel, let's take another look." About twenty-five men stood at the entrance to the temple. We do not know who those men were, but they could have been priests. Twenty four courses or groups of priests served in the temple. Each course would serve a certain length of time, and then go home and be replaced by another group. The twenty-five priests (?) in the vision might have included the High Priest. Thus, most all priests would have been represented.

The men stood "between the porch and the altar." Thus, they had their backs turned away from the altar of sacrifice, and they looked toward the sun rising in the east. Their eastern gaze indicated that they had turned away from God. They worshiped the sun instead of the living Lord and God.

Let's step back in Hebrew history to the time of King Manasseh. 2 Kings 23 recounts the horror of what had taken place in God's house before the reformation under King Josiah. Look at a partial list of abominable acts that the Hebrews had been carrying on in God's house. They burned incense to Baal, to the sun, moon, planets, and all the host of heaven. They had placed "groves" for immoral worship in the temple area. Adjoining the temple they had houses for sodomites (2 Kings 23:7). A place for child sacrifices had been a part of their rituals. King Manasseh had placed altars for pagan worship and immoral acts in both courtyards of the temple. Josiah broke the backs of those corrupt, abominable acts. But that good king died in 609 B.C. Faster than words can tell the story, the Israelites returned to the maniacal madness of Manasseh.

In his visions, Ezekiel witnessed a renewed performance of the wicked abominations by God's people. The priests who handled the sacred had turned away from God and had beccme corrupt. They worshipped the creation instead of the Creator, and they forfeited all rights to be God's servants. God asked Ezekiel a question that could have been an exclamation mark. God asked, "Have you seen this, O son of man?"

Another question fell upon the prophet's ears, "Is it a light thing to the house of Judah that they commit the abominations which they commit here?" (Ezekiel 8:17). A "light thing" would mean something that has no importance, no significance. But when God's people forsake Him and go the route of abominations in His house, the entire affair has become a spiritual tragedy. When people turn away from God, they keep doing wrong. The result of not following God is that of filling the land with violence (v. 17).

An added word about the conduct of the priests is alarming, too. They "put the branch to their nose" (v. 17). This may reflect the practice of Babylonian sun worshippers with the strange ritual in which they held a twig or a small plant to their noses to filter out any unclean breath they might exhale in order not to contaminate their sun god. If so, The Yahweh (Lord) worshipers were performing a ritual of the ancient Babylonian sun worshipers. On the other hand, it may mean something like "thumbing the nose" at God, as an expression of contempt for Him (Cooper, p. 124; Taylor, p. 100). In summary, as the Israelites performed the ritual of ancient sun worshippers, they insulted God by their idolatry.

A warning is given before judgment falls upon Jerusalem. God said in Ezekiel 8:18 that He planned to turn His fury loose on His people. He said that He would not spare any of the guilty sinners, nor show pity on them. Even if they cried with a loud voice, He would refuse to hear.

V
A Portrait of God's Fury
(9:1-11)

Keep in mind that these visions of pagan worship in the temple took place in 591 B.C., about six years before the Babylonians would attack Jerusalem and ravage the land. Ezekiel had a vision of the abominable acts of the Israelites that would usher in judgment.

The vision of the "six death angels" that Ezekiel saw represented God's judgment that He would bring through Nebuchadnezzar. The Babylonians would become "God's rod" to destroy Jerusalem. Each angelic being had a "battle ax in his hand" (9:2). Another person, "clothed in linen," accompanied the six who carried their weapons of destruction. This special person "had a writer's inkhorn at his side," with a "writer's case" equipped with pen and ink (v. 3). The righteous people of the city would have a mark placed upon their foreheads by the man with the inkhorn. Thus the six angelic beings would put to death the unrighteous ones who did not have the mark upon their foreheads. The people who "sigh and cry" (9:4) over the sinful condition of others would not face death. The ones with broken hearts are those who obey God. They are concerned about the spiritual well being of others.

In his book on Jeremiah and Ezekiel, A. J. Glaze states that the word for "mark" in Hebrew is taw which is the last letter of that alphabet (p. 138). Glaze writes that taw appears in the shape of a "T" or cross. Some Christians from the time of Jerome (fourth century A.D.) regarded this mark as a sign of the cross and resurrection, although the connection is only conjecture, as Glaze indicates. However, in Egypt the Israelites found safety as they had "blood sprinkled over the doorway" on the first Passover Night as God's death angel passed through the land (Exodus 12).

In Ezekiel's account, the angelic beings started their work at "God's sanctuary" (9:6). That is, spiritual leaders must give an account to God. Simon Peter wrote, "Judgment must begin at the house of God" (1 Peter 4:17). God's people who have works that are an abomination to Him are going to face severe judgment. Of course, God knows every case and always knows what decisions to make.

God's final judgment is going to be relentless. God's instructions to His messengers were understood by them: "Let your eye spare not, nor have any pity. Utterly slay old and young men, maidens and little children and women; begin at My sanctuary" (9:5-6). The man in linen who had an inkhorn by his side gave his report to God. He said, "I have done as You commanded me" (9:11). God's righteous people had nothing to fear. They had a mark for their protection. The unholy and rebellious ones without that mark had everything to lose. . .

Two camps of people stand before God. God shows mercy and pity to all who go to Him while the opportunity is open. The day comes when God says that mercy and pity have ended. The door to Noah's ark remained open until the day when judgment fell. Those on the inside were safe, and all others faced death. Those who stayed in Sodom and Gomorrah when Lot left faced fire and brimstone. Ezekiel's picture is old, but it has a message for today. The Bible says, "Flee from the wrath to come." Are we going to live or die?

Chapter 8

Count Down to Judgment
Ezekiel 10:1-12:27

—⟋w—

While in church one Sunday morning, a four-year-old boy
flip-flopped in his mother's lap. She tried to keep him quiet,
but he wouldn't behave. His mother said, "Shhhh, be quiet" several
times. Finally, she grabbed her boy and rushed toward the back
door. The little fellow knew what was coming. At the exit he yelled,
"Folks, pray for me!"

In Ezekiel's day, the Hebrews lived in rebellion against God.
Every report card they received had a failing grade. Jeremiah in
Jerusalem and Ezekiel in Babylon faithfully proclaimed God's
messages, but all the two prophets wrote and preached didn't bring
about a change in the lifestyle of God's people. Finally, the message
through Ezekiel came loud and clear: "The countdown to judgment
has started." An ancient message of judgment needs to be heard
today. The Bible states that everyone must give an account of himself
or herself to God. Chapters 10, 11, and 12 in Ezekiel underline judgment. Let's apply the message of judgment to our lives.

I
A Sinful City Faces Judgment
(10:1-22)

The city of Jerusalem has a long history. We remember that place
because of many events that unfolded there in bygone centuries.

Abraham carried Isaac to Mount Moriah, which is identified with Jerusalem in 2 Chronicles 3:1. David captured the city from the Jebusites and gave Jerusalem its name, "City of Peace." God's glory filled Solomon's temple as he dedicated it. However, across the centuries many Israelites had been unfaithful to God. Just as other prophets had done, Ezekiel announced that the city faced judgment because of its "abominable ways."

Chapter 10 of Ezekiel gives a fast review of the Throne Chariot scene already given in the first chapter. The cherubim are identified as heavenly beings. In chapter 10 their faces are those of a man, angel, lion, and eagle. The chariot has wings and wheels that move as the Spirit moves. Eyes show up all over the chariot, which indicate God's total knowledge. God is enthroned above the brilliant canopy or platform. The firmament glistens and reflects God's splendor and glory.

In chapter 10, the vision of "the man in linen" shows him taking burning coals from the cherubs on the chariot. In the previous chapter, "the man in linen" had placed a mark upon the foreheads of the righteous people. This time he has "burning coals" to scatter over the city. That act was a preview of things to come. Babylonian forces soon would destroy the city.

A vision of God's glory appeared once more in the temple, and the place became filled with the cloud of God's glory — the Shekinah of God's presence. The cherubim paused at the door of the temple. God's revealed glory was about to leave His dwelling place because the people had made flagrant transgressions against God and His temple.

Jonathan Edwards became one of America's great spiritual intellects. When he was 10 years of age, he stayed home from church one Sunday because of illness. After the family left, he walked into his father's study and picked up a black book that didn't have a name on the cover. When he opened the book, he gazed upon the words of 1 Timothy 1:17, "Now unto the king eternal, immortal, invisible, the only God, be honor and glory forever and ever." That young fellow said that those words overwhelmed him. He could hardly move for a few minutes as he meditated upon what he read. Edwards said he felt as though he was actually in the presence of the King Eternal. In those moments he believed conversion took place in his life.

Jonathan Edwards finished Yale University at seventeen years of age, graduating with highest honors. A few years later he began praying for a spiritual awakening in America. He once stayed in a solitary place where he prayed and fasted for three days. His prayer was, "Oh God, give me New England, give me New England!" When he returned to his church to preach following that time of being alone with the Lord, the people said his face glowed like the face of an angel. God heard the prayers of Jonathan Edwards and sent revival to the early American colonies. Of course, George Whitefield became a flaming evangelist during those Colonial years, also.

God's people have experienced the breaking forth of God's glory many times. In Ezekiel's vision, God's glory filled the temple one more time before judgment fell. The people had shut God out of their lives. The throne chariot with God above the cherubim moved to the door of the temple on its way toward the mountain on the east.

The throne chariot paused briefly at the door of the temple as perhaps God took a look back at the city. For three hundred years the Holy of Holies had been the place where God revealed His glory (Kings 8:11; 2 Chronicles 5:14; 7:1). Finally, God's revealed glory was leaving the temple and Jerusalem because of the people's idolatry, and they would not have His protection any longer. A sad and emotional moment came to God and to His escorts. Judgment was going to fall. Four years seemed like a long delay, but Nebuchadnezzar and his soldiers were getting their war machinery ready. Judgment had started its countdown, and the people of Jerusalem learned, too late, that they couldn't push God off His throne. They learned the frightening lesson that sin brings God's judgment.

II
Civic Leaders Face Judgment
(11:1-25)

In chapter eight, the story of twenty-five "men" who may be priests is given. If they were not priests, they carried out that role. In chapter

11, the story of 25 civic leaders is given, and two of those are high officials. Those men may be the same as the twenty-five in chapter 8. They had been set apart to keep their city running smoothly. They had the opportunity of giving good counsel to the people in Jerusalem, but they failed in their duties. The biblical mandate is to follow the will of God and be on His wavelength, whatever the outcome may be. Jeremiah gave counsel to the leaders to submit to Nebuchadnezzar, but they put no confidence in his words (38:1-7). Instead, they cast him into prison for telling them to surrender. The twenty-five leaders of Jerusalem, along with most others, disregarded God's plans and pursued their own ways. Thousands died by "famine, pestilence, and sword" because they refused God's way.

The twenty-five civic leaders, speaking independently or by their own authority, declared, "The time is not near to build houses; this city is the caldron, and we are the meat" (Ezekiel 11:3). The time to build houses had not come for them. However, they felt that they would be as safe from the Babylonians as meat in a pot is safe from the flames. In others words, the civic leaders in Jerusalem were saying to the people that they did not need to fear the Babylonians. (Ezekiel, Taylor, John B, p. 109). The evil counsel given by those civic leaders caused death to their comrades. God said to the evil counselors that they were responsible for the "dead in the streets" (11:6). The people had a false sense of security. Ezekiel 11:3 states that the twenty-five said they were like flesh in a caldron. They thought the walls of Jerusalem would protect them like an iron pot would protect flesh from fire. The walls of the city, from their perspective, would save them from the Babylonians. The endangered people learned that the city was the caldron, and that the leaders were not flesh protected in the pot (11:7). God said they would be removed far from the city and would face the sword (11:8). They had trusted in the walls to save them, instead of letting God be their protection. They faced death "at the border of Israel" (11:10-11). The frequently occurring words come rapidly again, "Then you shall know that I am the Lord" (11:10, 12).

The scene changed to one of sudden death. Two among the twenty-five had their names flashed upon the screen as being among the "evil counselors" (11:1, 13). Pelatiah died suddenly. Perhaps his death came as a warning to others that it is never safe to run counter to God's will. Ezekiel had a soft heart and didn't rejoice when the news of Pelatiah's death came. He cried and talked to God about the matter. The prophet wanted to know if God had plans to obliterate the entire remnant. Ezekiel wanted to say, "Lord, don't let any more tragedy come to your people!"

God explained the scenario to Ezekiel, telling him that the worst elements had been left in Jerusalem. Those in the capital knew that Ezekiel and thousands of his fellow countrymen had gone into captivity. They concluded that those in captivity must have been evil and that they were the best. Those who remained in Jerusalem circulated the word that the land had been given to them (11:15).

God was saying to Ezekiel that the logic of those in Jerusalem was wrong. He declared that those in exile were His people. Then God gave a long list of blessings for the exiles in Babylon (11:14-21). God said He would be a "little sanctuary" ("diminished sanctuary") for His people in exile, even though He had scattered them. The city of Jerusalem and the temple would soon be destroyed. And yet, God said to those in Babylon, "I shall be a little sanctuary for them in the countries where they have gone" (v. 16). God seemed to say, "You can't beat this arrangement, Ezekiel, because you'll find that My Presence is your hope."

The story has circulated about a Red Cross worker who served in North Korea. As that man was walking down a crowded street one day, he heard a tune that caught his attention. He slowed his walking pace and looked around. Then the Red Cross worker saw a man cleaning the street, and he was humming a tune. He listened. Yes, the Korean was humming, "Jesus loves me this I know, for the Bible tells me so." In that communist land, a man had found God as his "little sanctuary."

We may not be in the midst of trials; we may be "on top of the world." And yet, whatever the circumstance in life, we need to know that God wants to be our sanctuary.

Some mothers face difficult days. They may have to care for their children alone. Divorce may have left them bereft of a spouse. Some have said good bye to their husbands who have entered military life. Work around the house never ends. Clothes have to be washed, the house has to be vacuumed, bills have to be paid. They struggle between work at home and maybe a job outside the home. Weariness sets in and questions pop up about how to keep going. But hope is on the horizon!

For everyone who struggles as well as for those without problems, God still wants to be our "little sanctuary." Thank the Lord that He is a refreshing oasis in the midst of life. Even as Ezekiel and the exiles heard the news of God's Presence in Babylon, God is with us today. Look up, celebrate, and thank God for being our sanctuary!

Good news from the Lord of grace and glory kept pouring in. That happened to the captives along the banks of the Chebar canal after the tragic loss of their city. God gave the promise that He would restore a remnant following the destruction of Jerusalem, and gather the scattered remnant again (Ezekiel 11:17).

God's prophet had a word for his exiled kinsmen (11:15). The future of Israel lies with the exiles, and not those left in Jerusalem. Another blessing for the restored people was that they would be stripped of their idols and idolatry forever (v. 18). No more will Baal tempt them, nor would they give a second look at Tammuz. Ashtaroth will be burning in the city dump. The idolatrous practices of the world will not control God's ancient people again. Those images and idols from the time of Joshua until the rise of the Persian Empire became stumbling blocks for them. But never again! No more would they break the second commandment. They were going to fall in love with God and never run after obscene idols again — free from those abominable things! (11:18-19).

Ezekiel gave the Israelites more wonderful news: they would have a new heart and new spirit (11:19). They needed to be removed from Jerusalem where God would take them into the surgical ward and do the heart transplant they desperately needed. The Eternal Healer would give His people a New Heart, and they would have excellent health. The new life would have a "new spirit" also. The new spirit is related to the new heart. That stony heart has gone and the new spirit replaces the spirit of rebellion. God's people would become sensitive to His voice because of a new heart and spirit.

A new conduct would be given to God's people so they would walk in His statutes. They would begin to practice the words of Micah 6:8 about doing justice, loving mercy, and walking humbly with the Lord. For a long time, Ezekiel struggled to tell them about a new conduct, but they didn't practice that life until God gave them life (11:20).

A reminder comes as almost a postscript. For those who don't like the new way of life and want to return to their detestable ways, God will let them have it! The abominable ways are open for all that demand them. That unwholesome way will be their recompense and will come down upon their own heads (11:21).

Years ago Robert Peel served as Prime Minister of England. He had an invitation to attend an evening dinner where other distinguished guests would gather. During the time in that luxurious house, some started telling ugly jokes about the Christian faith. In the midst of those slurring remarks, the Prime Minister asked the host if he would ring the bell for a butler. England's distinguished man said to the butler, "Go for my horse and carriage, please." To the startled host, he said, "I am a Christian, therefore I will go." A new way of life comes from God because He gives us a new heart and a new spirit.

Ezekiel has a final vision of the departure of the glory of the LORD from Jerusalem. The heavenly beings "lifted up their wings" with God's glory above, and the presence of the Lord moved up and over the city and stood on the mountain just east of Jerusalem. The Chariot Throne waited for a time. Perhaps at that moment, the Lord looked and remembered His people that He had nourished through the years. They had rejected God and lost their resource of protection. God's glory departed from Jerusalem and their house was "left unto them desolate." Write the word "Ichabod" over Jerusalem because "the glory of the Lord departed."

Then a swift trip took place for Ezekiel. In visions, he had been in Jerusalem. God's Spirit carried him back to the exiles. He had watched the judgment on Jerusalem unfold, and now he had the job of telling that story to his fellow exiles.

III
The Judgment Story is for Everyone
(12:1-28)

If we want to be informed about God's judgment, don't consult wizards and fortunetellers. Go straight to God's Word where He declares that everyone must give an account of himself or herself to God. The exiles in Babylon heard Ezekiel's story about Jerusalem's soon-to-be judgment.

A few days before judgment fell, a false prophet spoke up. He said, "Look! Settle down! I've told you before that the Babylonians are not going to touch us! We are in the sacred city. God is going to protect us. If anything happens, it will be years from now. We are going to be safe!" Another false prophet chimes in, "You can never trust Jeremiah as he speaks from prison or Ezekiel preaching in Babylon. We don't need to surrender to King Nebuchadnezzar. We are not cowards, and we are not going to submit to that general, no matter what Jeremiah keeps telling us. Let's stand our ground." Hananiah speaks words that are recorded in Jeremiah 28, stating that Jeremiah didn't tell the truth, and that the people didn't need to be afraid of Nebuchadnezzar. Jaazaniah and Pelatiah, two princes, gave bad counsel to the people in Jerusalem, assuring them of their safety (Ezekiel 11:4). No more words came from the false prophets. God would interrupt the topsy-turvy scene. His delay in bringing the forces of Babylon to Jerusalem was not a denial of the catastrophic event, but it meant that disaster would be the end for the rebellious people in Jerusalem.

Both groups, those in Jerusalem and the exiles in Babylon, suffered grave problems because they had lived in rebellion against God. They suffered from spiritual myopia and auditory nerve dysfunction. They had "eyes to see and ears to hear" but they neither saw nor heard (12:2). Since the plainly spoken words about the judgment story of Jerusalem would not be understood by those in exile, God told Ezekiel to perform a pantomime of those happenings. Ezekiel may not have had classes in acting in his earlier years as he studied for the priesthood, but he knew how to get the attention of his fellow exiles and show them what was taking place in

Jerusalem through his pantomimes. Let's raise the curtains on the stage and watch Ezekiel!

Let's run for our lives (2 Kings 25:4; Jeremiah 52:8). That message came from King Zedekiah of Jerusalem when he realized his time was up. Ezekiel's pantomime gets an A plus. Ezekiel told his fellow exiles what he was going to do. They gathered around. He took some clothes, something to sleep on, a handful of food, and stacked all that stuff in front of his house. The goods stayed there all day, as though he might have been expecting someone to come and help him move. That night the exiles watched in amazement as Ezekiel pretended to be King Zedekiah. He cut a hole in the wall of his house, and climbed through that hole, dragging his stuff behind him, putting all that he could carry on his back, and perhaps speaking in low tones, "Goodbye! My family and my soldiers are leaving town, and we are getting away from the Babylonian army that's breaking down the walls. Run, folks! Enemy troops are coming down the street now!" (An imaginary scene from Jeremiah 52).

Ezekiel acted out his part well. The exiles understood the message. But they may have wondered, "Is this really going to happen?" Yes, when the Babylonians camped around Jerusalem for eighteen months, King Zedekiah stayed inside Jerusalem as long as he thought he was safe. When the news broke that Babylonian soldiers had entered the city, the king grabbed a few possessions and said to his family and soldiers, "Let's get out of this place as fast as we can!" As the darkness of the night enveloped the city, they slipped through the broken down city walls, and away they ran as fast as they could go (Ezekiel 12:13-14). (Here is a brief explanation of the scenario of King Zedekiah and his group: 2 Kings 24:18 states that Zedekiah was twenty-one years of age when he began his 11 year reign. 2 Kings 25:2 and Jeremiah 52:5 state that in year eleven of his reign Jerusalem fell. Zedekiah along with his family and a few soldiers escaped from the city, but were captured within a short time).

"Not so fast, King!" A few miles away on the plains of Jericho, the run-away group heard the word, "Halt!" Babylonian soldiers captured Zedekiah and his entourage (Jeremiah 52:1-11; 2 Kings 25:4). The Babylonian soldiers quickly made their decision. They killed the sons of 32-year old King Zedekiah. Then they gouged out his eyes, bound him in chains, and led the blind king to Babylon as exhibit one of their victory over the Israelites.

For a few months, mealtime in Jerusalem does not win a kosher prize (12:17-20). Banquet tables are not set and music is not playing. Servants don't stand around, waiting to refill wine glasses. False prophets finally have become quiet, and no one is lined up to give toasts to King Zedekiah. Babylonians with battering rams keep hammering on the city walls. No one has eaten a good meal for several days. The hungry Hebrews look at their dirty dishes and know that they may never have another meal.

Look at their uncouth eating habits. They rush about grabbing moldy bread, passing a few pieces to small children and to aged grandparents. Their hands tremble as never before as they try to "gobble down" the bread. A few pick up water glasses. The wine has long since disappeared. Half the water is spilled because shaking hands can't hold the glasses to their lips. Everyone shakes as though they have palsy, and the trembling and quaking won't stop. They know that tragedy is about to happen. Is there a word from God for them? Heaven is silent and all hope has faded. The end has come!

Two times in Ezekiel 12:28 we note the appearance of "Lord God," indicating His emphatic message. "The word which I speak will be done." Don't expect another postponement, the Lord declares (v. 28). Jerusalem didn't have another opportunity. Their end had come, and harsh judgment like the storm of the first vision had come upon them. The Israelites in Jerusalem had bypassed the day of God's grace. God calls people in every generation to repent and return to Him. What's our response going to be?

Chapter 9

False Prophets
Ezekiel 13:1-23

—⚏—

One of God's preachers of this generation is Charles A. Tope. This man served as a missionary in East Africa for more than a quarter of a century, having served earlier as pastor of several churches. Since "retirement," he is a teacher in the Schools of Evangelism with the Billy Graham-Franklin Graham Evangelistic Association.

Most of us know the names of pastors, evangelists, and laity from many backgrounds who would be considered excellent servants of the Lord. God always has faithful people who honor Him with their service. But we also know leaders who betray their calling and speak messages that harm their listeners.

Jeremiah, Ezekiel, and Daniel are three prophets who served faithfully. During those years, however, false prophets seemed to outnumber God's true prophets. The prophets who challenged Ezekiel and Jeremiah were primarily Israelites, not pagan prophets. They were God's people "gone bad." They had access to the temple and religious training as others did, but they were not true to God. Their identification is not always easy. The Old Testament never lays down a complete definition for them, even though Deuteronomy 18, Jeremiah 28, and Ezekiel 13 speak directly to this issue. Ezekiel does not call them "false," and this seems the best way to describe them.

Before "zeroing in" on specific traits of the deceptive Israelite prophets, let us define them as those who proclaimed Jerusalem's inviolability. That is, they repeated their message that Babylon would *not* conquer Jerusalem. They argued that Jeremiah and Ezekiel were preaching a message of "gloom and doom" in contrast to their message of peace and security for all of God's people. They "white-washed" the tragic events of 722 B.C. when Assyria defeated the Northern Kingdom of Israel. They overlooked Nebuchadnezzar's invasion of the Southern Kingdom of Judah when he carried thousands captive to Babylon in 605 B.C. They also failed to understand that the capture of leading citizens of Jerusalem in 597 B.C. indicated that any other rebellion against Babylon would mean total disaster for the Southern Kingdom. Even when enemy troops surrounded Jerusalem in 587-86 B.C, these prophets proclaimed that God never would allow the enemy to conquer His people, despite all their transgressions. Now look at specific traits of those Israelite prophets who were not proclaiming God's message.

I
False Prophets Parade among God's People
(13:1-16)

False prophets speak their words, not God's. God has not given them authority to speak. They "prophesy out of their own heart" (v. 2). "Heart" in some translations of Ezekiel 13:2 appears as "imagination" or "mind." In 1 Samuel 13:14 Samuel told Saul that the Lord "has sought for a man after His own heart." The only time this expression is used in the Old Testament is in relation to Saul and his failure to be God's man. Acts 13:22 states that David was a "man after My (God's) own heart." The false prophet has the resource of man's wisdom, but he is not tuned in to God. No person can render service to God if his heart is divorced from God. Jeremiah 17:9 states, "The heart is deceitful above all things, and desperately wicked; who can know it?" False prophets have their own philosophies. Their life and work centers on self that is alienated from God. They substitute their words for God's word. (See Jeremiah 23).

94

False prophets are foolish. This is God's definition of them. Verse 3 states, "Thus says the Lord God: Woe to the foolish prophets." Webster's dictionary says the foolish person is one who is absurd or ridiculous. He has lost his composure. This one fritters life away on trifles. A closely associated idea of a foolish person is one who makes evil decisions or actions. In Ezekiel 13:3 they are called "Nabals" like Ammon in 2 Samuel 13:13-17, 1 Samuel 25, and Jeremiah 17:11. In Ezekiel 13:3 the reference probably means "high-handed and arrogant" (Tate).

The Old Testament word for fool relates to a wicked person, an evil character, or one who is "shamelessly immoral" (ISBE, v. 2, p. 1124). Also, the idea is of one who is hasty, impatient, self-sufficient, and one who despises advice and instruction. He is quick to become angry, thereby causing strife. Also such a person is careless, conceited, indifferent to God and His will, or one who is known for brute stupidity (ISBE, ibid.). Such persons are on a collision course with disaster. Such a man in the Old Testament had the name "Nabal" which means "fool" in Hebrew. First Samuel chapter 25 has the story.

Nabal owned a sheep ranch in the hill country of Judah. Once when David and his men camped out in the area as Saul pursued them, his small army exhausted their food supply. David sent a request to Nabal for help, but that man refused any support, accusing David of being a runaway servant. Nabal's wife heard about her husband's critical reaction to David's request, and she carried food to them. During that time Nabal became intoxicated, and when he awakened from his stupor and learned what his wife had done, he became so upset that he had a stroke or a heart attack, and died shortly thereafter. Like Nabal, false prophets have foolish hearts.

False prophets follow their "own spirit" (v. 3). Such people absorb the world's culture and atmosphere and they let the spirit of the world be their guide. They make their own decisions, instead of letting God direct them. One pastor had a funeral service of a lady who was about sixty years of age. She had requested special music at the funeral service. That song was, "I'll Do It My Way." False prophets, as well as countless others, go their way, not God's way. They follow the spirit of the world and their own spirit, not the Holy Spirit.

False prophets have false visions. They "have seen nothing" (v. 3). Of course, they may have visions, but not "visions of God " (1:1). For a brief moment, let's look at an example from Jeremiah's life (Jeremiah 27 and 28). Jeremiah pleaded for the Israelites in Jerusalem to submit to Babylon because he knew that it was the Lord's will. He illustrated his message by taking a yoke that a farmer might put around the neck of an ox, and put it around his neck, saying, "This is how Nebuchadnezzar is going to have our nation in subjection. He is coming and will put a yoke around our necks and we will be under his control. However, if we surrender to him, our city will be saved." A prophet named Hananiah rushed up to Jeremiah, yanked the yoke off his neck, and broke it to pieces. He said that just as he had broken the yoke of wood, so God would break the yoke of Babylon from Israel's neck. He declared that within two years the king and all who had been taken into captivity would be back in Jerusalem (Jeremiah 28:2-4, 10-11).

Jeremiah's response to Hananiah was that God could bring back everything if He wanted to. However, God's word through Jeremiah was that the Babylonians would put an iron yoke around the necks of surroundings nations, and they would serve the Babylonians. Jeremiah also told Hananiah that he would die within a year, and a few days later, he died (Jeremiah 28:6-17; Ezekiel 13:9).

False prophets are as deceptive and useless as a jackal, a fox-like animal (v. 4). "Jackals" is the correct translation, but the idea of a "fox" is not far removed from the text. Both animals have similar behavior patterns. One day I walked down a trail through a wooded area and saw a fox jump into the trail about one hundred yards ahead of me. Since the animal did not see me at that moment, I walked quietly behind him. When the fox stopped, turned around and stared at me, I stood motionless. The cunning red animal couldn't decide what he was seeing. He cautiously moved about ten more yards down the trail, turned, and looked at me again. We played a game for three or four more minutes until the animal "smelled me out," and into the woods he ran. Ezekiel knew the habits of jackals and foxes that live in hollow logs, holes in the ground, or run-down buildings, but they never remodel any place they live.

False prophets deceive with pretensions. In centuries gone by when a wall of a city was broken down, repairmen restored the wall so everyone inside would be safe; they repaired the gaps (v. 5). When spiritual walls are broken down, however, false prophets don't repair the walls. Like jackals, they may be "among the ruins," but they don't restore the broken places (13:4-5). They are shoddy workmen who see a wall that is broken and needs to be repaired, but they only "whitewash" the walls. They don't have good material to build a wall, or fix what's broken. The superficial coating without mortar will fall away when the wind, hail, or rains come. The poorly built walls will come crashing down (13:11-13).

False prophets don't know anything about spiritual walls of repentance or a holy life. The discipline of prayer, fasting, and living God's word are bypassed by them. They don't know anything about the kind of life that Ezekiel had. The shabby work of the false prophets won't stand "in the day of battle" (13:5). Their lives are devoid of spiritual elements that guarantee their survival. In the day of God's fury their shabby work would come to an end (Ezekiel 13:5, 10-12).

False prophets suffer a big loss because God is against them (13:8). They will not be recognized as belonging to God's people. They will not have their names in God's registry. They have no inheritance among God's people. Again, a statement of warning is issued about false prophets who will learn that Jehovah is the Lord (13:9).

Look at another chapter in Jeremiah's life. He had been forced to go into Egypt by his Israelite countrymen when Babylon was about to capture Jerusalem. God's prophet had warned them about pagan worship as they gathered wood, built fires, and made cakes to a pagan goddess called "The Queen of Heaven." The men rejected Jeremiah's warning, declaring that they would burn incense and pour out drink offerings to the "Queen of Heaven." Jeremiah said the result of their idolatry was desolation all across their land plus death by the sword and famine to the Israelites in Egypt who would never return to Jerusalem (Jeremiah 7:18; 44:17-19, 25-27).

False prophets give a false message. They seduce and lead people astray as they say, "Peace! when there is no peace" (v. 10). Time and time again Ezekiel and Jeremiah had told the Hebrews that Babylonian forces would come and smash their city and leave everything in ruins. The false prophets said the prophets who gave such words of warning didn't know what they were saying. Instead, they declared that nothing would happen to Jerusalem, despite the fact that Assyrian forces had carried their people into captivity in 606 and 597 B.C. God's response to false prophets must have shocked them. He declared that He would consume them in His fury and destroy any work they had done. Everyone who didn't accept the message of God's true prophets would suffer His wrath, and they then would know that He is the LORD (13:14-15). God put an end to the weak, wobbly walls of the ones who assumed visions and authority for themselves. He would show that His true prophets had spoken His message as He had commanded. God states that He is angry with the false prophets who speak in His name. His anger and wrath will be poured out upon them.

God said He would judge the wicked prophets along with their shabby work. The blazing words shine on Ezekiel's scroll again: "Then you shall know that I am the Lord" (13:14). As a postscript to what had just been declared, a further word is given from the Lord. He stated that the walls would not be any more, nor the workers who plastered them, nor the ones who declared peace when there was no such thing (13:15-16).

II
False Women Prophets Stroll Around
(13:17-23)

After giving a TKO to prophets who lived under the guise of being true servants of God, Ezekiel had words of condemnation about women who use prophesy while pretending to be God's servants. A good word needs to be injected about marvelous women who serve in God's kingdom. Bible history mentions the name of Miriam, the sister of Aaron and Moses. She led the Hebrew nation in praise to God after He drowned the army of Pharaoh in the Red Sea (Exodus

15:20-21). Deborah has her name written in blazing light in the book of Judges. She gave one of Israel's soldiers courage, and together they marched with their soldiers, and saved their nation from their enemies (Judges 4-5).

Also put Huldah's name in the ranks of preeminent spiritual people. She took a quick look at God's document that had been lost and told King Josiah that the rediscovered writing was God's book (2 Kings 22:14). Read the New Testament and see the four daughters of Philip who were prophetesses. Romans chapter 16 gives a long list of those who worked with the apostle Paul. Among them was deaconess Phoebe (v. 1) and about a dozen other devoted sisters in the Lord who made an impact in Rome for Christ. The mother and grandmother of Timothy instructed him and had an important role in causing him to be the man he became (2 Timothy 1:5). Joel 2:28-32 declares that God would "pour out His Spirit upon all flesh... sons and daughters would preach." Peter echoed that truth in Acts 2:16-18.

A big stain fell across Ezekiel's scroll because he didn't find women who demonstrated loyalty to the Lord. Instead, wicked women strutted across the stage under the guise of being God's prophetesses. They were a deceptive group who duped the hungry souls that came to them. They pretended to speak God's word and carried captive many who visited them for counsel. Ezekiel throws light upon the prophetesses and their tricky ways in their demonic dungeons (13:17-23).

Like false prophets, false prophetesses "prophesy out of their own heart" (v. 17). This phrase describes those who speak in the name of God, even though He has never spoken to them. They put up their placards, but God condemned their religious practices of extortion. They duped their clients by giving them cushions or pillows to lean upon. As the gullible clients reclined comfortably on the pillows, those patrons became more relaxed as they listened to the deceptive words of the teachers who misguided them.

The women prophets also provided magical charms for their customers. That practice also used "magic bands" for their arms and wrists. Those Hebrew prophetesses had picked up some Babylonian witchcraft practices, and acted as mediums and sorceresses, leading people astray. The prophetesses covered the heads of their clients.

They had closets filled with veils to drape over the heads of anyone who walked into their places of business. The young and the old, the weak and the strong, the men as well as women became their clients, and had their heads covered. The size of the customers presented no problem, because they had veils of every description that could fit everyone. With the head covered, the clients became duped for a "spiritual experience." They possibly passed through "mind altering rituals" that took them into the spirit realm, because the magic bands and veils were used to deceive. The clients suffered from an altered mental state as the false teachers "hunted for souls" to destroy them (13:8).

In the Amazon area of Brazil a lot of trees are being cut down to clear the land for more farms. In some places where trees are piled up, birds fly into the places to roost during the night. Sometimes hunters go to those places with lanterns and torches, shake a pile of brush, and the birds fly out. The excited hunters have brooms made of brush with which they knock the birds to the ground and catch them. The birds are not aware that as they fly out of their roosting places, they may become victims of the hunters. In symbolic terms, Ezekiel states that some listen to false teachers who use the light of their little torches to lure the gullible into their nets.

False prophetesses polluted God's name. With the pretense of doing work in God's name, they deceived God's people. They did their evil work for a handful of grain and a few pieces of bread, just to keep themselves alive (13:19). The result of paying a cheap price for that religious ride proved to be death to many of God's people (13:19). That religious racket did not come to an end in a long-ago world. Fortune tellers and palm readers keep going with their magic religion for the spiritually blind. Such practices are rampant across the world today. People stumble along in spiritual darkness because they have not come to the One who is "the Light of the world."

False leaders bring death to those who need to live, and they keep alive those who need to die. They do their evil work by lies and twisting the truth, and are often convinced that God is on their side and that their work is true, not always aware of their false messages

(13:19, 20). Indeed, their evil work makes the righteous sad as they see damage to God's cause (13:22). While the prophetesses did their deceptive work, the hands of the wicked became stronger (v. 22).

With all the preaching on radio, television, and in books, how do we "sort out" the good and the bad? Some who write and preach may grab a microphone and declare they are proclaiming God's Word with the insinuation that those outside their camp are suspect, and perhaps even unfaithful to God because they don't dot every "i" and cross every "t" as they do. Vawter and Huppe share a wise observation: "When he (Ezekiel) says they (prophets) purveyed 'lies,' we must bear in mind the scriptural meaning of a lie, which is not that a thing is not factual, but it is used in a 'pernicious' way" (Ezekiel, p. 85). There may not be a lack of facts, but after a quick one, two, three argument, an audience may be led to wrong conclusions. One may take truth and turn it into a perversion. One may use administrative skills or logic to manipulate facts, giving power and prestige into their own hands. People may become "masters of manipulation." Most of us want to convince everyone else that we are right, that we are good apologists who defend the truth. We garner the facts, but lead others to wrong conclusions. Sometimes we don't let it be known that we have our own personal agenda, no matter what happens as a result. Perhaps what all God's people need is a good dose of repentance in order that God may be magnified and His eternal kingdom stabilized by His power and grace.

Ezekiel closes chapter 13 by stating that the divination would end. God declared that He would stop the religious tricksters in what they were doing. Their fabrications would stop under God's stroke of wrath. God will deliver His people from the hands of the professional prophets who pretended to be God's ministers, but were not. When salvation comes, God's people realize that He is God. Even those who reject God will learn that Jehovah is God. In Ezekiel 13:21, 23 the message is given, "You shall know that I am the Lord." False religion with its deception won't give life. That which God demands is faith that gives a "new heart, new spirit, new conduct." Rituals won't regenerate or revive a person. All must have a personal relationship with the Lord where we love

God with all our hearts, and our fellowmen as ourselves. Ezekiel hits close to home for all of us. Are we ready to walk the road that he traveled?

Chapter 10

Idols in the Heart
Ezekiel 14:1-11

—ᴍ—

S everal years ago radio stations and magazines carried publicity about inexpensive wedding rings. The ad stated something like the following, "Genuine imitation diamond rings only $9.95." A lot of gullible people bought those rings because they thought they were buying valuable items.

Some members of churches may be "imitation Christians." Other words to describe make-believe people of God might be phony, hypocritical, fraud, sham, or counterfeit. One day a group of elders visited Ezekiel at his house on the banks of the Chebar canal. They wanted to know something of God's plans for His people in Jerusalem as well as for those in exile. God spoke to Ezekiel, telling him to be alert to those leaders who had come to ask questions about the events of the day. God wanted Ezekiel to know that He would not answer those who had come with their questions, because they were not honest with Ezekiel or with God. God will not answer people who try to deceive Him.

I
Deceptive Elders
(14:1)

Anyone may place an idol in his or her life. Idols cover a big territory. Unwarranted pleasures, possessions, popularity, power, pride, positions, or plans may become idols. Verse 3 states that the elders "set up their idols in their hearts." Nebuchadnezzar had taken a large number of Israelites into captivity in 597 B.C. Most of those who were taken into exile probably did not take any idols from the temple with them; however, even in a foreign country where they had become physically separated from their idols, they still worshiped them because they kept them in their minds. They made a personal, deliberate choice of "establishing" idols in their lives. Just as a person might spend a lot of time choosing an automobile, selecting a suit, building a house, or planning a marriage, in similar fashion the people had set their minds on idols. Each one makes his or her decision and becomes responsible for the action that is taken.

A shocking event took place after God delivered His people from Egyptian slavery. While Moses was on the "holy mountain" with God for forty days, Aaron and other Israelites made an idol (Exodus 32). When Moses came down from the mountain and asked how that had happened, Aaron said he didn't know how the golden calf appeared. He said they threw some gold and silver in a fire and the calf came leaping out! Aaron didn't tell the truth, because they planned and worked to produce that idol. They set up the golden calf and had a big party around the thing. People with "idols in their hearts" have them because they make plans for them.

II
God Sees Hidden Idols
(14:2-3)

No person can hide his or her sin from God. He knows all about wrong deeds that are planned and carried out. When the elders sat before Ezekiel, they never imagined that their sin would be revealed to the prophet. They looked at Ezekiel and had made full preparation to ask him questions, hoping for an answer that would have been in accord with their wishes. But they had not counted on God telling Ezekiel, "Beware of this group, son of man!"

The Lord knows what people tuck away in their hearts. Most people do not parade their evil plans publicly, but rather resort to the age-old habit of hiding them. In the New Testament era, Ananias and Sapphira worked out a scheme to impress people with their contribution of property. They kept hidden in their hands and their hearts an "idol of greed." God stepped into the picture and showed that trying to deceive others through pretense is a dangerous thing (Acts 5:10). The Bible states that none can hide his thoughts from God (Psalms 94:11; 139:2; Luke 12:2). If the elders could not get by with their sly maneuvers, do you think we can hide anything from God today?

III
Dangers of Idols
(14:4-5)

Any idol that a person carries in his heart becomes a stumbling block for that person. An idol catapults the idol carrier into iniquity (v. 3). The word "iniquity" means a grave injustice, vicious act, or wickedness. The word "iniquity" appears forty-two times in the book of Ezekiel (3:20; 14:10; 33:8, etc.) Who wants to have the charge of iniquity placed against himself? And yet, God places the charge of this guilt against everyone who tramps around with idols in the heart. A lot of stumbling goes on among God's people because of idols that may not be on display, but are real.

The Apostle Paul met an unusual situation in the church in Corinth where some people made sacrifices to pagan deities. Following the sacrificial event, the idol worshipers sold some parts of the animals to meat markets. When Christians visited those markets, they often would buy meat from animals that had been offered to idols. On occasions recent converts to the Christian faith had negative feeling about eating meat that had been used in pagan worship. Paul said that eating meat or not eating meat that had been offered to idols should not disturb a Christian. However, he wrote that if eating meat that had been offered to idols became a stumbling block in the way of another believer, then it would be best not to eat that meat. We may not have a visible stumbling block that will cause another believer to stumble. However, invisible idols in the heart that no one else knows about, will cause the person to stumble who has it in his or her heart.

We need to be careful about visible as well as invisible stumbling blocks that can cause anyone to fall into iniquity.

Idols in the heart cause the idolater to become estranged from God (vs. 4-5). Vital fellowship with God becomes dimmed or eclipsed when a person does not allow God His rightful place in life. Friendship, love, or affection for the Lord will be displaced when some big or even insignificant-looking idol takes over. As an example, consider an automobile. The vehicle may be new. Power brakes, power windows, power everything may be all over the automobile. A person may pay fifty thousand dollars for the automobile and people may say "Wow!" when they see it. And yet, a small ten-cent item like a screw or nail can stop an automobile when it causes a flat. The size of an idol doesn't always determine the suffering that may come. Any idol can severely damage fellowship with God.

The text mentions that God will judge a person "according to the multitude of his idols" (v. 4). The problem that may seem minor may soon become major as idols get added to life. Take the case of a person's heart. One artery that is twenty percent clogged may not be bad. However, if three or four arteries become ninety percent stopped up with fat and cholesterol, that person faces danger. Spiritually, everyone needs to understand the dangers that idols bring.

IV
God's Answer to Idolatry
(14:6-8)

Repentance is God's recipe for spiritual recovery. Verse 6 says the guilty person needs to "turn from" his idols. The text states that one is to turn from "all... abominations" (v. 6). The command comes from God to say goodbye to every idol that infiltrates life. When the message of John the Baptist is read from Matthew 3:8, we find the word "repent." John preached that a person must turn from the wrong way to the right way of living. Each one must bear fruit that shows a changed life because no person can depend upon an inherited religion to help (Matthew 3:9). Repentance calls for a change in life. One who has been involved with abominations and has been going away from God shows that he repents as he leaves his sin and goes to God for cleansing.

If a person fails to repent, God deals with that one. Ezekiel 14:8 states that God answers the unrepentant idol lover, "making him a sign and proverb, and I will cut him off from the midst of My people." God deals with apostates! Hebrews 10:27 speaks of "a certain fearful expectation of judgment, and fiery indignation which will devour the adversaries" of God. We need to remember the words from Ezekiel as well as those from the book of Hebrews. Jesus also expressed three potent words in Luke 17:32 as a sign or proverb, "Remember Lot's wife." The story of Lot and his wife is given in Genesis 19. Sodom and Gomorrah could not be saved from God's wrath because ten righteous people could not be found there. God's messenger told Lot and his family to flee from the place without looking back. After God sent fire and brimstone down upon the cities, Lot's wife turned and looked back. Perhaps Sodom had become an idol in her heart, because she died suddenly and became a "pillar of salt" (19: 26). Hebrews 10:31 states, "It is a fearful thing to fall into the hands of the living God." If a person does not want to become a sign or proverb along the path of life, God's word about repenting must be put into practice.

V
False Counselors Judged
(14:9-11)

Ezekiel gave a frightening word about a person who goes to another for counseling. Ezekiel states that if a person is guilty of sin and goes to someone to have that evil condoned, the one who give support to the evil also becomes guilty. God acts in the life of a counselor who does not tell the truth, and causes that one to be deceived. God opens the way for the prophet/counselor to go wrong if that one is not willing to be truthful. The prophet is free to do what he wants to do, and at the same time he is responsible for his actions. "He is deceived and it is the Lord who has deceived him. He is deceived because he has lost his spiritual perception. He fails to detect the insincerity of his inquirer and he works up some answer, as the false prophets of chapter 13 did, without a true divine inspiration" (Taylor, Ezekiel, p. 127). The "counseling corner" is one that's loaded with danger. A person may excuse his or her sin, stating that another has caused the problem, and that even a wrong course of action is justified. One may say, for instance, that he or she knows what is happening is wrong, but that the sin is the convenient way for that one. This particular reference in Ezekiel may be "played out" in a dozen ways. It is clear that a "prophet" or counselor who condones wrong becomes guilty and will face God's judgment.

If one is "induced to speak anything" that's wrong, the Lord allows it (v. 9). That is, because of a person's stubborn and rebellious heart that leads him down the trail of wrong, God eventually lets him have his own way. In that sense of the word, the Lord brings about this seduction. The "prophet" who agrees with the one who fails to use "spiritual logic" becomes as guilty as the one who seeks counsel.

God disciplines both parties who share the wrong in order that His people may stop straying from Him. God allows chastening or punishment to come to the rebellious person in order that others may learn the lesson of being true to the Lord, and not be contaminated with their transgressions (v. 11). Through this experience, God says His people become His people and He will be their Lord (v. 11).

VI
The Penalty of Unfaithfulness
(14:12-21)

Persistent unfaithfulness to God brings catastrophic punishment (v. 12). A person may stumble and fall, but if he continues in the path of unfaithfulness, God's wrath comes down upon him. God said He would judge Israel because of their iniquities. The last section of chapter 14 of Ezekiel gives a clear picture of a few of God's judgments. Those dangers are listed several times, indicating the nature of the judgment (5:12; 12:16; etc.).

Punishment and discipline may come at the level of starvation. God said His people would face famine. Ezekiel 14:13 states that everyone, including animals, would suffer because of the lack of food.

The people in Jerusalem faced such difficult times that they turned to cannibalism, children eating parents and parents eating children (4:13). The armies of Nebuchadnezzar encircled the Hebrew capital for nearly two years, and death from starvation claimed almost one-third of the people.

Punishment may come by means of wild beasts (14:15). The Hebrews had exploited the land for four hundred ninety years, without any of the territory being given a seventh-year rest. When the Assyrians carried the 10 northern tribes into captivity and Babylon carried Judah into exile, the land received rest. During those seventy years when little farming was done, lions and other wild animals invaded the place. Death came to many people in villages and small communities because of the lack of protection. Beasts may attack as a chastening rod from God at any time. To spiritualize the animals, we may say that the beasts are false leaders and demons are drugs, crime, etc. that destroy people.

Punishment may come through warfare (14:17). God said the sword would come against Jerusalem. No one knows how many of God's people died from Babylonian swords, but the number was large. Any retelling of those events shows that the sword was an awesome weapon of destruction that the Babylonians used against God's people. Conflicts still arise in many places as a result of unfaithfulness to God.

Punishment may come through pestilence (14:19). When famine strikes, coupled with beasts, and death from the sword, then pestilence invades and strikes hard at any survivors. Disease germs multiply and cause a plague when the environment becomes polluted. The story of suffering and death because of diseases in centuries gone by is an unending one. Bubonic plague has wiped out millions. The Black Plague that hovered over Europe in centuries gone by killed about one-fourth of that continent's population. Diabetes, cancer, and other illnesses bring death to people worldwide. Death for many may not be the result of one's own wrong, and yet the Bible declares that nations as well as individuals reap what they sow. We may reap later than we sow, and we may not see the results of all the good or bad that we sow, but the sowing and reaping process goes on (Galatians 6:7). Someone rightly said that a person should never sow wild oats and pray for a crop failure. Year after year Israel sowed "wild oats" and hoped they would reap a good harvest despite all their evil doings. Let's not try to bury this story in ancient history, thinking that the lesson has no application for today.

VII

**Persistence in Idolatry Makes Prayer Ineffective
(14:14, 17, 20)**

People who keep idols in their hearts may be placing themselves out of the reach of prayer. At least, those who persist in the camp of idols face stiff problems. God spoke a strong word through the prophet Hosea about His people and their idolatry. Hosea 4:17 states, "Ephraim is joined to idols, Let him alone." A time comes when the Lord tells people who have become saturated with idols that He will let them go.

The prayer habit should be kept alive, but at the same time, a balance must be kept in all spiritual equations. Isaiah 59:1 states that the sins of God's people brought about a separation between them. Psalms 66:18 declares, "If I regard iniquity in my heart, the Lord will not hear me." If idols become enthroned in a person's life and the habit continues, that person faces a critical danger-zone.

Let's not ask any lightweight people of prayer to come and rescue transgressors. Let's go for the well-known giants in the faith. The Lord says look at a few of them. Let's go first to the text in Jeremiah 15:1. God said, "Even if Moses and Samuel stood before me, My mind would not be favorable toward this people. Cast them out of my sight, and let them go forth." Wow! Consider Moses for a moment. After Israel's idolatrous act of making an idol at the foot of Mount Sinai, he returned to the mountain and fell down before God and prayed for God to save those people, or take his own life (Exodus 32:32). God answered that prayer and forgave the sins of the people. Look briefly at Samuel who was a man of prayer. He said in 1 Samuel 12:23 that he didn't want to sin against God in ceasing to pray for the Israelites. Surely the people of Ezekiel's day would have another chance with Moses and Samuel praying for them. But God said, "No!"

Think about three names that God gave to Ezekiel: Noah, Daniel, and Job. Their names stand out in bold letters in Ezekiel 14:14, 20. Noah built an ark for the saving of his family. As a man of faith, he must have prayed many times, asking for wisdom in his work. But Noah's praying did not save the sinful people from the flood, nor would it have saved them in Ezekiel's day. What about Daniel? Questions have been raised about the identity of the Daniel in Ezekiel 14:14, suggesting that this man might have been another Daniel of ancient times. However, Lamar Cooper states, "There is enough justification...to warrant the identification with Daniel, the contemporary of Ezekiel in Babylon" (Ezekiel, p. 262). To me it would seem that if Ezekiel had meant another person other than the prophet Daniel, he would have given a definitive word to that effect. The Bible indicates that Daniel was a man of prayer who habitually raised the window in his room three times each day as he looked toward Jerusalem and prayed for his nation. And yet, Daniel's praying would not have saved the Israelites from Babylonian forces.

What about Job? He was "perfect and upright," presenting "burnt offerings" to God, and interceding for his family of ten children every day (Job 1:1-5). No other person on planet earth at that time matched Job for his righteousness. That trio of towering giants evidently had seen many answers to their prayers. They knew the meaning of James 5:16 that referred to Elijah as a man of prayer. They knew that "the effective, fervent prayer of a righteous man avails much." Prayer would not be heard for the idolatrous Hebrews, even if Moses and Samuel were to appear on the scene and intercede, or if Noah, Daniel, and Job came back and started praying for them. The case for calling upon God had closed because of the idolatry of the people God would not hear them, no matter how much they would pray.

VIII
God's Remnant
(14:22-23)

From the motley crew of idolatry-soaked people, God reaches in by His grace and saves a remnant. Ezekiel 14:22 has an awakening word, "Behold, there shall be left in it a remnant who will be brought out." God did a work of salvage, even though Jerusalem lay in ruins. When all hope seemed to have faded, God still intervened to speak about those He would save for "His name's sake."

John Wesley became a miracle of God's grace. Ruffians burned down the home of Samuel Wesley, the father of John and Charles Wesley. All members of the family rushed out of that small, burning house in Epswich, England. The parents began to count the children and discovered that John was not among them. They looked up at the second story of their small house and saw the five-year old child as he was looking through a window. One man stood on the shoulders of another and pulled the frightened boy to safety. Later, the father said, "He is a brand plucked from the burning."

God's remnant was a brand that He carried through the crucible of suffering and death. Their salvation came about because of Divine love, mercy, and grace. He let His people go through purging in order that everyone might see "their doings and their ways." That cleansing showed that God corrected their evil ways. Their salvation gave comfort to God's people, knowing that He does everything right. Genesis 18:25 gives a question that Abraham asked God, "Shall not the Judge of all the earth do right?" God saved a remnant from Sodom, and He intervened to save a remnant from Jerusalem. The Lord makes no mistakes in His actions. God has a right and He has a reason for what He does. How do we stand before Him?

Chapter 15

An Analogy of a Useless Vine
Ezekiel 15:1-8; (John 15:1-8)

—ᴍ—

The fall 2003 edition of a Baptist magazine entitled "Open Windows" has a story written by Becky Singer Carr of Missouri. One day her son, Joe, came in from their orchard and said, "Mom, I guess I'll have to wear my bike helmet to mow the yard. Look at what fell on my head!" He held up the worst looking, worm-eaten pear that a person would ever see. Becky said her pride fell about their orchard as she looked at the tree from which the pear had fallen, and at that very moment the tree split apart and fell to the ground. The leafy green tree looked all right on the outside, but it was dead and rotten on the inside.

Ezekiel said Israel had a critical problem. He compared his nation to a vine that possibly looked good from a distance, but was rotten and fruitless. Israel was God's vine and people; however, a vine is no good if it does not produce fruit. We can analyze the parable of the vine and learn great lessons.

I
A Great Potential Lost
(15:1-8)

Any person or nation should be pleased to have had the start that God gave Israel. Throughout the Old Testament, God told about

His blessings to Israel, His vine. Psalm 139:17-18 states that God's thoughts to His people are precious and beyond the number of the sand. Look at a few blessings that Israel received to put her on the road to greatness.

Look at Israel as a vine of God's planting. Jeremiah 2:21 states that the nation came from good seed of the highest quality and stock. They looked back to Abraham as their father. God called him and gave him and his descendants rich, everlasting blessings.

Look at Israel as a vine of God's deliverance. They had been in Egypt for several centuries. Exodus 19:4 declares that God brought them out "on eagles' wings." That transportation was better than supersonic flights today. The times that God saved His people from enemies who were stronger and more numerous, showed that He kept His eye upon them, and continued to bring them protection unlike any other nation on the face of the earth.

Look at Israel as a vine under God's rules. He gave them the commandments which were easy to understand and that were for their wellbeing. God's guidance is always unexcelled.

Look at Israel as a vine rooted in choice land. Deuteronomy 31:20 reminded the Hebrews that they would live in a land flowing "with milk and honey." They inherited the best.

Look at Israel as a vine blessed with choice teachers and prophets. Of course, God as their "vine dresser" gave them protection and care as long as they allowed Him to do so. Leaders such as Moses, Joshua, Samuel, David, Isaiah, Jeremiah, Ezekiel, and many others endeavored to give the Hebrews the best of guidance. The writings and teachings of their prophets and other leaders are unexcelled in all world literature. The list of quality leadership that God gave Israel is an enviable one, despite the false prophets that appeared among them. They had a unique opportunity to become a great vine for God's glory.

II
A Downward Spiral
(15:1-8)

Despite Israel's bountiful beginnings, a flaw appeared in their story from the outset. The sons of Jacob sold their younger brother into slavery. The nascent nation slipped into idolatry in the slave fields of Egypt, as well as on the slopes of Sinai. For more than two centuries, during the time of the Judges, they continued to sink deeper into idolatry and immorality. During those "Dark Ages," the record states that "every man did what was right in his own eyes" (Judges 17:6; 21:25).

When Samuel served as judge and prophet, the "sons of Jacob" demanded a king to rule over them, emulating the heathen nations on every side. After the time of the monarchy of Saul, David, and Solomon, the nation traveled down a crooked, downhill road. Nineteen kings served in the northern tribes and all of those were bent on evil. Twenty kings served the two southern tribes, and only two of those had a good record, Hezekiah and Josiah. The kings moved the divided kingdom further and further away from the Lord, and closer and closer to destruction. Thirty-seven idol-bent kings with only two good ones spell disaster for any people.

III
A Parable of Judgment
(15:1-8)

In chapter 15, the message from God through Ezekiel stated that Israel was like a worthless vine. God's prophet states that the transgressions of Israel were bringing judgment upon them (v. 8). The word "transgressions" in this text has the idea of broken faith or treachery as the nation pretended to worship God, while their hearts had become addicted to idols. God made a covenant with Abraham, spelling out that he and his descendants through Isaac would be true to Him. Another covenant was made at Sinai as Moses and Israel committed themselves to be faithful to the Lord. And yet, rebellion after rebellion occurred in Egypt, the wilderness, and in the

Promised Land. Those transgressions of abandoning God for idols and immorality became so accelerated that God had to bring catastrophic judgment upon them. This time Jerusalem and everything related to the people and institutions had to be consumed by God's holy fires of wrath. The vine would be burned. The vine would have to go!

The design had been for Israel to be a missionary people, but they did not do a good job in that area. When God called Abraham, He declared that through him and his descendants the world would be blessed (Genesis 12:1-3). Later on, God told Moses that through Israel's priestly ministry, they were to be a holy people for His name's sake (Exodus 19:5-6). Wherever God led the Israelites, they were to be a "light to the Gentiles" (Isaiah 49:6). As a vine, they were to be fruitful among all people where they would live.

The vine became fruitless and useless. Ezekiel gave good descriptions of wood from a vine. That wood, compared to the trees of a forest, would not be good for anything except for fruit bearing (15:2-3). It would be too small and fragile to be used for a house or ship. Neither would furniture manufacturers give an order for wood from a vine. The vine's wood often would not have the size and strength to serve as a peg to hold a pot from the kitchen (15:3). People don't gather vines for firewood, either. That kind of fire from fragile vines is short-lived, and heat from it is minimal (15:4). What would God do with a useless vine that represented Israel? Burn it — temple, city, and everything. Jerusalem became like a vine burned on both ends and scorched in the middle. For three years Assyria waged an unrelenting war against Samaria, and the capital of the Northern Kingdom finally fell in 722 B.C. Babylon completed its destroying work of Jerusalem in 586 B.C. As woodcutters bring in wood from the forest for fuel, so God would let fire devour Jerusalem (15:6). God did not protect His vile vineyard.

Some wanted to escape from God's judgment, but could not. Those who survived famine and pestilence within the city met the sword as they squeezed through the broken-down walls of the capital. Even the surviving remnant that missed the conflagration became decimated, leaving only a "remnant of the remnant." More than a century before Ezekiel's day, Amos described the impossibility of escaping judgment. His story relates to a man in a field who escapes from a lion, only to be chased by a bear. The fellow reaches his house, totally exhausted. He puts his hand against a wall to rest, and a serpent bites him. There's no escape from God's judgment. Jeremiah 11:10 states that judgment would fall upon God's people because both Israel and Judah broke the covenant with God. They reveled in their iniquities as they turned their backs upon God. Ezekiel declared thirteen times in Chapter 7 that "the end has come." God's vine faced judgment. Since Day One, the vine had not fulfilled its purpose and would not serve any longer.

IV
The Vine Fulfilled

Let's recognize a central biblical truth: God cannot be defeated. Even before the creation of the cosmological order, God had an eternal purpose to redeem man (Ephesians 1:4; Revelation 13:8). If God had chosen any other race or tribe of people, those people would have failed Him, too. The Israelite nation did as everyone else does by sinning and coming short of the glory of God (Romans 3:23). God knew what would happen to Israel, but He used them, despite their failures, as a conduit for Jesus, despite the risks. He chose Israel to be His vine to give His message to the world; they failed, but God did not fail. He stays on track with history and His eternal purpose for all of creation.

Since Israel failed in being fruitful, God discarded them as His vine. The worthless vine in Ezekiel 15, a metaphor for Israel, fell under divine judgment. He did not protect Israel as His vine, but brought a powerful enemy against them. However, God's eternal plan for mankind could never fail. Near the close of His earthly ministry, Jesus who embodies Israel, spoke "ear tingling" words, saying, "I Myself am the true vine" (John 15:1). He came as the restored, replenished, renewed vine that Israel had a chance to be. The disciples of Jesus are the branches that are connected to Him and receive life from Him. As God's vine, Jesus gives the life-flowing Spirit to all who come to Him. Wonderful results take place in every branch that has a vital relationship with Him.

The vine gives the potential of fruitfulness to the branches. Jesus stated that the branches connected to Him will bear fruit, much fruit, more fruit, and abiding fruit (15:2, 5, 16). These words should echo over and over again in our ears and result in a harvest that brings unending joy to all of God's people. When we are connected to the life-giving Vine, we become a fruit-bearing nation for God.

In 1960 while our family was in language school in Costa Rica, Donald Grey Barnhouse came to the school and thrilled the students with his message. Barnhouse tells about a grapevine in Hampton Court, England, that is almost one thousand years of age. Those branches grow to be one hundred feet in length as they extend themselves from the trunk of the vine that is about two feet thick. The vine reportedly produces tons of grapes each year. The branches are productive because they are connected to the vine's trunk, and they are pruned and carefully attended all year long. England's remarkable vine fulfills what Jesus mentioned in John 15 about being productive.

While I served as pastor of a fledgling mission work in Cordoba, Argentina, we had the joy of seeing Adela and Marta Diaz along with their mother become a part of the mission family. Pastor Daniel Annone followed me in that new church and recently sent a letter, telling about this family that he has guided across the years. Adela became an attorney and her husband, Miguel Font, is an engineer. In 2003, they have visited with Daniel Annone, telling that God is calling them into full-time ministry. Both were ordained in November and serve together in a church in the province of San Luis. They are a part of the "much fruit that abides." In the same mission work, Susana Alvarez and most of her family received Jesus as Savior. Susana later married Fernando Lopez, and they have continued to serve faithfully as pastor and wife in God's vineyard in Argentina.

Rick Davis served as Director of Evangelism in the Baptist Convention of Texas, before re-entering the pastorate. He tells about a night in 2003 when he arrived back at the airport in Dallas and took a taxi to his car that had been left a few miles from the airport. As they traveled through the traffic, Dr. Davis asked the taxi driver, "Have you heard about Jesus Christ?" The taxi driver responded to Rick Davis, "Are you a Baptist?" Davis answered, "Yes, I'm a

Baptist Christian, but why do you ask?" The fellow said he had been in America for three years and the people who always talk to him about Jesus are Baptists! When we talk to others about the Savior, we become fruitful.

Vine branches should bless others with joy. Fruit from the vine not only sustains life, but also changes the environment where one lives. One "fruit of the Spirit is joy" (Galatians 5:22). An interesting parable is related in chapter 9 of the book of Judges. The trees of a forest had a conference and decided they wanted a king to rule over them. They spoke to an olive tree, asking the olive if it would come and be their king. The olive said that it had a job of producing oil and could not leave its work. The trees spoke to a fig tree. The fig tree said, "Why should I leave my work of producing sweetness to serve as your king?" They asked the grapevine if it would come and be their king. The grapevine answered, "Why should I leave my place of making wine that makes the heart of God and man merry to rule over you?" God's people are to make the heart of God and man "merry." The fruit of the vine should add joy to life. The words of chapter 2:13 in the Old Testament book entitled Song of Solomon states that pleasant vines with tender grapes give a good smell. We are to be like costly perfume that makes every place we go "smell good." If we are productive, we'll give joy to others and help change the environment from gloom to gladness.

Jesus performed His first miracle at a wedding in Cana of Galilee (John 2). The attendants at that place had an even greater celebration as the supply of wine increased. Lest anyone become too carried away with a reference to wine, perhaps it is appropriate to remind ourselves that Solomon wrote, "Who has woe, sorrow, contentions, complaints, wounds without cause, redness of eyes? Those who linger long at the wine... Do not look on the wine when it is red, when it sparkles in the cup" (Proverbs 23:29-30)! Our joy-giving lives, however, need to continue. God can cause His joy and fragrance to be reflected through us, wherever we may go.

God's vineyard needs workers who sweat and get dirt beneath their fingernails. Vine keepers and dressers may stay on the job from dawn to dusk, carrying out orders that the owner gives. Vines and vineyards are normally protected and given a lot of care. They take a long time to grow and require much work of fertilizing, watering, pruning, etc. As branches on the vine, and even while we work in God's vineyard, we should have the kind of life that models the life that Jesus lived. If so, that will be a life of duty, love, forgiveness, healing, mercy, sacrifice, restoration, joy, danger, and even death. His "grapes" have to be crushed to produce fragrance. Are we ready for the risk-taking of discipleship and allegiance that God wants from us?

Jesus told about a man who had two sons. He asked one to go work in his vineyard. That son said he would not, but afterward repented and went. He asked his second son to work in his vineyard and that son said he would, but later did not go (Matthew 21:28-31). Unending work needs to be done in God's vineyard. As branches on the vine and as workers in the vineyard, we have the opportunity to honor God as we are a part of His vine. What are we going do in God's vineyard?

Chapter 12

Jerusalem's Spiritual Biography
Ezekiel 16:1-63

—⟁—

A biography of Billy Graham appeared some time ago with the title, Just As I Am. Biography comes from two Greek words, "bio" and "graph." "Bio" means life and "graph" means write. If someone were to write a story of our lives, most of us would want the writer to be selective, putting in everything that is complimentary, but leaving out ugly events.

Ezekiel spoke a spiritual biography of Jerusalem in Chapter 16 of his book. He gave as complete a story as possible about that city in one chapter. Ezekiel traced the history through a long, winding route from their first day to future time. He didn't seem to leave out much that related to their sordid story, telling about their corrupt lives as well as about the good that took place when God intervened and changed them. God struggled long and hard with His people then, even as He works with people today. Let's try to understand this biography as we look at Jerusalem in four ways: Jerusalem: The Abominable Foundling, Jerusalem's salvation, Jerusalem's degradation, and Jerusalem's restoration. Chapter 16 gives emphasis to all four areas, showing that God is present in all events of life.

I
Jerusalem's Desertion: The Abominable Foundling
(16:1-5)

Many older and younger married couples have pictures that remind them of joy-filled days when God blessed their union with children. Sometimes homes look like an art gallery with photographs of children from birth through school years, marriage, and beyond. We oftentimes delightfully smile and say "ah" over family portraits.

The reader receives a shock as he or she scans Ezekiel's description of God's Jerusalem, especially in her early years. Instead of beautiful, complimentary words, the prophet uses words that are harsh, hideous, and repulsive to the core. God spoke to Ezekiel, telling him to tell Jerusalem about her abominations (16:3). Ezekiel did not dodge the issue, but spoke directly to Jerusalem about her sins. He wrote about the marriage bond between God and Israel, using language relating to a foundling child being picked up by an eastern (Asian) traveler. Ezekiel does not give a refined description of Jerusalem. He jabs and stabs today's readers as well as the original readers with stark, uncouth words about their condition and behavior. In reality, he calls Jerusalem a fatherless child. A softer word may be "foundling" that describes a child that is cast out into a field by parents who do not want it, and therefore abandons it. That "foundling" is left to die alone in an open field.

Past relationships indicate Jerusalem's abominable state. The Israelites had an addiction to pointing to Abraham as their ancestor. Ezekiel gives shocking news for them as he delves into their genealogy, connecting them to the Ammonites and Hittites (16:3, 45). Their past history gave the people of Jerusalem a disturbing view of history which they didn't want to hear. Ezekiel reminded them that their roots could be traced back to Noah and his grandson, Canaan (Genesis 10:1, 6). Two nomadic groups of Amorites and Hittites came from Canaan's family (Exodus 3:8, 17; Deuteronomy 7:1; 26:5). The Amorites lived in the Dead Sea area, and the Hittites occupied the area from Asia Minor to northern Mesopotamia for centuries.

Isaac and Rebecca became sad when their son, Esau, married two Hittite women, and they feared that Jacob might go the same route (Genesis 26:34; 27:46). The chief god and goddess of the Amorites were Baal and Ashtoreth — the Babylonians, Greeks, and Romans had other names for Baal and his consort. The Hittites and Amorites became known for their degenerate lives. Their religion led them to child sacrifice, and sometimes they placed sacrificed children in the walls of new houses as "good luck" (Halley's Bible Handbook, p. 166). Those tribes had become so corrupt that God warned Joshua not to let the Hebrews go the way of their abominations (Deuteronomy 18:9-14). Since the Hebrews thought they should be exempt from national catastrophe because Abraham was their father, Ezekiel told them that their father was an Amorite and their mother was a Hittite. To further insult them, Ezekiel declared that their behavior was worse than the way of the Canaanites. The Israelites emulated those groups, practiced child sacrifice, resorted to witches, put pagan idols inside the Temple, and became involved in scandalous conduct. The history of Jerusalem was more revolting to God than were the heathen tribes near them (1 Kings 14:22-24; Ezekiel 5:6).

Ezekiel reminds the Israelites that at birth, no person came to aid them by cutting their umbilical cord (v. 4). They lay "kicking and screaming" with no one to wash or cleanse them. To see them as helpless, newborn infants was a revolting experience. No one showed pity or compassion, and they faced certain death. Indeed, Jerusalem was like an unwanted baby whose parents cast it into a field to die alone at birth. Without God's help, they were castaways, and were hated the day they were born (16:4-6).

The "abominable foundling" was without present resources to help it (16:2-5). They had seen their land invaded by foreign troops. Their former way of life of peace and prosperity had disappeared. The connections they had with surrounding pagan nations and those farther away such as Assyria, Egypt, and Babylon did not help. They cut themselves free from any genuine commitment to the Lord when as a nascent nation they rebelled against God. Centuries before, when they languished in misery as a beginning nation in Egypt, Pharaoh gave orders to the midwives to kill all boy babies at birth (Exodus 1:6). For about four centuries, Israel struggled to get away from their "foundling predicament," but could not. God's intervention gave them a new beginning (Amos 2:10: Joshua 1:4).

Of course, not everyone is a "foundling case" today. And yet, the condition of countless people catapults them into a helpless state such as the one that Jerusalem experienced until God intervened. People in third-world countries, as well as those in nations blessed with abundance, find themselves struggling with problems because of a lack of resources. The need for more economic, physical, and other resources helps drive many to dungeons of desperation. Also, the disturbing message is that everyone apart from the grace of God is caught in a "web of abominations" (16:2). Since Job 25:5 states that "the stars are not pure in the sight of God," what else can people alienated and separated from God expect other than condemnation? Jerusalem's "foundling story" is for everyone who refuses God's grace. The bad story changed to a good one for Jerusalem, and that same message is for today.

II
Jerusalem's Salvation
(16: 6-14)

Ezekiel shocked Jerusalem with bad news, but then he gave good news. Verse 6 comes from the heart of God, "When I passed by you and saw you..." The Lord didn't turn His head when he saw that deserted child, but showed unlimited compassion. Others did not care, but God did. He was not like the Levite and priest who passed a man who had been robbed, beaten, and left for dead on the road to Jericho (Luke 10:33). The Israelites were about to be trampled upon and polluted in their own blood, but God didn't pass them by. He is always ready to stop and help anyone who accepts Him.

The Lord redeemed His people. He reached them when they could not reach out to Him. God saw them in their ugly estate, and said, "Live!" That one word "live" in Ezekiel 16:6 is worth more than anything in the world. God intervened when Jerusalem languished in her worst condition, and He let her know that she could have life. With God looking on, Jerusalem had a reprieve; she had a great word from God, and that was a word of command, "Live!" God's grace fell upon the ears of a struggling people who had no hope. Jerusalem came out of her field of death because God brought her out.

God gave the luxury of life. When no one else washed and cleansed the foundling, helpless child, God did (v. 4). The salt helped cleanse and purify the Israelites who then would be clothed or swaddled. Paul echoed this truth in 1 Corinthians 6:11 as he wrote, "…Such were some of you. But you were washed, but you were sanctified, but you were justified…" Redemption is real in the lives of those who respond to God's grace and love. Just as Jesus called Lazarus from the grave, He calls to life those who respond to His invitation. Just as God's Spirit breathed upon the valley of dead, dusty bones of Ezekiel 37, so the Spirit of God blows upon and brings life to people of any century. Anyone can hear that ancient word making an echo in ears that will hear, "Live!" Salvation is available to everyone. Isaiah 55:1 reads, 'Ho! Everyone who thirsts, come to the waters; And you who have no money, come, buy and eat. Yes, come, buy wine and milk without money and without price." The Bible message is that everyone may have life if they accept God's message and walk with Him.

The Lord rewarded His people with growth. Note that God caused His ancient people to "thrive like a plant in the field" that grew, matured, and became very beautiful (16:7). Verse seven gives a description of Israel. The nation grew as a young woman grows and arrives at full maidenhood. Actually, Jerusalem was not a "beautiful lady," but she matured sexually and God prepared her for marriage. Those words should have been kept in the minds of God's people forever. God's grace is amazing!

The Lord related to His people. He claimed them as He married or "spread My wing (skirt)" over them (v. 8). When Naomi returned to Palestine after being in the land of the Amorites, her daughter-in-law came back with her. Ruth followed the instructions of Naomi, and visited Boaz who had gone to sleep in his grain barn. When Boaz awakened, Ruth asked him to spread his skirt over her, thereby paving the way for their marriage relationship. Boaz did that, and soon the marriage took place (Ruth 3:9). The Lord welcomed His ancient people into a covenant relationship with Himself. God was the husband and Israel became His wife. Those descriptive terms of God and His people are used a few times in the Old Testament (Isaiah 54:5; Jeremiah 31:32, etc.). God declared in Exodus 19:5-6 that He brought them out of Egypt on "eagles' wings" and promised if they would keep His covenant they would be His special treasure. He promised to make them a "kingdom of priests and a holy nation" (1 Peter 2:9; Revelation 1:6, etc.) God has "one family" that is composed of sons and daughters where there is neither Jew nor Gentile, male nor female (Galatians 3:28). That same figurative language is used with Christ as the bridegroom and the Church as the bride. Everyone may have the reward of a relationship with the LORD.

The Lord replenished His people with a regal wardrobe. He took away the "old garments" and gave new ones. Ezekiel 16:10-14 seems incredible. God clothed Adam and Eve with fig leaves from Eden, but He clothed Jerusalem with royal robes. The outfitting that God does parallels the story of the Prodigal Son that is recorded in Luke 15. God gives His people "robes of royalty." He has a wardrobe that excels every other.

Look at the details of what God has waiting for those who come to Him. Ezekiel states that God gives the best of clothes — embroidered work, fine linen...silk. The finery listed in this passage reflected the lavish life of oriental royalty. Fabulous jewelry awaits "the daughters of Zion." The list includes bracelets, necklaces, nose rings, earrings, and a crown for the head. More than a century before the writing of Ezekiel scroll, Isaiah spoke about some provisions that God makes for His people: "I will greatly rejoice in the Lord... for He has clothed me with the garments of salvation, He has covered me with the robe of righteousness, As a bridegroom decks himself with ornaments, And as a bride adorns herself with her jewels" (61:10).

When Abraham sent his servant in search of a bride for Isaac, he sent expensive gifts for her. Genesis 24 tells that when the servant found Rebecca, he presented her with those gifts. Among those expensive items were bracelets for her wrists, nose rings, clothes, and vast amounts of jewelry of silver and gold, as well as expensive gifts for her brother and mother (Genesis 24:22, 47, 52). God placed ornament after ornament upon His people, giving them matchless beauty and glory.

God refreshed Jerusalem with a royal banquet. "Fine flour, honey, and oil" indicated that the provisions which God made for His people were plentiful (16:13). Moses wrote about God's "royal bounty" in Deuteronomy 32:13-14, stating that Israel had "honey from the rock...oil...milk of the flock...fat of lambs...the choicest wheat...the blood of the grapes." God's provision for His people outstrips the food that one gets in the world. David wrote in Psalm 23 that God "prepares a table before me in the presence of my enemies." Divine provisions are far better than the devil's delicacies.

The Lord gave recognition to His people. Verse 14 states, "Your fame went out among the nations because of your beauty, for it was perfect through My splendor which I had bestowed on you, says the Lord God." God brought His people to the epitome of beauty and glory. During the reign of Solomon, the Queen of Sheba visited him. That luxury-laden queen almost fainted as she saw the glories of Solomon and his kingdom. She said not one-half had been told her about Solomon (1 Kings 10:1-9). No one can overstate the fortune, fame, and future that God has for His people.

The Bible states that one day the King of Glory is coming. God's glory will then fill the earth and every kingdom of the world will become His (Revelation 11:15). The renown of that everlasting kingdom will stretch from shore to shore and never will fade. God wants us to get a glimpse of the eternal beauty that He has for His people. God's assurances to Jerusalem should remind us of what He has for the redeemed of all ages.

III
Jerusalem's Degradation
(16:15-34)

Life sometimes "turns sour." Backsliding can take place among the best of God's people. Noah did wrong, and so did David, Solomon, Simon Peter, and Paul. Write in large letters the truth that Jerusalem, "the apple of God's eye," lost her glory. The people committed abominations that startle any reader. Take a look at a part of one page from God's Book about the transgression of the Israelites. 2 Kings 23:3-9 lists a few of their sins: They placed idols in God's house and had priests who burned incense to pagan deities, as well as to the sun, moon, and stars. There were booths for Sodomites adjoining the Temple! Ezekiel 16:15-17 tells of the harlotry lifestyle of many, and a record stands about the "unmentionable" sin that probably related to "phallic images" and fornication in God's temple. Is it any wonder that the older rabbis didn't want younger people reading this book? From the heights of God's marvelous salvation, Jerusalem plummeted to the depths of shame. Sin can blot out the glory of life that comes from God. The Scripture from Ezekiel shows the route of degradation.

Pride caused God's people to fall. Ezekiel 16:15 declares that God spoke to His people saying, "You trusted in your own beauty, played the harlot ("whored" or "fornicated") because of your fame. They forgot that their blessings came from God's hand of grace and love. Instead of letting their confidence continue in God, they had a misplaced faith. They put confidence in themselves. Proverbs 16:18 states, "Pride goes before destruction, and a haughty spirit before a fall."

Aesop, a Greek writer who lived about the time of Ezekiel, wrote a fable about a frog that wanted to move from a dried-up water hole to one with water. He saw two ducks and asked them to take him to a new location. When they told the frog that they had no way to take him, the frog said that they could take a stick in their beaks and he would get between them and hold on to the stick with his mouth as they flew to a place where water could be found. They agreed, and everything went well until a farmer looked up and saw that unusual sight. He said, "I wonder who thought of that trick?" The frog croaked, "I di-i-i-i-i-d!….." Pride caused Jerusalem to stumble, too.

Prodigal living caused God's people to fall. Ezekiel 16:15-19 tells how the Hebrews "played the harlot" with all that passed by (v. 15). They prostituted their gifts and privileges, paying their paramours to have relationships with them. They moved idols of heathen deities into God's temple. They took their "garments of glory" that God had given them and used their wardrobes to decorate their idols as well as the houses of prostitution on every high hill around them (v. 16). They took their silver and gold and made images, playing harlotry with them (vs. 17-18). They took food and incense and gave that to pagan gods as a sweet-smelling savor (vs. 18-22). They gave their meat offerings as a "savor of rest" to the idols of wood, expecting the idols would then be at peace with the worshiper! Jeremiah 19:5-13 and Ezekiel 16:19-21 state that God's people sacrificed their children by tossing them into the fire of pagan gods and giving incense to those pagan deities. Prodigal living brings degradation to God's people in every age. A vast array of activities that never honor God leads people into places of shame they may never think possible.

God's people became spiritually corrupted and petrified. In the sixth century before Christ, the degradation to which the Hebrews sank caused their hearts to become like stone. Their national conscience seemed as hard as a petrified forest. Calloused and cruel, they took their own children and continued to offer them as sacrifices to foreign deities. Take one example of their spiritual hardness and corruption from Jeremiah 7:31 and 2 Kings 16:3. King Ahaz led the way as "He made his son pass through the fire, according to the abominations of the nations whom the Lord had cast out from before the children of Israel."

When a child or grandchild becomes ill, the parents or grandparents can hardly rest until that the child becomes well. Musicians, pastors, Sunday School teachers, and many others often are bombarded with calls about someone who faces a critical illness. We spend hours talking to God about those who have physical pain and ailments. Can we imagine another scene? A beautiful Israelite child has reached the age of two or three years. The parents have become addicted to a Canaanite god. They grab their child, run with him toward the place of sacrifice, look upon a roaring fire beneath the outstretched arms of a grotesque god, and hurl the screaming child onto that god's arms. They watch as the child goes down to death as a sacrifice. Demonic practices continued for a long time near the holy hill of Jerusalem. Blinded by heathen practices, the hearts of the people became like stone. Horrible acts of sacrifice continued until God put an end to those cruelties by using other nations as a rod to chasten and purify them. God said that He would bring such calamity that "both...ears will tingle" when the story was heard (2 Kings 21:12). The people provoked God in such measure that He promised to wipe Jerusalem as clean as a dish and turn the city upside down (2 Kings 21:13).

Pollution poisoned the people of God. Efforts to save the environment from pollution continue in many countries. Fines are applied to companies if they fail to meet Environmental Pollution Agency standards. Cars have to pass tests and food has to be tested and meet certain standards. The list goes on for curtailing and evading dangers of a polluted environment. We often overlook spiritual pollution that ruins life. Ezekiel 16:15-34 gives strong emphasis of the wasted lives of the Israelites.

God's people adopted the immoral practices of the Canaanites, Assyrians, and Babylonians. They degraded their lives through acts that would have caused the people of Sodom and Gomorrah to blush with shame. Unabated and shameless activities continued "under every green tree" and "upon every high hill" (Ezekiel 6:13; Jeremiah 3:6). A "house of sodomy" was located beside the Temple in Jerusalem. That unbelievable story is related in 1 Kings 14:24; 15:12 and 2 Kings 23:7. Even when Jeremiah and Ezekiel warned about judgment, God's people kept on sinning. Sin continues its course today, just as in ancient history.

Punishment fell upon God's people. When mankind turns its back on God, evil takes over. Eventually, God brings sinners to face the day of fearful reckoning. God said that the lovers with whom Jerusalem had politically and spiritually aligned themselves would rob and strip her of her clothes and jewels. They would stone the Israelites, and thrust them through with swords (16:40). Their houses would be burned and judgment would be executed by those whose gods they followed (v. 41). More than 100 years earlier, Assyria had carried into captivity the best of the ten Northern Tribes. After Israel's punishment, the two southern tribes should have learned that they would face judgment unless they repented, but they kept on with their abominations.

A shocking report is given about the people of Jerusalem and the two Southern Tribes. Ezekiel 16:42-52 repeats the previous story that the father of the Israelites was an Amorite and their mother a

Hittite (16:2, 45). The "elder sister" was Samaria, the former capital of the ten Northern Tribes. God had destroyed Sodom, and yet that city was called the younger sister of Jerusalem because of their abominable living. A knockout blow came as God said the sins of the Israelites were worse than those of Samaria and Sodom (16:42-52). Finally, the walls of Jerusalem came tumbling down, and the shrieks and screams of agony and death echoed all over Mount Zion. Punishment that measured up to the sin of the people came, and they learned too late that "the wages of sin is death" (Romans 6:23). Have we learned this lesson that Jerusalem failed to learn?

IV
Jerusalem's Restoration
(16:53-63)

The promise of restoration that God gave to the "whole house of Israel" flashes across the pages of the Bible. Webster's Dictionary defines "restore" and "restoration" in several ways, including the idea of being rebuilt, renewed, or returned to an original or former state. The idea is also to bring to an improved condition or make new.

The term in Ezekiel 16:53 about God "bringing back their captives" may be translated, "restore the fortunes" or "restore to well-being" (Tate). Cooper states that Ezekiel's message about restoration gives emphasis to the work of God after judgment that would come to Israel. Even though Judah had become a "byword" with her pagan nations, God would bless His people as well as Gentile nations (Cooper, p. 177).

The Bible lists several cases of restoration, such as David's prayer, "Restore to me the joy of Your salvation" (Psalm 51:12). A rich tax collector by the name of Zacchaeus told Jesus that if he had taken anything falsely from anyone, he would restore it fourfold (Luke 19:8). Simon Peter preached that Jesus returned to heaven after His resurrection "until the times of restoration of all things" (Acts 3:21). God frequently spoke about restoring the Hebrew nation. Jeremiah 27:22 refers to the vessels in the temple, but also related to the Hebrews: "They shall be carried to Babylon, and there shall they be until the day that I visit them...Then I will bring them up, and restore them to this place."

After Ezekiel wrote about Jerusalem's "foundling years," he told of their salvation and degradation. Then he closed this longest section of his book which seems to be a summary of his entire writing. This final section of chapter 16 has the news of God's restoration of His chosen people. God Himself would bring them back from Babylon and restore them. "He will renew the bond that faithless Jerusalem has broken and the renewed covenant will be everlasting" (Blackwood, p. 111). The restoring of the covenant reminded the people of their sin and shame. It also emphasized that God made atonement (forgiveness) for His people and gave them an enduring peace (16:63). Despite all their failures, God initiated and carried out His plan for the restoration of Israel, and will continue until the "restoration of all things" (Acts 3:21; Isaiah 65:17; Romans 11:11-33; Revelation 21:22).

Restoration came through the eternal covenant that God made with His people. Jeremiah 31:31 and Ezekiel 16:60, 62 give emphasis to a restored covenant with Israel. Prior to Ezekiel's time, God promised David that the kingdom through his descendants would last forever. That promise-covenant pointed beyond David and finds fulfillment in the "Son of David," who is Jesus the Christ (Luke 1:31-33). This divine kingdom has been established and will rule eternally over all other kingdoms (Daniel 7:13-14; Revelation 11:15).

The nation of Israel violated the covenant that God made through Abraham, affirmed through Moses, and reaffirmed through David. Israel no longer carried out their purpose as the conduit through which the Messiah came, and therefore God punished them, but not rejecting those who would trust Him (Isaiah 54). Paul asked in Romans, "Has God cast away His people? Certainly not! For I also am an Israelite, of the seed of Abraham...God has not cast away His people whom He foreknew" (11:1-2). Paul wrote that "all Israel will be saved" (11:26). That is, Jew and Gentile make up the "new Israel of God," and God accepts all who return to him (Galatians 3:7, 9, 29). The salvation of Jews, like that of the Gentiles, comes through the new covenant in which God provides a new heart and a new spirit. The renewed covenant and the new heart go together (N.T. Wright, Jesus and the Victory of God, p. 283). When Jesus came, He regarded those who identified with Him and responded to His call as "restored Israel" (Wright, p. 316). God gave the Temple with its rules, rituals, and regulations, but it had fulfilled its purpose, and was redundant and was on its way out. Jesus certainly had no idea of seeing another temple constructed of brick, mortar, and wood (Wright, p. 426; Revelation 21:22).

It is important to keep in mind, however, that Jesus did not come to destroy the old covenant, but to fulfill it. He gave fresh meaning and life to that which had become stagnant, dead, and fruitless. He welcomed all who came to Him in repentance, and accepted them as members of His new fellowship. He ate with publicans and sinners, talked to the elite like Nicodemus, and showed a Samaritan woman that she, too, could drink of "the water of life." Briefly, Jesus opened the door to all who were tired of the old life and longed for regeneration, renewal, and new life. One day someone told Jesus that His mother and brothers were nearby waiting for Him. He answered that those who do the will of God in heaven become His sisters, brothers, and mother (Matthew 12:46-50; Mark 3:31-35; Luke 18:29-21). The new covenant came at a cost, and Jesus was ready to pay that eternal price so that everyone might have life.

On the night of His betrayal and arrest, Jesus met with His disciples in the Upper Room for the Passover meal. He said to them, "With fervent desire I have desired to eat this Passover with you, before I suffer" (Luke 22:15). He expressed His strong desire to bring about the new covenant through His death. During the Passover meal, Jesus said to His disciples, "This cup is the new covenant in My blood, which is shed for you" (Luke 22:20; Matthew 26:28; Mark 14:24). Jesus confirmed the new covenant by His violent death on Calvary's cross (Luke 23:32-33; Psalm 118:22-24). He gave His life a ransom for lost humanity, opening the door of salvation for everyone to accept pardon and have life. Jeremiah 31:31-34 also gives the story of the new covenant. Restoration comes through the everlasting covenant.

George Mueller of Bristol, England, died in 1898. At sixteen years of age, authorities imprisoned him for theft. While he was a student in the university, he began a life of alcohol and prodigality. God soon stepped into the life of Mueller, saving him when he was twenty-one years of age. His autobiography of four large volumes recounts the ways that God answered his prayers repeatedly. He established an orphanage and cared for thousands of homeless children for decades as God miraculously provided for them food, clothing, and shelter. God regenerated, restored, and renewed Mueller's life. In the post-exile years God restored Israel and continues that restoration work through Christ. Restoration and renewal take place every day when people open their lives to the good news of salvation through Jesus. Let's keep telling the story of God's redeeming power, shall we?

Chapter 13

An Allegory: God and His People
Ezekiel 17:1-24

—w—

John Bunyan, a Baptist preacher, spent twelve years in jail in Bedford, England, because he didn't have a license to preach. While he was in prison, Bunyan wrote Pilgrim's Progress. This writing is an allegory or a symbolic story of Pilgrim who traveled from "The City of Destruction" to "The Celestial City." The book is a figurative description of John Bunyan and his Christian pilgrimage.

Ezekiel wrote a beautiful allegory. Chapter 17 has two great eagles that represent Babylon and Egypt. A cedar tree that changes into a vine represents Judah. More details in this three-fold allegory or parable show up as this story unfolds (v. 2).

I
Nebuchadnezzar: Eagle Number One
(17:3, 11)

The great eagle with big, colorful wings filled with feathers is presented in Ezekiel 17:3, and is defined in Ezekiel 17:11 as Nebuchadnezzar. A lot of background material on Nebuchadnezzar is found in the book of Daniel, 2 Kings 24, 2 Chronicles 36, and Jeremiah, chapters 37 and 52.

Nebuchadnezzar became king of Babylon in 605 B.C. He had defeated the Egyptians in Carchemish in 612, on the upper

Euphrates river near the Assyrian and Asia Minor (Turkey) frontier. He inherited the throne from his father, Nabopolassar, and became one of the notable kings of ancient history. When Babylon forces carried Daniel into captivity in 605 B.C., he lived during the rule of King Nebuchadnezzar. Later in the life of Babylon's king, Daniel gave a description of the king when he was dethroned and lived in the wilderness like an animal, eating grass for survival. His hair, fingernails, and toenails grew long like those of an animal (chapter 4). In Ezekiel 17, Nebuchadnezzar appears under the symbol of a great eagle.

The eagle is the king of birds, the greatest among flying creatures. From 605 until 562 B.C., Nebuchadnezzar ruled as king of Babylon. He built the famous "Hanging Gardens" which became one of "The Seven Wonders of the World." The wings of the eagle give a picture of the empire over which this king ruled. The "great wings" as well as the eagle's description as "longwinged" symbolized the power and prosperity of the Babylonian Empire (17:3). The feathers with many colors represented the languages, cultures, and habits of the people over which he ruled. His kingdom included one hundred twenty-seven provinces, making his dominion "worldwide."

Nebuchadnezzar is pictured as making his flight from Babylon to Lebanon, a symbol for Jerusalem (17:3, 12). Jerusalem is pictured as the land of Lebanon because Lebanon was known for its cedar trees (v. 3). During the reign of Solomon, he had so many cedars shipped from Lebanon to Jerusalem that the temple was called "the forest of the house of Lebanon."

The reference to "the forest of the house of Lebanon" is used five times: 1 Kings 7:2; 10:17, 21; 2 Chronicles 9:16, 20. When Nebuchadnezzar symbolically landed on a "cedar tree" in Jerusalem (17:3-4, 12), he took the highest branch of the cedar and broke off the top of its young twigs (17:3-4, 12-13). The "young twigs" from the cedar refers to King Jehoiachin and the young princes of the land. Jehoahaz, the twenty-three year-old king son of King Josiah, ruled only three months because Egypt took him to that country, and made Jehoiakim king in his place (2 Kings 23:31). In 597, Babylon took Jehoiachin into captivity along with Ezekiel and other leading people of the land (2 Kings 24:8-15; 2 Chronicles 36:9-10). Those captives were taken to Babylon, "city of merchants" (17:4, 13; 2 Kings 24:14, 15). Nebuchadnezzar left the untrained masses in Jerusalem.

Before Nebuchadnezzar returned home to Babylon from Jerusalem in 597, he placed Zedekiah on the throne to rule in the place of Jehoiachin who had ruled only three months when he was deposed (17:5, 13-14). Zedekiah was in a "fruitful place" in Jerusalem (17:5, 13-14) and Nebuchadnezzar made a covenant or agreement with him. The contract stated that Judah's king and his subjects in Jerusalem would be loyal to Babylon. They could live and be prosperous in their own country, but their well being would be determined by their loyalty to Babylon (Ezekiel 17:13; Jeremiah 37:5-11; 39:1; 2 Kings 24, 2 Chronicles 36:11-21).

Zedekiah "grew and became a spreading vine of low stature" in Jerusalem (17:6, 13-14). For nearly 10 years, Zedekiah remained loyal to Nebuchadnezzar (2 Kings 24:20). But troubles began because Zedekiah appealed to Egypt to help him in his rebellion against Babylon, even though neither he nor Egypt had the resources to successfully rebel against that eastern country who controlled them. Before looking at the tragic Zedekiah-Nebuchadnezzar confrontation in 587 BCE that brought on the total destruction of Jerusalem, look at the "second eagle."

II
Egypt's Pharaoh: Eagle Number Two
(17:7, 15)

Egypt appears in the text in allegorical terms as the second "great eagle." However, in the time of Moses (1400 B.C., circa), Egypt lost most of her glory. That nation became blighted through the 10 plagues, and her army drowned in the Red Sea. In 605 B.C., Egypt's status as a superpower suffered another setback when the Babylonians defeated them in the Battle of Carchemish. Pharaoh-Hophrah and his Egyptians learned that they were not equal to Nebuchadnezzar. But when a new pharaoh came to the throne, he seemed attractive to Zedekiah.

Judah's king looked at the attractive "eagle" immediately south of him. Pharaoh Psammatichus II (594-588 B.C.), the Egyptian king, looked good enough for Zedekiah to rely upon, and he was ready for an alliance with any power to protect Jerusalem from the Babylonians. The wings and feathers of Egypt appealed to him, and he sent ambassadors to visit the new Pharaoh with the purpose of obtaining soldiers to help him rebel against Nebuchadnezzar (17:7, 15). Pharaoh reluctantly considered some appeals from Zedekiah, but when the testing time came, Egypt declared that they would not be able to give Jerusalem the help they needed. Egypt's men and horses would never be able to stand up against Babylon's power (17:15).

God asked a question concerning King Zedekiah. Will his plan of revolting and rebelling against Babylon work (17:15)? The LORD answered His own rhetorical question: "in Babylon he will die" (v. 16). Since Zedekiah decided to break the contract with Babylon, his act of rebellion and his fragile alliance with Egypt was going to be costly for him (17:9-10, 15-21). God's word to Zedekiah was that payday was coming because he had broken his covenant with God and with man. As a result, he would be taken into captivity, and would die in Babylon. A brief rehearsal of that soon-to-be tragedy in Jerusalem helps one remember the event.

Zedekiah, along with his family and a contingent of soldiers, tried to escape from Jerusalem when the forces of Babylon broke through the walls of their city. Zedekiah was captured, his sons were killed before him, and the Babylonians gouged out his eyes, and took him to Babylon where later he died (17:20-21; 2 Kings 25:6-7). An oft-repeated message from the Lord appears in Ezekiel 17:21: "You shall know that I the Lord have spoken it."

III
The Highest Branch of the Cedar
(17:22-24)

By means of the Babylonian forces, God would take the "highest branch of the cedar tree" that was in Jerusalem (17:22; 2 Kings 24:8). That "highest branch" at that moment might have been interpreted by some as Zedekiah (or his nephew, Jehoiachin, who was in exile in Babylon). However, the essential meaning through the symbol is of the royal house of David, meaning that God would provide a new type of David-like king, the Messiah. Babylon's action continued (with God's behind-the-scene control) as he took a "tender twig" from the top of the branch and planted it "upon a high mountain," Jerusalem. On that highest mountain, God's people would prosper and flourish as they had never done before (Cooper, pp. 182-184).

The fruitful limbs or boughs from the new tree would be a place for every kind of bird to dwell beneath its shadow (Ezekiel 17:23). That new tree in God's purpose provides security and sustenance for "the birds" that rest beneath its shadow. When that prophecy will be totally fulfilled is still moot, but eventually all trees of the field, or all nations, will recognize that "tree" as God's appointed and anointed Messiah (Ezekiel 17:24; Matthew 13:31:32).

In many symbols, the stories of God's Messiah and Branch appear in the Old Testament. For instance, Isaiah 2:2, 4:2; 11:1, 53:2; Jeremiah 23:5; 33:15; Zechariah 3:8; 6:12; and Micah 4:1 are prophetic of a Messiah who had been promised. New Testament references about the activities of Christ appear in Luke 1:51-52; 23:31, etc.

IV
Some Conclusions

We can learn some basic, revolutionary truths as we read Ezekiel's allegories.

1. God is sovereign. No matter what happens in history, God remains the Lord of history. He is above all events, and He is in control. He never abdicates.
2. God uses any nation or individual He chooses as His instruments in bringing about His purposes in human history and in eternity.
3. We are responsible for the commitments we make. Promises are to be taken seriously.
4. Judgment comes to those who are unfaithful to God and to one another.

5. The future for God's people is secure. We don't have to worry. The LORD is God!

6. Two concluding questions need to be answered. Do we have a personal relationship with the Lord of the universe? Are we faithful to God and to one another in daily life? How do you answer these two questions?

Chapter 14

Personal Responsibility
Ezekiel 18:1-19:14

—⁀w—

A sixty-year old lady worked as a cook in a small town in Texas. While on the job one day, she fell and broke an elbow. Someone said that the floor in that civic center kitchen was always slippery, and that caused the fall. The woman had been on a ladder, and she thought she was on the first step of the ladder instead of the second when she stepped off and took a tumble. The floor was not the cause of the accident. We always look for a scapegoat for our problems, don't we? Most people blame someone else for their mistakes. Flip Wilson had a saying, "the devil made me do it." All the way back to Adam, we look for a culprit for our crimes.

In Ezekiel's day, the Israelites blamed their troubles on their parents and grandparents. They had a refrain, "The fathers have eaten sour grapes, and the children's teeth are set on edge" (Ezekiel 18:2). The Lord declared that He would stop people from blaming others for their faults. Since everyone belongs to Him, those who sin must give an account unto Him (18:4). The basic thesis is presented in verses 5 and 32 of this chapter. The declaration is given that a just person does what is right and one who is not doing right needs to repent and live, because God has no pleasure in the death of the wicked (18:23; 33:11), but the person who sins will die. Ezekiel Chapter 18 gives some cases to consider.

I
A Look at the First Case
(18:5-9)

Ezekiel writes about a just man, but who is such a person? The one who is "just" is basically the person who has a right relationship with God (Marvin Tate). The righteous person walks in God's way and responds to God's directions for life. Of course, a person who has a personal relationship with God may sometimes show up as a "rascal." Think of Noah and his one-time drinking spree, or consider David who sinned grievously. And yet, sinful saints have a personal relationship with God and repent when they do wrong (hopefully!). The just person has become righteous through faith and is called "just" because God declares him/her righteous. Like Abraham who "believed God, and it was accounted to him for righteousness" (Genesis 15:6; Romans 4:3), the just person receives life from God. The lifestyle of a person shows whether he is just or not.

The just people live separated lives. That is, the world does not control or dominate them. They do not "eat upon the mountains." In Ezekiel's day, many Israelites gathered at celebration feasts on the mountains in worship of pagan gods (v. 6). The just person refrains from that lifestyle. In modern society the people of God sometimes become so mixed in the world's culture that it's hard to tell which camp they belong to, God's or the devil's. The music, language, and habits of the world squeeze us into its mold. First John 2:15-17 warns about the lust of the eyes, the lust of the flesh, and the pride of life. One poet wrote, "The world is too much with us, late and soon. Getting and spending, we lay waste our powers."

The just person refuses to worship idols, and does not "lift up his eyes to the idols of the house of Israel" (v. 6). Hosea 4:13 gives a clear warning about idolatry, and the message about sacrificing to idols needs to be emphasized. The second commandment forbids idolatry, and yet that ancient word from God is bypassed so often today. Ezekiel's word for "idols" is "detestable things" (20:8). Idolatry may be defined as worship that is given to some physical object as a god. An idolatrous person is one who lets some object, animate or inanimate, come between himself or herself and the Lord.

The wickedness of idolatry is to give to something else the devotion and allegiance that belongs to the Lord God. The just person — the one with a right relationship with the Lord — worships the living God and rejects idolatry. God's people need to examine life continually see if they are guilty of idolatry.

The just person is upright or ethical; he is morally clean. He does not commit adultery or fornication. He keeps his marriage vows, does not steal, lie, and lives in a way that honors the Lord. English poet Tennyson had Sir Galahad saying, "My strength is as the strength of ten, because my heart is pure." Psalm 24:3-4 declares, "Who may ascend into the hill of the Lord? Or who may stand in his holy place? He who has clean hands and a pure heart, Who has not lifted up his soul to an idol, nor sworn deceitfully."

The just person does not oppress others (v. 7). Oppression means the exercise of cruel power over another. Sometimes people cannot defend themselves, or someone may take advantage of them by oppression. This verse is a clear call to be gracious and kind to others. When the prophet Samuel was old and gray, he had an interesting meeting with hundreds of Hebrews (1 Samuel 12:1-5). He asked them to tell him if he ever had oppressed or had taken advantage of them. The people answered the prophet, saying that he never had defrauded, oppressed, or taken advantage of any of them! We would say that Samuel lived a "just life."

A modern-day example of oppression is Saddam Hussein. The stories that have come out of Iraq are nothing short of a litany of tragic and inhumane treatment of multiplied thousands of Iraqi people, and anyone else who dared cross that dictator's path. But what about our oppression of others? What about the history of oppression of about every nation on the face of the earth? Oppressors can be found among large and small corporations, within denominations and churches, and within families. Some people may be so dictatorial that they demand or expect their own way in everything. A righteous or just person refuses to oppress others.

The just person does not harm others by violence (v. 7). He keeps away from robbery. Read any metro newspaper and you will see a long list of robberies that keep taking place. Violent actions against others may happen anywhere, anytime. The person who is "right with God" should not be violent or harm others. Unfortunately, Christians sometimes have been or may be involved with activities that are questionable. What about slavery, racism, war, child labor, and a long list of other social wrongs?

The just person "has restored to the debtor his pledge" (vs. 7, 12). A pledge is some security that is given for a future payment. If a person buys an automobile, he might be asked to show some collateral — the property he owns, his income, or other indications of worth as protection for the one who is the lender. To require a pledge or guarantee from another for a debt is not wrong. However, a lender is not to take advantage of another in the dealings that might go on between them. Deuteronomy 24:12-13 mentions a poor man who may have a need, and he leaves his coat as a pledge to the lender that the payment will be made. However, if the night is cold, the person with the coat should return the garment to the owner so that he won't suffer. Furthermore, when payment is made to the lender, both should understand that the man who has been helped will get his garment back and not lose it. The idea is to be considerate of anyone who faces a desperate condition, and not take advantage of him.

The just person supports those who face critical needs and becomes a humanitarian with a spirit of charity. Ezekiel states that he "has given his bread to the hungry, and covered the naked with clothing" (v. 7). At the close of the war with Iraq, many nations have gone to the rescue of those people who have been under the heels of oppression for a quarter of a century. Various nations have sent thousands of tons of medicine, food, and clothing to help alleviate the suffering and death that the nation faces. A charitable spirit is godlike.

The just person shows kindness with loans (v. 8). In Old Testament times, God's law forbade usury or the lending of money with interest to those within the Hebrew community (Deuteronomy 15). Some took advantage of others with high interest rates. Business practices today require that interest rates be charged for the use of another person's money, but the principle of fairness and integrity still remains. Exorbitant rates should never be charged, although some companies take advantage of others with 20 or more percent interest rates on loans. People and businesses that are "just" will be fair in their dealings with others.

The just person sets his course of life in God's Word (18:9). He is to walk in God's statutes and judgments. Disobedience to God's is wrong because the Lord has set before us the way to live and relate to one another. The just person should live as God's word challenges us to live. One example from the Bible is Micah 6:8, "He has shown you, O man, what is good; and what does the Lord require of you, but to do justly, to love mercy, and to walk humbly with your God." God gives His people instructions on how to live, thereby demonstrating that they are righteous. We are responsible individually and personally for the way we live.

God declares in Ezekiel 18:9 that the one who is just "shall surely live." God's people have life now and eternally. They have abundant life. God invites everyone to trust Him, do right, and live!

II
A Look at the Second Case
(18:10-13)

The second example relates to an evil son who has a just father. Examples abound in families where a father is just and good, but the son does evil. Two cases from Scripture illustrate this story of a good father and an evil son.

Take the case of King Hezekiah. Isaiah 36-39 and 2 Kings 18-20 gives the story as well as 2 Chronicles 32. When Hezekiah heard that he was going to die, he turned his face toward the wall and asked God to extend his life. The prophet Isaiah prayed for the king, too. God gave Hezekiah fifteen more years of life. Some time later Hezekiah had a son, Manasseh, who became king , and he ruled fifty-five years. Manasseh's reign became the most evil of any king in Judah. He brought idols into God's house, had children sacrificed to pagan gods, plus a long list of other abominations. Manasseh, the son of a righteous king, became unjust.

Josiah, the grandson of Manasseh, set an enviable record as king. He served from 639 to 609 B.C. Josiah destroyed the idols that had been brought into the land, restored true worship, and had one of the greatest Passover Celebrations that Israel ever experienced (2 Chronicles 30; 2 Kings 23:22). He walked with the Lord.

Jehoahaz and Jehoiakim who ruled for a brief time as kings of Judah were both evil. Both were sons of Josiah who ruled thirty-one years. What's the lifestyle of one who is unjust or evil? That one's life may be partly reflected in the terrible description related in this chapter of an evil life. We understand that not all the litany of evil applies to everyone. The list of unrighteous deeds in the second case includes robbery, murder, idolatry, immoral living, oppression of the poor, and other abominations. One person probably is not guilty of every sin, but the life that has no room for God is not one that becomes a role model for anyone.

The unjust person has the sentence of death hanging over his head. God says such a person will not live. He may have a righteous father, but no one inherits a right relationship with God from his or her parents. God does not have grandchildren, only sons and daughters. The message comes loud and clear again that everyone must give account of himself unto God. Righteousness is not inherited. Of course, a good example may encourage a person to honor God, but no one can automatically become righteous because of parents who follow the Lord. Each one is responsible for his own actions.

III
A Look at the Third Case
(18:14-20)

The remarkable case of a bad dad and a saintly son is presented here. Normally, one would think that an evil father would see the son walking in his footsteps. However, a son may look at the way the father lives, realize the fallacy and futility of that way, and choose another route to follow. The son may scrutinize the long list of evil deeds of his father, and then say, "That is not the way I want to live my life."

The righteous son does not bear the guilt of his father. Neither can the wicked father be saved by the life of a righteous son. The son is not condemned because of a bad dad, and the fickle father cannot be delivered through the goodness of the son. We return to the basic premise that is given in Ezekiel 18:4. God says that the one who sins must pay the price for his own sin. Each person is responsible for himself or herself. That truth can never be more plainly stated than Ezekiel does in this Scripture.

IV
A Look at the Fourth Case
(18:21-23)

The story of one's lifetime spent in wickedness gets the attention of a lot of people. That kind of person will probably die sooner than expected, if an undisciplined life continues. For instance, any person may abuse his body with detrimental habits such as the use of illegal drugs, overeating, smoking, taking unnecessary risks, refusing to give the body adequate care, abusing others, and the list goes on.

However, something wonderful can happen. The wicked person may suddenly have his eyes opened, and have a change of heart. Perhaps one day this person looks at a funeral procession. He sees the hearse taking a deceased person toward a cemetery, and he may begin self-examination. He says to himself, "Self, you are going to die just as this person did. And when you do, where are you going?" The man decides that he doesn't want to end life without hope. He turns to God, and he receives a new life. When a wicked person turns to God and leaves his wickedness, God pardons him. He learns that when he is converted that God never remembers his sin. He says, "Wow! You can't beat this deal any way you try!"

Take the case of the two thieves who died when Jesus was crucified. One of those thieves mocked Jesus. The other had a repentant attitude and confessed that they were both dying because of their sins. The second thief turned to Jesus in faith, saying, "Lord, remember me when you come into Your kingdom" (Luke 23:42). Jesus gave the thief the assurance that they would be together in Paradise that day.

In the church where I serve at the moment of this writing, we have one member who came from Guatemala. While Jorge Garcia and I visited together one day, he told me about a past life that was not beautiful. One day he awakened to the realization that he needed hope for the future. Six years before we met, Jorge repented of his evil life and began to follow Christ. He has lived for God's glory and witnessed for Him from the day of his conversion. In this chapter from Ezekiel, God said that He takes no pleasure in the death of anyone (18:4, 32). God is ready to forgive the most hardened criminal, if that one will turn from his evil ways and place his life in God's hand. God says, "Turn!"

V
A Look at the Fifth Case
(18:24)

What about a righteous man who lives and does good most of his life, then changes? That is, if a good man turns from the way that is right and spends the rest of his life doing evil, what happens to him? The text states that such a man dies. The basic truth is that that when such a person comes to the end of his physical life and dies, he loses all the good that he may have done. He dies and suffers the result of his deviate life. Several interpretations have been given to this particular case, but this writer believes that the case is not difficult to solve.

The "just person" who does good and changes to an evil way of life probably has been a hypocrite. He may have ceremonial righteousness, but not a heart-righteousness that has made a real difference in his moral life and conduct. He depends upon his own good deeds as a show of what he is, and this kind of person has reckoned on what He has done through his own goodness to make him acceptable with God. He does not rely on the righteousness which is by faith, and he turns from his own righteousness, not that which he could receive from God.

The self-righteous man gives a picture that was explained by Simon Peter as he wrote about wells without water and hogs that go back to wallowing in mud (2 Peter 2:22). (Calvinists will love this!). The self-righteous person, therefore, does not have the graces that a godly person has, but is destitute of them. He returns to "all the abominations that the wicked man does" (v. 24). That list includes murder, adultery, theft, profanity, oppression, adultery, idolatry, etc. But did David, Noah, or Simon Peter ever become guilty of such evils? The truth is that they did, but they turned from those evils. They repented, and had a lifestyle that was godly.

The Scriptures make the truth clear that God's people have a righteousness that comes from Him, they demonstrate that righteousness, and therefore they live. The case of a man who starts out well in life, but detours into abominations and stays on an evil course shows that such a person is destitute of life that comes from God.

VI
God's Defense of His Plan
(18:25, 29-32)

The Lord of creation knows what He is doing. No one can bring a truthful charge of unfairness or injustice to the righteous God of eternity. He will judge "the house of Israel" honestly and fairly. The Hebrews faced judgment according to each one's ways, not the way their fathers lived. The ways of God are right! Look who charges God with guilt. The Hebrews who refused to keep God's word and who continued to rebel against him began to scream against God and His ways. They declared that God was not just in His treatment of the people, even those who became vile in their deeds. However, the Lord is right in His judgments, and is never wrong. Everyone needs to know this truth.

God gives a wake-up call to everyone. He says, "Repent, and turn from your transgressions, so that iniquity will not be your ruin" (18:30). God prepared to bring the forces of Babylon against Jerusalem, but He allowed Israel the time and opportunity to change. They had the opportunity to cast off their idols and stop their abominations. They could turn from their own ways and go God's way. The invitation to walk a new direction was extended to them time and time again. God says that iniquity is not destined to ruin a person, unless that person decides to stay on that route.

God's call went forth several times for His people to turn from their evil ways and live. Ezekiel 18:30 records God's message as He said, "Repent, and turn yourselves from all your transgressions; so iniquity shall not be your ruin." Verses 31 and 32 of this chapter again calls for action on the part of the Hebrews. The Lord declared,

"Cast away from you all the transgressions…and get you a new heart and a new spirit. For why should you die?…I have no pleasure in the death of one who dies…Therefore turn and live." The Lord gave His people the opportunity to turn and live, but they declined the offer. People can still turn and live. The decision rests with each person.

A fascinating story appears in Jeremiah 38. The prophet had been in a cistern and by the goodness of Ebed-melech, had been lifted out of the place that would have meant his death. King Zedekiah had given permission to the servant to have others help him lift the prophet from the miserable place. When he was in the "court of the guard," the king called for Jeremiah to meet him. The situation had become critical as Babylonian forces were near. Jeremiah told Zedekiah that if he would go and surrender to the Babylonians that he and his family would live and the city would not be destroyed. The king said he was afraid of what the people might say about him if he were to surrender. Jeremiah assured the king that nothing would happen to him by surrendering, except that he would live. However, King Zedekiah made his choice to keep on holding out against the army of the enemy just as others did. Zedekiah would have lived if he had done what Jeremiah told him to do. And yet, he was afraid of what others might say or do to him. He made his own choice as many people did at that time and as they do today. The message to all the people was simple. They could repent and avoid national and personal disaster, or they could refuse to obey God's word and die. They chose to die. People have the same opportunity today to live or die according to the decision they make.

God offers a "new heart and a new spirit" to everyone (Ezekiel 18:31). God replaces the old heart of stone for a heart of flesh that palpitates with life. The old spirit of rebellion is taken away and in its place God gives a new spirit, His Spirit, that leads one in joyful obedience to God. The new heart and new spirit implies a spiritual regeneration. The new life that comes from God is freighted with love and holiness. The repentant person has a heart that reverences, esteems, fears, loves, worships, and follows God. A repentant person finds joy in his or her obedience to God, in doing His will. The alternative to death is life. The alternative to sin is repentance.

God says the choice lies with us because the invitation to live is for everyone (v. 32).

VII
A Quick Glance at Sinful Judah
(19:1-14)

Ezekiel relates the appalling story of Judah under the figure of a lioness and a vine. Here the prophet resorts to symbolism again. Chapter 19 is a dirge or a lament over the death of Judah's kings or princes. The first picture is of a lioness who has two cubs. This is really a parable of Judah. The first king mentioned in this passage is Jehoahaz who ruled only three months in Jerusalem (609 B.C.) He did not prove to be a good king. The Egyptians took him in chains to Egypt where he spent the rest of his life (2 Kings 23:33).

The second king was Zedekiah. He ruled in Jerusalem from the time that Ezekiel was taken captive into Egypt until the fall of Jerusalem (597-586). 2 Chronicles 36:6 gives something of his story. His sons were slain by the forces of Nebuchadnezzar and the king's eyes were gouged out. He was sent to Babylon where he stayed until he died.

The second picture in Chapter 19 relates to a vine. The vine appeared to be good, but God had that vine plucked up in His fury. None of the princes or kings that served in Jerusalem proved worthy of God; hence, they were rejected. That vine had no strong rod as a scepter to rule; therefore the lament over Judah's rejection. God would supply the future messiah who would rule. God's plan can never fail. Have you and I allowed God to make us a part of His eternal plan?

Chapter 15

Rebellions of Israel
Ezekiel 20:1-21:32

—⁂—

School is one institution that has blessed the world since the beginning of civilization. School teachers seek to instruct, give guidance, and help students in every way possible. We may think of Ezekiel as being a "teaching prophet." He carried out to some extent the role of pastor and interpreter of God's will for the Israelites.

The elders or older leaders of the exiles in Babylon visited Ezekiel in his home on various occasions to "inquire of the Lord" (20:1). The expression about inquiring of the Lord is a technical term for seeking a message or an oracle from the Lord. However, the Lord said He would not let that group of men inquire of Him because of their transgressions. God told Ezekiel to confront them with their "detestable practices." Therefore, he reminded them of the transgressions of previous generations as well as their own rebellions (20:4). Their grades had varied from an A with Abraham to D's and F's with most of them across the centuries. The lesson is that those who rebel against God suffer.

I
The Story in Egypt
(20:5-9)

The beginning of the story in Egypt for Israel started as Joseph's brothers sold him into slavery. The sons of Jacob later went into

Egypt to buy food and found their brother serving as Prime Minister there. During those years of famine, Jacob's family returned to Egypt to live. They multiplied in that country and soon found themselves as slaves of a new Pharaoh.

For about four centuries they prayed and asked God to lead them out of Egypt and back to the Promised Land. Three times God "raised His hand" to show that He was their Lord, and that He would save them (vs. 5, 6). During the time that the Hebrews lived in Egypt, they started worshipping the gods of Egypt. God almost destroyed them during those years. However, He gave them the promise to bring them out.

What a liberation the Hebrews had! God may have opened up the Red Sea for a distance of twenty or more miles in order that six hundred thousand men plus their families could leave Egypt in one fast-moving event. I suspect they didn't get water on their clothes or mud on their feet as they rushed through the dried-up sea. Behind them, the army of Pharaoh drowned in the collapsing waves of the Red Sea. And yet, the Israelites did not get rid of their idols, but they rebelled against God and refused to listen. God brought them out of the land for "His name's sake" (v. 9). God didn't want His name profaned among the people where His people lived. The Israelites should have remembered the Lord and been true to Him forever for His gracious acts, but they rebelled.

II
The Story in the Wilderness
(20:10-27)

The wilderness wandering of God's people lasted forty years. The book of Numbers contains the details of those events. Ezekiel gave a hurried review of those 40 years in this section of his book. Soon after crossing the Red Sea, the Hebrews moved to the southern area of the Arabian peninsula.

At Sinai, God called Moses to meet Him on top of the mountain where he received the Ten Commandments (Exodus 20:1-17). During the time that Moses stayed on the "holy mount" with God, the people in the valley made a golden calf. Moses came down from the mountain and saw what had happened. When he asked Aaron about the event, Aaron evaded the truth. He said, "We don't know how this happened! We tossed some gold and silver in a furnace and out came this golden calf" (Exodus 32:19-35). Aaron lied to Moses.

God gave Israel the statutes or commandments to guide them in their daily lives, but they despised God's teaching. He gave them the Sabbath to rest and remember Him, but they polluted those days (20:21). God gave them instructions about the tabernacle where the people could come and worship together and learn more of Him, but they desecrated that place. They proved unfaithful to God in the wilderness wanderings, even when God provided food and drink for them as well as the cloud of His glory to guide them by day and a fiery pillar to keep them safe by night.

Two hundred fifty men rebelled against Moses, saying they wanted to go back to Egypt to live (Numbers 11:2, 31). The people had prayed for centuries, asking God to save them from the slave fields of Egypt; and yet, in the wilderness, they made plans to return to Egypt. That would have been impossible! How would they have crossed the Red Sea? What would Pharaoh have done with them that time? God stepped into the picture, opened up the earth, and let the rebels fall into that "big hole" and die.

Twelve spies made a trip into the Promised Land (Numbers 13-14). Their anticipated country had been described as "a land flowing with milk and honey, a place to be desired" (Exodus 3:17; Deuteronomy 6:3; 26:9; Ezekiel 20:6, 15; etc). The prospects of their future blazed across Hebrew history time and time again. However, after the spies surveyed the country, ten of them gave bad reports, saying that giants lived in the land, and the Hebrews seemed like grasshoppers when they compared themselves to the Canaanites (Numbers 13:33). Rebellion took place again. Instead of walking directly into their heritage, the twelve tribes wandered in the wilderness for 40 years until the rebels died. God showed His power again as the Israelites arrived at the Jordan River. The Lord stopped the water from flowing until they crossed into the Land of Promise.

III
The Story in the Promised Land
(20:28-30)

The Israelites could not overlook the deliverance that God gave them from Egypt and the Sinai wilderness. He brought them out of the "house of bondage-slavery" and carried them into the country that He had promised Abraham (20:28).

The "Dark Ages" in Hebrew history lasted from about 1300 B.C. until about 1050 B.C. (dates vary). During those two hundred fifty years, they overlooked God's gracious acts on their behalf. Near the very outset of their time in Canaan, Achan disobeyed God at Jericho and brought havoc to the people (Joshua 7). Even Joshua's leadership role didn't win their favor for long. He won thirty-two campaigns against pagan groups, but the Israelites fell prey to the pagan worship (Judges 2:17).

The book of Judges gives a summary statement at the end of that time in their history, stating, "Everyone did what was right in his own eyes" (17:6; 21:25.) Their idolatry in those extended years involved all twelve tribes. Ezekiel 20:28 gives a shocking introduction into the idolatrous practices carried on by the Lord's chosen people. They sacrificed unto pagan deities in the "high places" called "Bamoth" (v. 29). They persisted in practices of child sacrifices and immorality.

The beginning of the kingdom era didn't see improvement in their lives either. They demanded in the time of Samuel that they have a king like the nations around them (1 Samuel 8:4-8; Acts 13:20). During the centuries from Saul, David, and Solomon on down to the time of Zedekiah (Israel's last king), the Hebrews "played the harlot after the gods of the peoples of the land" (1 Chronicles 5:25). Their modus operandi was written briefly with three words: idolatry, immorality, and infidelity. A fourth related word might be added: rebellion. It is the expression that covers the unfaithful ways of the Israelites in general. They had the title of "rebels" almost from the outset of their history down to their last days.

IV
Ezekiel's Update in the Promised Land
(20:31-44)

God stepped directly into the prophetic and teaching ministry of Ezekiel again. Verse 31 of chapter 20 states that God didn't want the elders asking any more questions! He had endured enough of their pretensions. They didn't want to know the truth. They tried to deceive Ezekiel and the Lord by their questions, without any intention of being honest. Consequently, God said, "I will not be inquired of by you" (v. 31).

Despite their idolatrous practices of serving gods of "wood and stone" (v. 32), God said He would rule over His people; He was going to redeem and refine the Israelites until they finally recognized Him as Lord (vs. 33-37). He would bring them out from all the places He had scattered them until they learned that He was the Lord (20:44).

V
The Story of Chastening
(20:45-21:17)

The ancient people of Israel had to experience God's chastening hand because of their transgressions. Hebrews 12:6 reads, "whom the Lord loves He chastens." In Ezekiel's day, Israel was going to have catastriophic chastening, even though they didn't believe it!

Chastening by fire awaited the people of the Lord. God said, "I am about to set fire to you and it will consume all your green trees...the blazing flame shall not be quenched, and every face from the south to the north shall be scorched by it" (20:47). The elders looked at Ezekiel as they sat in his house in 590 B.C., and the date is recorded: "seventh year of their captivity, the fifth month, and the tenth day" (20:1). The hour could have been 10:00 a.m. or 3:00 p.m. Those elders sat quietly during the message of God's faithful prophet, without interrupting him, even though they probably squirmed as he spoke about God's fiery judgment against those who had committed idolatry. A fiery judgment, literal and symbolical, was going to take place throughout Jerusalem. Everyone was going to see Nebuchadnezzar's forces at work among them (20:48). The day of God's vengeance was fast approaching.

Ezekiel had used harsh, non-complimentary language with the exiles. Evidently they responded to him with looks of resentment, if not despair. The prophet spoke to the Lord about his confrontation with the exiles, stating, "Ah, Lord God! They say of me, 'Does he not speak in parables'?" A little later, Ezekiel would hear their rumor about him as the exiles would say something like the following, "Lord, they look at me as though I were a clown! They say that I'm speaking in parables that they don't understand. They say they're okay, and ask why I talk to them the way I do" (33:32). And yet, Ezekiel knew that God's word to the exiles was "right on target." He warned his fellow Israelites time and time again that judgment was coming to Jerusalem. Have we learned that God's chastening is not reserved only for the ancient people of God? Simon Peter wrote that judgment begins at God's house (1 Peter 4:17). We must give an account to God for ourselves. We can't dodge personal responsibility.

Chastening by the sword awaited the Hebrews. Ezekiel mentioned God's "sword of judgment" more than a dozen times in Chapter 21. Who could miss such a "sharp warning" as this! Chapter 21 states several times that the sword is furbished, glittering, sharpened, and taken out of its sheath against all people. Ezekiel made the sword story unforgettable as he continued to describe that deadly weapon.

The prophet told the elders that in Jerusalem the people's hearts would melt, their hands would tremble, and their knees would become as weak as water (21:7). Their enemies would soon be brandishing their swords at the city gates, and fear and panic would grip the land (20:12-16).

VI
Signs in the Middle of the Road
(21:18-27)

The elders needed more instructions to understand the fire and sword judgments of God.

True to God's command, Ezekiel demonstrated his message again with a sign in "the fork of the road." One sign pointed toward Jerusalem. The other sign pointed to the small country of Ammon that helped King Zedekiah in his rebellion against Nebuchadnezzar. The elders wondered what Nebuchadnezzar's route would be as he marched from Babylon to Jerusalem. Ezekiel said, "Let me tell you more about the soon-to-be invasion. We will have three demonstrations."

The first demonstration involved two arrows. One had the name of Jerusalem on it, and the other, Ammon's capital. "Let the first arrow that we take out of the bag be the one to show the route of Nebuchadnezzar," Ezekiel said. As they picked up that arrow, it had the name of Jerusalem on it. The second demonstration went the route of pagan religion. The king of Babylon consulted the teraphim, which were the images of Babylonian ancestral worship, and the message indicated Jerusalem as the king's target.

The third demonstration delved more deeply into pagan mysteries. The liver of a sheep was consulted. The colors or marks on the liver in some mysterious way indicated Jerusalem. King Zedekiah who led his country in a rebellion against Nebuchadnezzar would become the target for Babylon. The end of that unwise and helpless king was near. Ezekiel 21:25 stated that the "profane wicked prince of Israel" had come to the end of his day. His diadem would be removed, and his crown stripped from him.

Three times in Ezekiel 21:27 the statement is given about the end of Zedekiah and Israel's kings. The statement reads that "a ruin, a ruin, a ruin" has come to Jerusalem ("overthrown, overthrown, over-thrown" spells out total destruction). The end had come to Zedekiah and the corrupt people of Jerusalem. But the end of Zedekiah had a new chapter. Ezekiel 21:27 has a word about a coming messiah. (The usual reading is to contrast Zedekiah, the "wicked prince," with another ruler. The immediate context seems to suggest Nebuchadnezzar. At least, the established rule of Zedekiah would be overthrown). And yet, a new and everlasting reign would begin, and Zedekiah's kingdom "shall be no longer, Until He comes whose right it is, and I will give it to Him" (Ezekiel 21:27; Genesis 49:10; Luke 1:52). The Messiah from David's lineage would receive the scepter and "wear the King's crown." He would come and begin His eternal reign. The "Desire of all nations" would come (Haggai 2:7). The Lord God would give to the "new king" the staff and crown, and He would rule (v. 27).

VII
Adios Ammon
(21:28-32)

Ammon was a small country east of the Jordan River, north east of the Dead Sea. The people of this country had helped Zedekiah in his rebellion against Nebuchadnezzar. The final history of Ammon soon would be a reality. God asked His prophet to say to Ammon, "A sword, a sword is drawn, Polished for slaughter" (v. 28). God's indignation would be poured out on Ammon. The Lord declared, "I will blow against you with the fire of My wrath...You shall be fuel for the fire...You shall not be remembered" (v. 32). Judgment would fall on Ammon. The Israelites would finally understand God's message, "For I the Lord have spoken (v. 32). We need to learn this lesson, don't we?

Chapter 16

A Day of Reckoning
Ezekiel 22:1-24:27

—⚏—

In times of war, invasions and attacks are not usually announced. The attacking forces want to catch their enemies unprepared for any defensive action. However, God let His people know well in advance that the Babylonian army would attack Jerusalem. Jeremiah and Ezekiel preached for more than ten years that the Babylonian army would destroy them, but the warnings of God's prophets fell on deaf ears.

God's people in Jerusalem, as well as the exiles in Babylon, refused to believe that their city would be destroyed. Since God had chosen the Israelites as His special people, they argued that nothing evil would happen to them. Besides, several prophets told them that Jeremiah in Jerusalem and Ezekiel in Babylon continued to give false messages about any attack upon Jerusalem. Even though God had declared His message about Jerusalem's "Day of Reckoning," the people refused to turn from their evil ways. The world is responsible for what it does. Everyone is responsible for his or her actions.

I
Jerusalem's Sins
(22:1-31)

Ezekiel reminded those who heard and read his messages that his words came from God (v. 1). God also reminded Ezekiel that he was a "son of man" (a human being), and that eliminated any boasting on his part. The message for Ezekiel was that Jerusalem's detestable acts were going to bring doom to the city (vs. 2-3). Their sins of idolatry and murder, linked to other transgressions, meant that their days were fast coming to a close. Because of all their hideous crimes, they would become a laughingstock to other nations. People far away and near at hand would mock the city filled with turmoil (vs. 4-5).

Look at the sinful princes who are mentioned in 22:6. The political leaders or princes of Israel should have been role models for everyone. However, their litany of sins became scandalous. They had become guilty of oppression of the poor and widows, desecration of holy days, bribes, extortion, and immorality (22:3-4, 7-8, 15, 25). The crowning sin that brought on their depravity was their forgetfulness of God (22:12). The behavior of the politicians helped bring on famine (vs. 23-24). The princes, symbolically, became like lions that ripped apart their prey (v. 25).

Caesar Vallerotto and I made a mission trip to Mina Clavero, Cordoba, in Argentina. As we drove across the mountains, Mr. Vallerotto pointed to a cabin. He said that a few years before a couple had lived in the little cabin. A lion roamed by the place one day, saw a one-year-old child in the yard, grabbed the helpless baby, and bounded off into the rough mountain terrain, never to be seen again. In parabolic language, Ezekiel said the politicians had devoured helpless people. God struck his hands together as an expression of anger and disgust because of the behavior of the princes, and said He would scatter His people among the nations because of their sins. Finally, they would learn that the LORD is God (v. 16).

The people faced severe punishment. Before Ezekiel addressed other culprits in Jerusalem, he told of their upcoming punishment. God's people were nothing more than dross or waste products. They were like copper, tin, iron, and lead — not good silver (22:18). God was placing them in a furnace where He would blow fiery blasts of wrath upon them. They would be melted down in the fire that was being prepared for them.

Near where I grew up, Will Fautheree had a syrup mill. We stripped the sorghum with wooden paddles during the hot days of

June or July. After cutting down the stalks of sorghum, we hauled the cane to the syrup mill. A mule pulled a pole around and around as we stuck the stalks of sorghum into the rollers of the mill. The juice flowed into a barrel, and as more sorghum juice was needed, the valve would be opened to release the juice into the three by eight feet copper-like cooking pan. A roaring fire was under the pan, and the juice was cooked for a certain length of time. Constantly, someone would scoop up the skimming from the pan of juice and put it into a fifty-five gallon barrel. Some people made cheap alcohol or rum from the skimming after it fermented. Often the skimming was poured into a trough near the mill, and pigs would drink it and become drunk. But the cooked juice became good syrup. The skimming was a byproduct and was of no value — except for boozehounds!

In a parable, Ezekiel declared that God's people were like the skimming. They were dross that had no value (22:19-21). This was a shocking word for God's people. The Apostle Paul had a similar word in 1 Corinthians 9:27 about being a "castaway." God's people need to be careful!

Look at the priests (22:26). Everyone expects those who represent God to be the epitome of virtue. A different story emerges from the book of Ezekiel. The Old Testament priests converted the sacred things of God into unholy things, teaching that no difference existed between the two. They desecrated the Sabbaths, and thereby caused God to be profaned among them.

The Old Testament priests, as well as most of Christ's apostles, married and had families. That has been God's design for the human race. The Catholic Church has faced many problems because of unmarried priests and nuns. The January 8, 2003 issue of <u>Dallas Morning News</u> had an article, stating that forty percent of USA nuns have suffered some kind of sexual trauma or rape. The evangelical churches face serious problems among the clergy who have moral breakdowns; thus being married does not necessarily solve sexual problems. Other religions commit immoral acts, too. God says judgment falls upon His people when leaders violate God's commandments.

Look at the prophets (22:25, 28). Normally when reference is made to biblical prophets, we think of God's servants who are always faithful. And yet, the shocking truth is recorded that many unfaithful prophets lived in Old Testament days. Jesus stated that many false prophets were among God's true prophets and servants (Matthew 7:22; 24:24). Jeremiah preached in Jerusalem while Daniel and Ezekiel served in Babylon, and they were faithful to God and their constituents. And yet, many who professed to be God's prophets were not. They did not have a word from the Lord. They spoke when God had not spoken to them.

The false prophets are in business for their own gain — mega-bucks and mansions. Even though they whitewash their work, they face judgment (vs. 28). An evangelist, pastor, or lay person may be tempted to "whitewash" that which is wrong. A teacher in a class-room may find it easier to speak pleasing words, rather than words of reprimand relating to that which is clearly wrong. We must not compromise the truth. We need to "speak the truth in love" (Ephesians 4:15); however, that which is wrong must not be glossed over.

Look at the land-owning people, the gentry (22:29). The ordinary citizens in that time turned into people of extortion and oppressed the poor and aliens. Those who had full citizen rights could easily tyrannize those who were not blessed as they were. They failed to be just in their dealings. The evil of being unfair to others is a temp-tation for many people. Only a few in Ezekiel's day escaped the charge of being transgressors. Everyone needs to ask several ques-tions like, "Am I right with God? Do I practice Christian ethics? Am I guilty of crimes? Do I practice what I preach?" Could it be that today's people may often be as guilty as the ancient Israelites who violated God's commands? A lot of heart searching needs to be done, don't you think?

God's people need to "repair walls" for protection against spir-itual attacks. If evil forces threaten their safety, someone needs to rush to repair the areas that have broken down. Chapter 22 closes with verses 30 and 31 with the Lord speaking: "So I sought for a man among them who would make a wall, and stand in the gap before Me on behalf of the land, that I should not destroy it; but I found no one. Therefore I have poured out My indignation on them..." God wanted someone to "stand in the gap" of their "broken down walls" so that He would not destroy the land. God did not want Jerusalem destroyed and His people captured, killed, or taken into slavery. However, He could not find enough righteous people to save the country.

God sent Jonah to Nineveh with a commission of judgment against them, but God determined to save them after they repented (chapters 3-4). He wanted the world to repent during the time of Noah in order that destruction might be avoided (Genesis 6). God was ready to save Sodom and Gomorrah, but ten righteous people could not be found (Genesis 18-19). God did not find enough righteous people to step forth and be the saving element for Jerusalem. God calls for people to "stand in the gap" today. He wants people to build walls of protection for family, church, community, and national life. God is interested in the well-being of everyone. If we fail, then God's chastening comes upon us as it did with the Hebrews in the time of Ezekiel (v. 31). Are we God's people who "stand in the gap" today? Let's consider another scene in this drama of Jerusalem's rebellions.

II
Two Adulterous Sisters
(23:1-49)

Let's have a brief review of Israel's history at this time. Abraham's son, Isaac, had a son named Jacob. God changed Jacob's name to "Israel" and gave him twelve sons. Those twelve sons gave their names to the tribes of Israel. Later, the time of the kings began with Saul in about 1050 B.C. After Saul's rule of forty years, David and Solomon served as kings in Israel. Soon after the death of Solomon in 931 B.C. (928?), the ten Northern Tribes made Samaria their capital. The two Southern Tribes of Judah and Benjamin had Jerusalem as their capital. Quite frequently both had the name "Israel," although the Northern Kingdom is frequently called Israel and the Southern Kingdom, Judah.

Israel lasted from 931 until 722 B.C. when Assyria captured them, leading most of their prominent citizens into slavery. The North had nineteen kings during its existence as a kingdom. Judah had twenty kings during its time as a kingdom until 586 B.C. Their demise came with the Babylonian conquest, and both groups were in the Babylonian-Assyrian areas. With this historical reminder, let's meet the "two sisters."

The capital of the Northern Kingdom, Samaria, received "Oholah" as her name (23:1-10). That name was given to the Israelites because they refused to return to the temple in Jerusalem to worship. The word means "her (own) tent" because they didn't worship at the temple in Jerusalem. Oholah's sin was her flirtation with Assyrian lovers, prostituting herself with pagan neighbors. Also, Assyria had an array of military might that attracted the attention of the Israelites in Samaria. The glory of their leaders and the multitude of gods for pagan worship appealed to the 10 northern tribes. As a result of their unfaithfulness, the Lord let Assyria conquer Samaria and strip her of her glory. The Israelites became a byword among the Assyrians.

Let's meet Oholibah, a new name for Jerusalem (23:11). Oholibah means "my tent (is) in her." The two southern tribes of Judah gloated over the fact that the temple was in their territory. Besides, they had not suffered the fate of the Northern Kingdom. Thus, they felt secure because God had not sent them into earlier captivity with the Israelites.

Oholibah saw horses, chariots, and well-groomed military people of Assyria and sent messengers to that country because they lusted for that kind of life. The language of Ezekiel is pornographic, showing the depravity to which the Lord's people had gone. Ezekiel reminded the exiles that Jerusalem had become worse than Oholah, their sister. Ezekiel said, "Woe to you, Oholibah." He said three small kingdoms had linked up with Babylon and at that time were preparing for an invasion of Jerusalem. The enemy would come with weapons, cut off their noses and ears, kill some by the sword, and stone others to death. The army from Babylon would burn Jerusalem, rob, rape, and kill the people without discrimination, leaving Judah stripped and ruined. Oholibah or Jerusalem would have to drink from the cup of suffering that her older sister had held in her hands more than a century before (23:32).

The people had forgotten God, putting Him behind their backs; therefore, they would suffer the consequences of their evil doings (v. 35). A list of the detestable practices of God's people doesn't sound too strange in modern-day ears. They robbed, stole, committed adultery, defiled God's house, became guilty of child sacrifice, and reveled in their idolatrous living (v. 36). They dressed as prostitutes and appealed to the Babylonians to come their way and enjoy a care-free kind of life with them (vs. 40-45).

Ezekiel stated again that God was going to let them be stoned and be killed by the sword (23:46-47). Their houses were going to be burned, and judgment was about to fall upon them. God said He would put an end to their lewd behavior (v. 48). Then the people would know that the LORD is God (v. 49). The price of the lesson that the Israelites learned was death, destruction, and desolation. Can we learn that when we exclude God from life, and put aside His word that we, too, face a horrible future?

III
The Parable of the Cooking Pot
(24:1-14)

This chapter is dated in the ninth year, the tenth month, and the tenth day, from the captivity in 597 B.C. The sun was soon to set for Jerusalem. Her end had come into clear view. Ezekiel needed to act out another parable to demonstrate to the exiles what was taking place back in Jerusalem.

Put on the cooking pot (24:1-14). This drama can be told quickly. Fill the pot with water and put the best meat in the water: the legs, shoulders, and best bones of the animal. Stack the wood around the pot, and set the wood on fire. Let the water start boiling, and let the meat and bones start cooking. Jerusalem's inhabitants were going to be in "God's pot." He said, "Woe to the city. I am piling the wood high around the pot." The fire is going to be roaring. The pot won't protect the meat that's being cooked, because the roaring fire continues beneath the pot. Even the pot would suffer a "melt down." The people of Jerusalem were going to face the onslaughts of Nebuchadnezzar's army and the people inside the city would be cooked. Roasted! Burned!

God said that He would not hold back His wrath. The day of their destruction would not be delayed another moment. Seven times God let the people know that judgment was being poured out upon them:

1) The Lord had spoken this word, 2) Judgment will come to pass, 3) He will do it, 4) He will not turn back, 5) The Lord will not spare, 6) He will not repent, 7) He will judge them (24:14). Seven sure words of judgment are spoken by the Lord in one verse! Woe to the people who had turned their backs upon God and had cast aside His Word! His wrath was going to be poured out upon them. Blackwood states that these repeated judgments had the intensity of a war drum that summoned troops to destroy (Ezekiel: Prophesy of Hope, p. 165).

IV
The Death of Ezekiel's Wife
(24:15-27)

Death came to the prophet's family. The only mention that is made of Ezekiel's wife is in chapter 24:15. She is called "the desire of his eyes." She died on the day of the invasion of Jerusalem. Without a warning, without any preparation for the event, God told Ezekiel that He was taking his wife away from him with one "stroke" (24:16). The Lord asked Ezekiel to "sigh in silence" at the time of his wife's death (v. 17). God also asked Jeremiah not to mourn at the time of Jerusalem's fall (Jeremiah 16:5-13). The death of Ezekiel's wife came as "one stroke." Cooper states that "one blow" in the Hebrew language describes death that occurs suddenly in battle or through some disease (Numbers 14:37; 25:8-9; 1 Samuel 4:17; 2 Samuel 17:9). The prophet's wife probably contracted some disease that was sudden and fatal.

The Lord used that occasion as an object lesson for the Israelites not to make a display of their grief over the loss of Jerusalem. Death for Jerusalem was necessary for restoration and new life to come (Cooper, p. 239). Jesus spoke about death (specifically His own), saying that a grain of wheat must fall into the ground and die in order that a greater harvest may come (John 12:24).

Ezekiel was told to keep doing his work as though he had not lost his wife. The exiles knew of the death of Ezekiel's wife, and they were puzzled as to why he did not express any grief. He answered them according to God's instructions. Jerusalem is coming under the sword of the Babylonians this very day. Don't grieve, don't eat the food of mourners, and don't dress as those who have lost loved ones. And yet, out of death God would bring life.

Another message came to those in exile: "You shall know that I am the Lord " (24:24). A new day dawned for God's people (24:25-27). A fugitive soon would arrive from Jerusalem to tell Ezekiel about Jerusalem's fall. God told Ezekiel that his mouth would be open and he would be free to speak, "and no longer be mute" (24:27). This big turning point in the book of Ezekiel comes with a renewed word from God that everyone will know that "I am the LORD" (24:27). Have we learned this lesson?

Chapter 17

Seven Ancient Nations Around Israel
Ezekiel 25:1-32:32 (also chapter 35)

—⟁—

As Ezekiel chapter 24 closes and chapter 25 begins, a new day had dawned for God's ancient people. Within eighteen months after the Babylonian forces invaded Jerusalem in 587 B.C, the city was smoldering in ruins. Thousands of people had died, and thousands more had gone into captivity. Ezekiel prophesied against Jerusalem throughout the first twenty four chapters of his book.

Ezekiel chapters 25-32 refer extensively about seven Gentile nations surrounding Jerusalem or Judah, giving the reasons for their judgment. Chapters 25-28 deal with six of those countries. Chapters 29-32 give the story of Egypt, the seventh one.

Interestingly, Ezekiel made no mention of Babylon in these chapters. One reason for omitting that nation may have been his own safety. Another reason may have been that God was using that vast empire as an instrument to punish Israel. Ezekiel listed the nations around Israel in a clock-like pattern. Across the Jordan River, in a northeastern direction was the small country of Ammon. To the east of Jerusalem, across the Dead Sea, was the land of Moab. South of Jerusalem was Edom, and west of Jerusalem along the Mediterranean Sea coast, was the country of Philistia. Up the sea coast to the northwest of Jerusalem lay the small country of Tyre. Twenty-five miles further north was the little kingdom of Sidon. A little more than one hundred miles southwest of Israel's border was Egypt. When a person draws a rough map, putting the land of Israel in the center of the map, it is easy to have a pictorial view of these seven nations that surrounded Israel.

In Chapters 25-28, Ezekiel's book several times has the words, "That they may know that I am the LORD." Perhaps, the meaning of the words about pagan nations knowing the Lord was in knowing God's judgment of them. Beyond doubt, God wanted the Gentile nations to learn that He was and is the LORD. In these same chapters, the prophet stated nearly fifty times, "Thus says the Lord." Again, the repeated emphasis about God speaking should have attracted the attention of those ancient nations.

We may learn some vital lessons about God and the nations of the world as these chapters are briefly reviewed. One, we can learn that God is sovereign. Not only was God the Lord of His chosen people, but He is the Lord of all nations. God exercises His final control over every nation. A second lesson we may learn from these chapters is that every nation must give account of itself to God. A third revolutionary truth is that God may choose any nation or any individual as His instrument to accomplish His purpose. Just as God chose Ezekiel to be His prophet, He also chose Babylon as His instrument to chasten Israel. God needs instruments and He looks for those who will help bring about His purpose.

Morality is important in the life of a nation, a family, and individual. This truth needs to be understood. God calls for high ethical standards on the part of everyone. As the story unfolds about the seven nations around Jerusalem, we learn that a proud, boastful attitude gets anyone into trouble. God condemned Tyre and their king because of their pride. We should learn a lesson in humility from those nations. Another lesson we can learn from these chapters is that we should never laugh at another's tragedy. If one pokes fun at another, he or she may suffer for that action.

I
A Prophesy against Ammon
(25:1-7)

The beginning of Ammon came out of a tragic moment in history. Sodom and Gomorrah had been destroyed after Lot and his family left Sodom. After the tragic loss of his wife, Lot was alone with his two daughters (Genesis 19:30-38). One night they gave their father wine to drink and the older one slept with him. On the following night, they caused Lot to be inebriated again, and the younger daughter had sexual relations with her father. The younger daughter had a son, Ben-Ammi, and he became the father of the Ammonites.

When Jerusalem was destroyed in 586 B.C., the Ammonites said in derision, "Aha!" or "Hurrah!" to Judah (25:3). Because of their scorn for the Lord, for the land of Israel, and the House of Judah, Ammon would be given to "the men of the East" (25:5). That enemy of Ammon would make their capital city of Rabbah "a stable for camels," and their land would be plundered by nations. God would destroy them (v. 7). That small nation in judgment would learn that "the LORD is God." Destruction would come to them.

II
A Prophesy against Moab
(25:8-11)

Moab's beginning came through Lot and his older daughter's relationship. He became the father of the Moabites. When Jerusalem fell, the Moabites said that Israel was like every other nation. They also looked upon Jerusalem in a scornful, despiteful way, overlooking the fact that they were the Lord's chosen people. God said that the same punishment meted out to Ammon would fall upon the Moabites (25:10-11). They would be conquered by the people east of them, and would cease to exist. They also would learn that the Lord is God.

III
A Prophesy against Edom
(25:12-14; 35:1-15)

The Edomites were descendants of Esau. Jacob and Esau had critical problems over their inheritance. Since Jacob received his father Isaac's blessings, Esau hated his brother (Genesis 25-27). Nearly five hundred years later, when Israel came out of Egyp, the Edomites would not let the Hebrews cross their territory (Deuteronomy 2). Esau's children still carried a hatred for Jacob's family. They continually took revenge on the house of Judah and, because of their sin, God judged them. They would lose their territory south of the Dead Sea, and they would die by the sword. They, too, would learn that God is the Lord.

Chapter 25 of Ezekiel discusses Mount Seir or Edom. Note, also, that chapter 35 of Ezekiel discusses Edom more extensively than does this passage in chapter 25. In the later chapter on Edom, the story is given about three sins they commited against Judah during Jerusalem's calamity: One, they had kept up an endless enmity against the Hebrews. Two, they slaughtered the Israelites with the sword when God's people were helpless. Three, Edom took advantage of Jerusalem when Babylon defeated them, declaring that the land belonged to them, and that they would possess it. The Edomites rushed into the vacuum that had been left when Babylon destroyed Jerusalem. Therefore, Ezekiel denounced Edom in Chapter 25 as well as in Chapter 35. Two times in Chapter 35 the words appear, "Thus says the Lord God" (vs. 3, 14). Four times in the same chapter the words are written, "Then you shall know that I am the LORD" (vs. 4, 9, 12, 15). In time, utter desolation came to Edom, and the nation no longer exists.

IV
A Prophesy against Philistia
(25:15-17)

The Philistines lived along the Mediterranean coastal area southwest of Israel. We remember the name of Goliath, the Philistine giant who fought David. The people from Philistia acted in vengeance against Israel. They hated both Judah and Israel. God said He would destroy them so they would know that He was the Lord.

V
A Prophesy against Tyre
(26:1-21)

Most people place the date on letters they write. Some sections of Ezekiel's book are frequently dated. Chapter 26 states that God's prophet spoke this section of his book "in the eleventh year, on the first day of the month." Thus, this writing about Tyre is dated, 586 B.C., immediately following Jerusalem's destruction.

Tyre celebrated when Jerusalem fell (26:2). Because this small nation on the Mediterranean Seacoast rejoiced over Judah's suffering, God said He would let Babylon destroy the capital city. As an added punch, the enemy would "scrape away her dust from her, and make her like the top of a rock" (v. 4). Alexander the Great in 332 B.C. finished the work of judgment on Tyre that Babylon had begun three centuries earlier. Tyre became little more than a place where fishermen spread their nets to dry. The people who lived on the mainland near the island capital died by the sword, and various nations plundered that land. Tyre, like other nations learned that the Lord is God (v. 6).

Ezekiel 26:7-21 gives a description of the attack upon Tyre. Nebuchadnezzar's army laid siege to the proud city, using battering rams to try to demolish the walls. He would try to take Tyre's wealth, destroy their costly houses, and leave the island capital and their mainland property in ruins. The princes would step down from their throne, sit in dust, and weep as they gazed upon the ruins of their once-grand kingdom. Eventually, God brought Tyre's glory to an end, even though Ezekiel 29:17-21 states that Tyre was not taken by the Babylonians, but it would fall later.

VI
A Lament for Tyre
(27:1-36)

The city of Tyre was a gateway to the world. Builders from many nations came to help make the kingdom great. The roll call of nations who sent builders reads like a modern-day United Nations gathering. The list included those from Lebanon, Cyprus, Persia, Spain (Tarshish, a seaport), Greece, Rhodes, Damascus, Arabia, Sheba of North Africa, and Haran in Assyria. The best workers from everywhere rushed to Tyre.

Ezekiel compared Tyre to a great ship that was well-built and well-manned. And yet, oarsmen would "abandon ship," and Tyre would find itself sinking into the depths of the sea. People from all nations would throw dust upon their heads, roll in ashes, put on sackcloth, and shudder over Tyre's ruin because that country would be no more (v. 36).

VII
A Prophesy against the King of Tyre
(28:1-21)

King Ethbaal III was the ruler at that moment in Tyre's history. Nothing specific is known of him other than what is described in Ezekiel chapter 28. Greenberg sums up the problem of the king with his pride that led to self-deification: "The leader's haughtiness springs from his success and prosperity, which puff him up to thinking he is equal to a god in wisdom" (Ezekiel, p. 573).

God had a special word of judgment for the King of Tyre because he had imagined himself as being a "god." He thought that he had become as wise as Daniel; and he had proved himself to be an astute man who knew how to manage and amass fortunes in gold and silver. His business acumen also opened the door for his pride and self-sufficiency; hence, God's judgment brought on his demise. Ruthless nations attacked the small kingdom, leaving the king totally defeated. Enemy swords would not stop until the beauty and wisdom of Tyre had faded into oblivion.

A new lament was made for the king of Tyre who had no future (vs. 11-21). He had been "the seal of perfection, full of wisdom and perfect in beauty" (vs. 12-13). He lost his coveted place in Eden. The precious stones that decorated his kingdom would now be gone. His position as an "anointed cherub" would be removed (v. 14). In disgrace, God cast the king from his palace, and he would be no more (v. 19). In Cooper's extended discussion on the king of Tyre, he states, "the conclusion that the figure behind the poetic symbol is the serpent...is a logical one...The real motivating force behind the king of Tyre was his adversary, the devil or Satan, who opposed God and his people from the beginning" (Ezekiel, pp. 268-269). The word "Ichabod" could have been placed over his name.

VIII
A Prophesy against Sidon
(28:20-26)

Sidon rested on the Mediterranean Sea coast about 15 miles north of Tyre. All hope faded fast for that small kingdom, too. Sidon, like all the others, would learn that God is the Lord (v. 22). Sidon's citizens had been like thorns in the side of Israel. Because of their actions against Israel, their blood would flow in the streets as enemy swords fell upon them. God repeated the message again. "They will know that I am the LORD."

IX
A Brief Reminder about Israel
(28:25-26)

The future for God's people is certain. God will gather His scattered people who have lived among all nations. Ezekiel declared several times that God would "scatter" His people, and 10 times he wrote that the Lord would "gather" them. They will live again in the land of their inheritance. They will prosper in the land that belongs to them. Is this a prophesy regarding "physical Israel" or "spiritual Israel?" Paul said all who believe in Jesus are the "sons of Abraham" and are "true Israelites." (Romans 9:6-7; 11:26; Galatians 3:7; 6:16). One day God will gather together all His people, and the Lord declares, "They shall know that I am the LORD their God" (v. 26).

Chapter 18

Messages against Egypt
Ezekiel 29:1-32:32

—ɯ—

Egypt is located in northeast Africa and southwest Asia. The Sinai Peninsula, south of Palestine, is located in southwest Asia, next door to Saudi Arabia, and is a part of Egypt.

Egypt is about one-fourth larger than the state of Texas. That African-Asian land is nearly eight hundred miles in width and almost seven hundred miles from north to south. Egypt's recorded history goes back to 3,000 B.C. — about one thousand years before the time of Abraham. This five thousand year-old nation has an ancient culture that matches the oldest nations of Asia. The twenty-first-century population of Egypt is nearly seventy million. The capital city of Cairo has approximately seven million inhabitants. Alexandria has more than three million and Giza more than two million population.

The Nile River runs on a northern, winding path through Egypt, emptying into the Mediterranean Sea, and is more than seven hundred miles long. The life of Egypt clusters along the river, extending out five to eight miles on the east and west. More than ninety percent of Egypt's people live in that corridor, and about ninety-five percent of the rest of the country is desert. The Sahara Desert extends across North Africa from the Atlantic into the Sinai Peninsula of Asia. Sahara in Arabic means "desert."

Today, ninety percent of Egypt's people belong to the Sunni Islam religion, and most of the others belong to the Coptic Orthodox Church. Arabic is the principal language of the country, although some speak English and French, as well as the Berber tongue. A few of the main products of Egypt include cotton, wheat, rice, fruit, beans, cattle, and fish. Tourism gives a big boost to their economy.

Ezekiel has seven messages that refer to Egypt. With the exception of one message, in Chapter 30, these messages have their dates listed. Because of Egypt's sin, God judged that nation, as He does all nations, stating that He would demote that nation and never let her rise to international status again. Let's consider an overview of the seven messages that Ezekiel wrote to the Egyptian nation.

I
First Note (587 B.C.)
(29:1-16)

We should have no trouble understanding God's message to Egypt. The Sovereign Lord said to Ezekiel, "Son of man, set your face against Pharaoh king of Egypt" (v. 2). The message was one of condemnation of Egypt for two reasons. One reason was their pride, and the second reason was their promise to help Judah or Jerusalem in their rebellion against Babylon, but they did not fulfill that promise. Hophra, the Pharaoh of Egypt, made a brash claim that he had created the Nile River, and that he owned it. The Lord called Pharaoh Hophra a "great monster who lies in the midst of his rivers" (v. 3).

Because of Hophra's pride, God would put hooks in his jaws and draw him out of the river, along with the fish that were stuck onto his scales. In this figure of speech, God said the smaller nations who had their trust in Egypt would be yanked out of the water with Pharaoh. God would drag the crocodile out to the desert where he would die, and birds and wild animals would devour him. Egypt would know who the LORD is (v. 6).

Egypt had another notable sin in that she promised help to Judah, but was unable, or unwilling, to fulfill the promise (vs. 6-7). Pharaoh Hophra, the grandson of Pharaoh Necho, encouraged

Judah to rebel against Babylon (2 Kings 25:3-8; Jeremiah 37). Judah rebelled in 597, but without success. When Egypt made an attempt to help Judah, that effort failed. Nebuchadnezzar quickly put down the rebellion, and the forces of Egypt left Judah stranded. The text in Ezekiel states that Egypt was only a weak river reed that Judah had leaned upon. The reed broke, and Judah suffered with a broken shoulder.

God promised to send a sword against Egypt, letting the nation become decimated by the sword of Babylon. Man and beast would be killed, and the survivors would be scattered. After forty years, God would let the Egyptians return to their homeland. After that time, however, Egypt would be a lowly kingdom and would never be among the leading world powers again. They would know that God is the Sovereign Lord (v. 16).

II
Second Note (570 B.C.)
(29:17-21)

After Nebuchadnezzar made havoc of Jerusalem, his forces attacked Tyre (26:7). That assault on this small maritime nation continued as a costly war for Babylon for 13 years, and the attack became a costly one for Babylon, because Nebuchadnezzar's forces didn't gain anything after those long years of assault — except bare heads and raw shoulders for all the soldiers! Later, the Lord promised to give Egypt to Nebuchadnezzar as payment for his labor and warfare against the powerful kingdom of Tyre (29:19).

The soldiers had worked their fingers to the bones as they tried to conquer Tyre. They had carried rocks and other materials and built a roadway into the Mediterranean Sea to the island's capital. Ezekiel's description is that "every head was made bald, and every shoulder rubbed raw" in that work (v. 18). Babylon didn't realize that they were working for God in their attack against Tyre. God knew what was happening and said He would pay Babylon for "bringing down Tyre." God let Babylon have a swift victory over Egypt, showing that the way God rewards nations may sometimes surprise us! Since God paid Babylon for doing His work, we know that He will reward His people today who work for Him. No one needs to be a reluctant servant of the Lord because everyone may do what God wants to be done.

God promised that He would cause Israel to prosper, even though that nation had fallen to Babylon in 586 B.C. His word rang out, "I will cause the horn of the house of Israel to spring forth." In the same sentence, the Lord said that He would "open the mouth" of Ezekiel and let him have freedom to speak (29:21). The twenty-two years of "dumbness" that God had imposed upon Ezekiel came to a close after the fall of Jerusalem, but no details of his work after 586 are given (3:26; 29:21; 33:22). The people heard important truth again: "Then they will know that I am the Lord" (29:21). Of course, Ezekiel's book does not end until his final words in 48:35: "The Lord is there."

III
Third Note: No Date Listed
(30:1-19)

Judgment time came for Egypt. The expression, "The day of the Lord is near" (v. 3), referred to the sword that Babylon brought against Egypt and their being robbed of their wealth as the foundations of the land were ripped apart (v. 4).

Egypt's idols and images were destroyed. Their cities from north to south fell into the hands of their enemy. Other nations such as Ethiopia, south of Egypt, and Libya (east of Egypt), would also suffer as Babylon pillaged Egypt. The sword and fire that wreaked havoc across that North African nation would show Pharaoh's land again that the Lord is on His throne and controls the affairs of the world.

IV
Fourth Note (586 B.C.)
(30:20-26)

God broke the arm of Pharaoh (v. 21). That setback for Egypt's leader came in 587 B.C. when he joined Judah in its attempt to repel Babylon's attack on Jerusalem (Jeremiah 37). God broke the other arm of Pharaoh when Babylon later came against Egypt (vs. 22-25). The sword fell from Pharaoh Hophra's hands and he became incapacitated to defend himself against Babylon. No one put medicine upon Egypt's broken arms, nor bound them up with a splint for healing. The nation groaned like a dying man (v. 24). God scattered the Egyptians, and they learned that He is the LORD (vs. 25-26).

V
Fifth note (586 B.C.)
(31:1-18)

The prophet gave a description of Egypt as one of the "cedars of Lebanon." He likened Egypt to Assyria. The tall cedar tree is described in poetic language. The tree towered above all others, birds rested in its branches, animals rested beneath its shade, the roots spread out to abundant waters, and it became the envy of other trees.

And yet, judgment came, and the nation fell. Pharaoh ended up in Sheol. All the nations of the ancient world trembled as they heard about the end of Egypt's greatness.

Sheol refers to the netherworld land. In his book Jeremiah and Ezekiel, A.J. Glaze states that Sheol is a place of shades (*rephaim*) or shadowy existence. Sheol is a place of uncertainty or iniquity (Glaze, p. 157). Egypt found her place in the pit. The small and the great who warred against God found themselves in the darkest corners of Sheol.

VI
Sixth Note (585 B.C.)
(32:1-15)

A note about Egypt's pride pops up again in Ezekiel. The people imagined themselves to be a lion in a forest and a crocodile in the Nile. Just as a crocodile sometimes thrashes around in shallow water, muddying a once-clear stream, so Egypt "muddied the waters" of the Nile. But God intervened and stopped that activity.

The Lord put a "net" around the crocodile. He hauled the water beast, figuratively speaking, to a desert. The animal died on the hot sand, wild beasts chewed away on the carcass, and birds came flocking to it. The end of Egypt came as the Lord spread their flesh upon the mountains and filled the valleys with their bones. Blood filled the valleys to the tops of the mountains, and ravines were filled with the flesh (vs. 5-6). The poetic, figurative language meant total destruction for that one-time proud nation. They heard, again, the refrain: "They shall know that I am the Lord" (v. 15).

VII
Seventh and Final Note (585 B.C.)
(32:16-32)

A final lament for Pharaoh Hophra sounded again (v. 16). Weeping and wailing took place at the demise of Egypt and her king. The nations of antiquity that preceded Egypt had gone to Sheol. This chapter gives a list of the powerful empires that preceded Pharaoh and his kingdom to that place of "shades and iniquity."

Assyria, the once-powerful nation, with Nineveh as its capital, heads the list of those who are there (vs. 22-23). Elam, a small country east of Babylon, found her bed in Sheol. Meshech and Tubal, north of Assyria, found their fateful place among all those who fell into disgrace. Edom and the Sidonians marched into their graves, too.

The hordes in hell watched as Pharaoh came among them. The end came for that nation as well as it does for all others who forget God. Yes, the death knell sounded. How can one know about the future of those who leave God out of life? Ezekiel 23:32 states the case clearly that the Sovereign Lord declares this truth.

Charles Spurgeon of England told about flocks of albatross and pigeons that crowded around ships as they came into harbor. A hook was baited with meat by a man who tossed the bait toward the birds. The birds rushed for the meat. The one who threw out the hook, pulled in the bird that grabbed the bait. Again and again as the man threw a baited hook among the birds, they continued to grab it. Even though many birds were being pulled in, the others never understood the danger of grabbing the bait.

The devil has plenty of bait that he tosses out to nations and individuals. Mankind is like senseless birds that try to gobble up what they think might be a great catch. We need to learn the lessons that ancient and present-day people find hard to accept: God is Sovereign and we need to bow to His purpose and will. Are we doing it?

Chapter 19

Watchmen on the Wall
Ezekiel 33:1-33

—ɯ—

Napoleon Bonaparte of France is remembered as one of the world's great conquerors. Following several years of schooling and military service, Napoleon became the Emperor of France. In 1815 Napoleon fought his final battle when the British and their allies defeated him at Waterloo. They sent Napoleon as a prisoner of war to the lonely Saint Helena Island in the Atlantic, off the coast of Africa. After Napoleon's death and burial in 1821, his few attendants returned to France. One of his friends, Sergeant Huber, refused to leave the emperor's grave, continuing to guard that tomb for nineteen years. When France removed Napoleon's remains to the dome of the Invalides beside the Seine River in Paris, Sergeant Huber stayed with Napoleon's body until it reached its final resting place.

If we think about faithful prophets in the Old Testament, the name of Ezekiel has to be in the list. God called Ezekiel to be a prophet in 593 B.C., telling him that he was going to be a "watchman for the house of Israel" (3:16; 33:7). Ezekiel lived among the exiles and did what God asked him to do as a prophet. The records don't tell the story of all his work, but what is recorded in Ezekiel's book does show his faithfulness to God. God has a work for His people in every generation. That work may be tough or easy, but whatever the work may be, we can be faithful watchmen while we do our job.

I
We can be Faithful or Careless Watchmen
(33:1-9)

Ancient cities had walls around them for their protection, with watchtowers on the walls. The people chose different men to serve as guards for their cities. A watchman stayed at his post during night hours, as well as during the day. If an enemy army approached a city, the watchman would see the troop movement. He had the duty of blowing a trumpet so that everyone might make defensive preparations.

Those who heard the trumpet knew that danger was nearby. If people prepared themselves, their lives would be saved. Those who heard the trumpet blasts, but didn't prepare themselves might be killed or captured. If the watchman slept on the job, or failed to sound a warning when an enemy approached, the people would not know to prepare themselves. If the enemy killed or captured those in the city, the watchman had the blood of the unfortunate victims upon his hands.

Even though we do not live in walled cities, we still need watchmen who will "blow the trumpet and sound an alarm" about dangers that come our way. A dozen ways may open for anyone to go an evil way. Those who "sound the trumpet" ("whistle blower") can warn everyone to live and do right.

We may become trumpet players or "watchmen on the walls" with our lives. Ezekiel didn't have any ugly stains or blemishes upon his life. We may assume that both the prophet and his wife were impeccable examples for all the exiles in Babylon. We should set good examples and live right, or we fail the LORD. Our daily life and conduct can become the sound of a trumpet, saying, "Walk in this way." If our lives fail to be the right example, we fail as watchmen.

A story has circulated about Francis of Assisi. He said to his students one day, "Let's go downtown, walk through the market-place, and preach to the people." A group of students followed him. After an hour or more, they returned home. One said, "Didn't you say that we would go out and preach to the people today?" Francis answered, "As we walked through the crowds in the city, our lives have been a sermon to all who saw us." We always preach with our lives.

The apostle Paul wrote to the Corinthians that God's people are letters that are read and known by all people (2 Corinthians 3:2). If we Christians understood that we are under the scrutinizing eyes of others, perhaps all of us would improve our conduct. The second stanza of the hymn, "Let others see Jesus in you," has arresting words:

> Your life's a book before their eyes,
> They're reading it through and through;
> Say, does it point them to the skies,
> Do others see Jesus in you?

We witness with our lips. Ezekiel certainly did! He continued to tell the people, "Thus says the Lord." Many times throughout his book, Ezekiel focused his messages upon God, calling his fellow exiles to be faithful to Him. Every Christian should feel comfortable in talking about God. We have the world's greatest story. We don't need to be ashamed to let others know about salvation through our Savior. Jeremiah witnessed in Jerusalem, and Ezekiel witnessed as a "watchman on the wall" to his fellow exiles by the River Chebar. As we study the lives of these two servants, we discover that they always proclaimed God's Word to the people around them.

We can take gospel tracts wherever we go, leaving those writings with people. The church where I serve at the moment of this writing has a two-by-three-inch tract with the picture of a man carrying a cross on one side of the card and John 3:16 written on the other side with a statement about confessing Jesus as Savior. We can leave tracts with people in shopping malls or anyplace we go.

When eating at a restaurant, I leave a tract with a tip. As I pass through immigration checkpoints on the South Texas border, I sometimes leave some of these easy-to-carry tracts with the immigration officers. As we speak courteously to people and leave some written word, they often express gratitude for the small gift. Church members can take dozens of tracts in a pocket or purse without any problem. On the back window of my automobile I have a small decal of a fish and the name "Jesus" within that design. We can be faithful watchmen by witnessing in many ways.

II
God Wants Every One to Live
(33:10-20)

The Israelites in the time of Ezekiel faced disturbing, self-made struggles. They had begun to wonder how they could live because they "pined away" in their transgressions (v. 10). They felt like they had begun to rot as a result of their own wrong doings. Previously they had cast the blame for their sinful condition upon their ancestors (18:2). At last, however, they started to admit their failures. Since they admitted their own transgressions had caused their grief and pain, God was ready to do something for them. Even though they confessed their wrong, they seemed to have a problem committing themselves to live in the right way. God answered them in their perplexities.

The Lord wants to forgive and restore His people. God finds delight in showing mercy and in forgiving those who go astray (33:11; Micah 7:18). He takes no pleasure in the death of anyone. He said to the "half repenting" people, "I have no pleasure in the death of the wicked, but that the wicked turn from his way and live. Turn, turn from your evil ways! For why should you die, O house of Israel" (33:11)? We may hear the pathos in the voice of God in the Scripture as He states two times, "Turn, turn." Ezekiel gave the message of life to everyone who would hear.

Centuries later, Jesus wept over Jerusalem, declaring that they would be saved, if they would only accept His words (Matthew 23:37). Simon Peter supports the truth of God's wish for everyone to return to Him because He is "not willing that any should perish but that all should come to repentance" (2 Peter 3:9). The problem of man's death can't be blamed on God because He wants everyone to turn and live.

Sinful people can repent. If a person could not change, God would not have made the appeal for the Israelites to return to Him, and have their life restored and blessed. The message "Repent" means everyone may return to God because He has outstretched, open arms.

Looking back to Jeremiah, we remember that he told King Zedekiah that he and the entire city would be saved if they would do what God said for them to do. The command was not hard to understand. Jeremiah said to the king that all he had to do was to walk out and surrender to the Babylonians and everyone would be safe (Jeremiah 38:19). Zedekiah said he could not do that because he was afraid of what others would think of him! He had his opportunity, but turned it down. People can repent, if they will.

A person shows his valid righteousness by the life he lives. He shows that repentance is more than a noun, it is a verb of action. Ezekiel 33:12-13 is a hard passage for some people because it says, "nor shall the righteous be able to live because of his righteousness in the day that he sins. When I say to the righteous that he shall surely live, but he trusts in his own righteousness and commits iniquity, none of his righteous works shall be remembered."

One approach to understanding the text is of a man who walks under the banner of being righteous or good, but turns to an evil way of conduct. The good that a man like this had done all his life would not be remembered, if that one committed some evil and died. Such a person could possibly be depending upon his own self righteousness to save him. The wicked man dies and shows by his non-repentant attitude that he has not really had a personal relationship with the Lord. If he had been a truly righteous man, he would have turned and repented, and thereby would have lived.

Consider the case of David. He sinned in a horrible way, committing adultery and having the husband of Bathsheba killed to cover up his sin. Even though David kept quiet about the sin for a long time, he faced his sin and confessed it. Out of his awful experience, David wrote his "penitential psalm" because he suffered with a broken heart after his wrong doing (Psalm 51). Later he wrote, "As far as the east is from the west, so far has He removed our transgressions from us" (Psalms 103:12). A shocking example is given of one who lived in an evil way, but turned at the last moment, and lived. The evil that the man had done would not be held against him, if he turned. As Jesus hung on the cross, one thief turned to him, saying, "Lord, remember me when you come into your kingdom." Jesus said to that repentant man, "Today, you will be with me in Paradise" (Luke 23:42-43). If we want to know how a miracle of forgiveness comes at any point in life, the answer flashes back, "The grace and love of God." One who repents has his sins forgiven and God does not remember them or charge them against him (Micah 7:19; Jeremiah 31:34; Hebrews 10:17).

The repentant person shows by his life that he has changed. Ezekiel said those who had taken a "pledge" from anyone needed to return it. For those who had been guilty of robbery, they needed to restore that which had been taken. The story of Zaccheus who climbed into a sycamore tree in order to see Jesus demonstrates true repentance. He told Jesus that if he had taken anything from another, he would restore fourfold (Luke 19:8). Our lifestyle shows that we belong to God, or we don't have a relationship with Him.

Repentance causes a person to walk in "the statutes of life, without committing iniquity" (v. 15). This statement declares that we are to live and do right. Our actions give a clear picture of life. We practice what we preach. God's people don't cover up their ugly deeds with words. We straighten up and become honest and fair with each other. God's people need a big dose of repentance. Most squabbles in denominational and family life would end if genuine repentance took place.

III
Jerusalem Has Fallen! A Fugitive's Report
(33:21-22)

Let's think again about the Israelites who were in Jerusalem. For about one and one half years, the Babylonian army had attacked the city. Many people died from starvation, illness, and the sword, and the city fell in 586 B.C. About a year after the fall of Jerusalem, a messenger arrived in Babylon to tell the story. We do not know why the trip of about 700 miles took the unknown messenger so long. Later on, Nehemiah made the trip from Babylon to Jerusalem in four months (Ezra 7:9). The messenger with the story of Jerusalem's fate might not have been able to leave immediately after the fall of the city. Most likely, Ezekiel heard a full account of the terrible holocaust.

The night before the messenger's arrival, God placed His hand upon Ezekiel again (33:22). The Spirit of God gave a fresh start to the prophet. He had no more hindrances about speaking. He no longer was "dumb" or restrained in proclaiming what needed to be heard by the people in exile (3:26). We would love to have the messages that Ezekiel preached after his somewhat "silent years." He had faced the elders who sat before him on previous occasions (8:1; 14:1; 20:1), and he had done a few "mime messages" (4:1-4).

One day God told Ezekiel to dig a hole through the wall of his house of mud bricks and drag his possessions through the broken place as an indication of how King Zedekiah would run through broken down walls of their city and try to escape (Ezekiel 12). Ezekiel may have started talking fast as he explained to his wife why he was digging through the bedroom wall! Soon his "dumb days" ended, and Ezekiel began to "bubble forth" his messages as never before. God's hand came upon him in a fresh way, and that must have been an ecstatic time in his life. Every Christian needs the experience of a fresh touch from the Lord. Have we asked God for an "Ezekiel renewal" lately?

IV
The Flawed Logic of Some Israelites
(33:23-29)

The struggling remnant back in the environs of Jerusalem began to deny the reality of the impending fall of the city and seek a rationale for their continued possession of the land. They had not been among the captives taken with Daniel to Babylon, nor had they been among the ones carried away with Ezekiel's "group." Moreover, they had survived the destruction that had come upon their capital city in 587-586. Hence, the surviving group seemed to have considered themselves privileged because they had escaped judgment. They worked out a good syllogism with its major and minor premise and conclusion. Their logic seemed reasonable to that motley multitude.

The argument began with Abraham who was their major premise. Their minor premise was that he inherited the land, even though he was only one receiving the inheritance. The conclusion was that since they outnumbered Abraham, they would inherit the land. Jerusalem and the whole area would become their possession.

God said to the group that they had a flawed logic. They had overlooked one essential ingredient. Abraham inherited the land because he was righteous. They would not inherit the land, because they were evil. Thus, God's word to the group straggling around in the Jerusalem area was simple: You are Abraham's physical descendants is the major premise. You are sinful is the minor premise. The conclusion is that you don't get anything! If the people wanted to know what they would receive, God had the answer. He said the sword, wild animals, and pestilence would be their heritage. Even if the people fled, Babylonian soldiers would find and kill them.

If they rushed into fields that had become overgrown with weeds and trees, wild animals would kill them. Lions, tigers, and bears would have their "banquet tables" with flesh and bones of the Israelites. If some sought refuge in caves, they would meet pestilence and disease. They would not survive, even with all the caves and dens that dotted the whole area of Judah. Death was on its way for those proud survivors, and they would not inherit the land. Everyone would learn that the Lord is God (v. 29).

V
The Talk of the Exiles
(33:30-33)

Many leaders think that most everyone thinks well of them. Ezekiel knew better! He had faced troubles from the exiles in Babylon, and God reminded him that he would not be placed on a pedestal. Even though he was changing his message from one of warning to one of hope for the future, Ezekiel still didn't win a popularity contest.

The Lord said, "Look, Ezekiel, they hear you, but the people go home and say things behind your back that they never say when you are with them. The exiles sit and listen, but go away unchanged." Some say, "The prophet has a pleasant voice, like one who sings love songs." Others think, "Ah, good music flows from his instrument, but..." "They hear your words, but do not do them" (vs. 31-33). A quick conclusion comes to Chapter 33. God said His people will know that a prophet has been among them (v. 33). The truth is that God wants all His people to *hear* His message and *do* what He says. How are we measuring up?

Chapter 20
Greedy Shepherds versus the True Shepherd
(34:1-31)

—ɯɯ—

W hen a person has a terrible toothache, he or she wants to see a dentist — fast! If the dentist says that the patient has a cavity, a broken tooth, or needs root canal work, the patient says, "Do whatever needs to be done, doctor. I need relief." God had spoken several times through Ezekiel, letting the people know they had serious problems. However, the people complained because the prophet told them that their sinful living had brought about their suffering and captivity.

Ezekiel found himself in a proverbial "mine field." The people became angry with him when he pointed out their transgressions. They wanted to hear a smooth message that everything was all right in their lives. God told Ezekiel to prophesy against shepherds who take care of themselves, rather than the flock (34:8). That group included both political and spiritual leaders. The shepherds were kings as well as priests and prophets. God said "woe" to those who failed in their responsibilities. Chapter 34 tells about the greedy shepherds, in contrast to the Good Shepherd. Ezekiel identifies the self-centered shepherds as well as the Good Shepherd.

I
The Greedy Shepherds
(34:1-10)

God has always had both good shepherds and greedy shepherds. Among the political leaders, we may remember David, Josiah, and others who appear in the camp of the trustworthy shepherds. Among the prophets and other religious leaders, we may recall the names of those like Miriam, Deborah, Samuel, Josiah, the four prophetic daughters of Philip (Acts 21:8-9), and others.

Elijah once told the Lord that he was the only one who had not bowed his knee to Baal, but God reminded Elijah that seven thousand had remained faithful to Him (1 Kings 19:18). The fact remains that God has good servants even while evil shepherds may be found in the church as well as outside. The Scripture points out some characteristics of bad leaders in any realm of responsibility.

Evil or false shepherds are selfish. Ezekiel 34:2-3 indicates that many shepherds are self-centered, thinking primarily of themselves. They are not concerned with the welfare of others. The shepherd who eats the best in the land, dresses himself with the wool from the flock, destroys those who are fed, and does not feed or care for those under his care, is a bad shepherd. An anecdote tells that once President George Washington sat down at a banquet, and soon was served fish. He asked the waiter, "How much did this chad cost?" The waiter responded that the price was $3.50. George Washington said, "Take it away. We are not going to have such an expensive meal served while others go hungry."

Greedy shepherds fail to help the hurting. Verse four of this chapter states that selfish leaders do not strengthen those who are weak, nor heal the sick, nor bind up those with broken limbs. Many people suffer from various illnesses in every country of the world. It is not possible to remedy all the societal problems that exist. Churches cannot take care of every need that people may have. And yet, when leaders, in the church or outside, fail to have compassion for the helpless, they have forsaken their leadership responsibility. Many people bring problems upon themselves. Those who go the route of drugs, alcohol, and immoral living can expect to "reap what they sow." It is not easy to restore a person who has been ruined by a deviate lifestyle. A person may find forgiveness for the wrongs that are done, but the scars remain. Those who go the downward route suffer from self-inflicted wounds; and yet, we need to have compassion on those who deliberately sin, as well as those who have unintentionally fallen.

Greedy shepherds rule by force and cruelty. Ezekiel 33:4 states that some fail to love and care for those under their rule. Saddam Hussein's torture chambers have been some of the worst in the story of the human race. Anyone who disagreed with the Iraqi president would lose his life, or be tortured so severely that he would wish himself dead. At the same time, such leaders as Hussein have lavished comforts and pleasures upon themselves. He had numerous palaces and other possessions that pictured a life of luxury, even though many of the Iraqi people languished in want. One of Hussein's palaces on the Euphrates River had a colonnade that extended for more than a mile. This scenario of being the "big boss" and being negligent of others takes place in many places. Keep in mind that the principle of "lording it over others" takes place in families, churches, denominations, giant corporations, small businesses, and wherever people live and work. Abuses take place on every continent and in every strata of society.

Look at the example of King Ahab and Queen Jezebel (1 Kings 16-18). They both had a life of pleasure and ease in their palace in Samaria. But Ahab wanted more. He failed to get the vineyard of Naboth, until Jezebel discovered his unsatisfied desires. An arrangement was made for the murder of Naboth, and his vineyard was confiscated. Jezebel and Ahab had no concern for those over whom they ruled. We may ask ourselves how we measure up when it comes to caring for those around us.

Greedy shepherds have no concern for those who are scattered. Ezekiel 34:5-6 refer to the invasions that the Babylonians made into Judah, as well as attacks by the Moabites, Ammonites, Edomites, and other "scavengers." God's sheep had no one to care or search for them (v. 6). Because of greedy leaders, one may sometimes wonder how families, churches, nations, denominations, and business ventures can avoid being more crippled and scattered. Some leaders may profess to care, but their actions don't show it.

Every church has scattered sheep. Who are the shepherds who will go after the hurting ones? Sunday School teachers should work to reclaim those who are away from the fold. Elders, pastors, and everyone who is a part of God's family have the responsibility of looking for hurting, scattered people. The question is, "Are we doing it?" Those who become victims of "the beasts of the field" need help (v. 5). The world, the flesh, and the devil deceive many. Our spiritual eyes should see those who need help, and we need to go after those who are scattered, no matter where they may be.

Greedy shepherds are blind to their own condemnation. Ezekiel 34:7-10 has a message straight from God about shepherds who fail in their ministry. The words are frightening and should awaken every person. Selfish shepherds will no longer take care of themselves and neglect the sheep. Luxury loving leaders in Ezekiel's day "shall not feed themselves anymore" (34:10). They were going to lose their flock, who paid their way. The Lord eventually stops the shepherd, political or spiritual, who thinks about his or her package of benefits and has no heartfelt concern for those they should be serving. In one way or another, God eventually strips greedy, money-grubbing, self-serving shepherds of their lordly positions. Ezekiel gave fair warning that God would deliver His flock from "their mouths" (34:10).

II
The Good Shepherd
(34:11-31)

Since most of the political and religious leaders failed on their jobs, God stepped in and declared Himself as the Good Shepherd.

The Good Shepherd searches for His sheep. An interjection is used in Ezekiel 34:11. God said, "Indeed I Myself will search for My sheep and seek them out." The sheep had been scattered far and wide. Many had been taken into Assyria in 722 B.C. The Babylonian forces had taken the Israelites into their country in 605 and 597 before their final attacks in 587-586 B.C. Jeremiah had been forced to go into Egypt (Jeremiah 42:6-7). The smaller nations, taking advantage of the bad circumstances of the Israelites, had carried some captives into their own lands. The Israelite exiles were helpless as troublous times continued upon them. The time of darkness and clouds "has eschatological overtones and suggests that this deliverance is to be the day of the Lord for Israel...the day when the Lord acts in salvation and judgment to usher in a new age of His righteous rule on earth" (Taylor, Ezekiel, p. 221; Ezekiel 34:12; Psalms 97:2; Joel 2:2; Zephaniah 1:15). Helpless sheep need the Great Shepherd to deliver them.

Jesus gave a beautiful picture of the Good Shepherd, in Luke 15. Ninety-nine sheep had returned to their fold. One didn't get back, and the Good Shepherd went in search of that one during a dark night on a lonely mountain. He found that sheep, put him on his shoulders, and took him to the comfort of the fold. God still searches for His people, takes them home, and cares for His sheep when He brings them home. Ezekiel 34:13-16 gives a wonderful picture of God's care for His people, stating, "I will bring them out from the peoples and gather them from the countries, and will bring them to their own land: I will feed them on the mountains of Israel...in good pasture...and their fold shall be on the high mountains of Israel. There they shall lie down in a good fold and feed in rich pasture on the mountains of Israel. I will feed My flock, and I will make them lie down." He feeds, folds, and gives them rest. Jesus said in Matthew 11:28-31 that He gives rest to all who come to Him. He heals the hurting, binding up their wounds, and gives them rest and health.

Think of the choice food that God gives His people. The books of Psalms, Proverbs, the prophets, the Pentateuch, the Gospels, and all the Scriptures are on God's "banquet table." God also gives rest that is better than any motel or hotel can offer. He nurtures and ministers to the total person. What a great God He is!

God disciplines those who need correcting. Ezekiel 34:17-21 states that God judges between the "sheep and sheep, between rams and goats." He sees those who gobble up what belongs to others. He watches those who devour the good grass and trample down what is left. God sees the animals that drink the clear water, and then muddy the water that others need. He watches those who hook and push others around. God knows those who scatter the diseased, and do not care for them. The analogy of these animals comes together in one picture. God knows the behavior of His people. The shepherds who fail in their responsibility will lose their sheep, and God will put an end to them (v. 21).

God will give His people the True Shepherd (vs. 23-24). That Shepherd will be His servant, the idealized David. God's shepherd will give Him delight, and eventually will triumph over all foes and unite His people in one sheepfold. John B. Taylor writes, "These features of the Messianic leader's person and kingdom are more significant to Ezekiel than the physical succession of the line of David's kings" (Ezekiel, p. 223). Jesus said, "I am the Good Shepherd" (John 10:11, 14). God promised one Shepherd and one fold, and Jesus has fulfilled that Shepherd role (33:23-24). The Shepherd is also the Messiah. Jesus said to the Samaritan woman that He was/is "the Messiah" (John 4:26).

God gives His people an everlasting covenant of peace. Ezekiel 34:25 speaks volumes in a few words. The statement reads, "I will make a covenant of peace with them." Jeremiah called the term used by Ezekiel as "new covenant" (31:31). Before Ezekiel's day, the Scriptures often made reference to peace that God would make available. God said to Moses that He was giving to Aaron's grandson and his descendants His covenant of peace (Numbers 25:12). God declared in Isaiah 54:10 that His covenant of peace would never be removed. Marvin Tate states that "*peace* is *shalom*, a word which conveys ideas of well-being, health, security, and good relationships with other people."

When mankind transgressed in Eden, the human race languished because of a lack of peace. For instance, soon after God banished man from His presence, Cain slaughtered his brother. That problem of bad relationships between nations, families, denominations, and individuals has persisted across the centuries. The world's peace conferences have never solved the critical problems of conflicts, nor ever will. And yet, the prophets could foresee a restoration of Edenic-like conditions as God would move into history with His 'Peace Initiative' called the 'Covenant of Peace'."

F. B. Huey states that the covenant of peace "describes an age of peace when people will live in harmony with God, with themselves, and with one another" (Ezekiel, p. 82). Numbers 25:12, Isaiah 54:10, Ezekiel 37:27, and Malachi 2:5 give strong emphasis to God's covenant of "well-being" for His people. God's people have His covenant of peace today, but we have not experienced the full results of that covenant in its total, eschatological meaning. Perhaps the analogy of sanctification may give insight into the covenant's realization. We never reach all the spiritual heights of sanctification in this life. The apostle John wrote in 1 John 3:2, "Beloved, now we are children of God; and it has not yet been revealed what we shall be, but we know that when He is revealed, we shall be like Him, for we shall see Him as He is." A present and a not-yet-possession is our heritage. We have not arrived because we are always on the way. Our pilgrimage is within the as-yet-unfulfilled covenant of peace.

God's peace gives marvelous results. Ezekiel 34:25 reminds God's people that they won't have "evil beasts" in the land to devour them (See Leviticus 26:22). They dwell safely and sleep calmly "in the woods." The word of peace gives security and calmness in the midst of the raging problems of life. The pictures in Ezekiel 34:25-31 is an Eden-like life, and the future is presented, as in Psalm 23. This vision of the future has overtones for today, doesn't it? Simon Peter slept calmly as that story unfolds in Acts 12, even though a death sentence hung over his head.

In addition to peace, showers of blessing come to God's people. One hymn states,

> There shall be showers of blessing:
> This is the promise of love;
> There shall be seasons refreshing,
> Sent from the Savior above.

Daniel Whittle wrote that hymn after the Civil War in the USA (1865). God's showers can make His people productive (vs. 26-27). Just as rain can make the grass grow on previously dry ranches and can cause seed to sprout and grow, even so God's blessings can be beneficial to those who respond to Him in the right way. The question is, "Are we walking with God and with one another?"

God's shepherd gives deliverance from the enemy through the covenant of peace. Verse 27 states that God would break the bands of the Babylonians and deliver His people from their hands. The Babylonian yoke no longer would be on their necks. God would give freedom, just as He would like to liberate His people from the destructive power of evil today. Heathen nations would no longer rule over God's people (v. 28). The "beast of the land" would no longer destroy them. In their dwellings, they would be safe and unafraid (v. 28).

God provides His people plenty of farming territory. Ezekiel 34:29 states that Israel will become a "plant of renown." Taylor (p. 224) states that this promise means that God will give His people plantations that will make them known among nations because of their abundant produce. Plantations of peace and prosperity without famine may be the idea. The truth is that God is ready to bless His people. We all need His favors, don't we?

Ezekiel 34:30 states that God's people will know that He is the Lord. The chapter closes with the words that God's people are the flock of His pasture, and that He is their God. How does one know these facts? Ezekiel wrote, "The Lord God says it" (v. 31).

If God makes these promises, and He does, isn't this enough for everyone to want to come beneath His victorious rule?

Chapter 21

The Dawning of a New Day
Ezekiel 36:1-38

—ɯ—

A number of years ago, farming people seldom needed alarm clocks. Roosters started crowing as soon as the first streaks of light flooded the world. Life started buzzing, in "overdrive," as darkness faded and a new day began to dawn.

Ezekiel became God's "alarm clock" to let the Israelites know that a new beginning was in store for them. After years of desolation and death, they had a word from God that life would change. Within a half-century, many of the survivors would be back in their homeland. God would do a miraculous work among His people in all lands where they had been taken captive. From chapter 33 until the end of Ezekiel's book, the visions of restoration replace the severe judgment scenes. God would prevail in His work of salvation, and evil forces would be defeated. Hallelujah time had come as God would give "the whole house of Israel" a new beginning (36:10; 37:11, 16; 39:25).

I
God's Message to the Land
(36:1-7)

In this section of the book of Ezekiel, God told the "son of man" to "prophesy to the mountains of Israel" (v. 1). The entire area soon would hear God's message – the mountains, hills, rivers, valleys, desolate wastes, and forsaken cities (v. 4). A few soul-stirring, uplifting words would be expressed by Ezekiel on behalf of God's people and their land. They needed that message!

God was going to cast out the enemies who had claimed the land. The nations who had come into Israel's territory during their captivity years had declared, "Aha! The ancient heights have become our possession" (v. 2). Those countries, and Edom in particular, now claimed the land and trampled the territory under their feet, making the place desolate (v. 3). As a result of the despised treatment of the land by Israel's enemies, other nations joined Edom in its slander of God's people. Those enemies had defamed Israel, making them a scandal upon the lips of others. Evil gossip continued, without doubt, for a long time against God's chosen people because the enemies had moved into the places vacated by the exiles. Their evil actions ignited the fire of God's wrath, and they would learn that the LORD can not be treated with contempt. He said, "Behold, I have spoken in My jealousy and My fury" (v. 6). The enemies would "bear their own shame" (v. 7). Edom, in particular, would become perpetually desolate (35:9).

God would claim again the honor of His own name. The Lord has a "burning jealousy" for His name (36:5). God spoke against His own people as well as the enemy in His "fury" (36:6). Several times before judgment fell upon Jerusalem, God said that He would "pour out His fury" on them (Ezekiel 7:8; 9:8; 20:8, 13, 21, 22:22). At last, Ezekiel had good news for the Israelites! God would gather His own people to Himself and "pour out His fury" upon the enemy. Those who had slandered God and His people would now come under the severe hand of judgment (v. 3). The Lord defends Himself, and His response of passion for His holiness comes from His own character. He would not be the Lord, if He would not or could not exonerate Himself before everyone. God gave a definite word about the punishment of Israel's enemies by stating, "I have raised My hand in an oath that surely the nations that are around you shall bear their own shame (36:7). When God raises His hand against His enemies, their day comes to an end!

Look again at the first words of this section of Ezekiel's book. God gave ear-tingling words in 36:1, "O mountains of Israel, hear the word of the Lord!" The message was about their liberation because freedom would come again. The land and the people now had a new message of restoration and life. God was bringing it about through His infinite love and grace. God's promises would never fail.

II
Divine Promise to the Mountains of Israel
(36:8-15)

God's promise of restoration to the mountains of Israel leaps out in stark contrast to the ruin that He would bring against the nations that harm His people. The mountains would have rich, divine blessings poured out upon them. They must have "leaped for joy" when they received that message of Ezekiel 36:8, "But you, O mountains of Israel, you shall shoot forth your branches and yield your fruit to My people Israel, for they are about to come." The Lord says those blessings come to "My people Israel." The use of the personal pronoun "my" indicates God's intimate relationship with them.

For about 70 years something like an empty echo had resounded across the valleys and mountains of Palestine. Many of their caretakers had gone, as well as the fruitful years for the mountains. However, God had not forgotten His creation. As Isaiah 35 had prophesized, "The wilderness and the wasteland shall be glad...the desert shall rejoice and blossom as the rose...They shall see the glory of the Lord...For waters shall burst forth in the wilderness, and streams in the desert. The parched ground shall become a pool, and the thirsty land springs of water; ... No lion shall be there, Nor shall any ravenous beast go up on it...And the ransomed of the Lord shall return, and come to Zion with singing, With everlasting joy on their heads" (Isaiah 35).

If anyone asks a question relating to the physical blessings for "the mountains of Israel," the answer is given in Ezekiel 36:9. The Lord declared, "For indeed I am for you, and I will turn to you, and you shall be tilled and sown." Since the earth is God's by right of creation, He can bless it when He gets ready to. The emphasis in

207

verse 9 is upon God as He said, "For indeed I am for you." The word "indeed" in this text is used as an interjection to stress God's support for His creation. No one should question that which God declares He is going to do. God declared that He was placing His blessings upon the mountains of Israel, and they would become productive (v. 8). God showed interest in the physical well-being of "the Land," and looked with favor upon it, promising that He would renovate the land that Israel would occupy again.

For years the Holy Land became free of any major farming activities. The exiles left much of the land desolate and uninhabited, with little cultivation taking place (vs. 9-11). The country became a wilderness. Desolation was widespread, and grain bins and houses must have fallen into disrepair and decay. Underbrush was everywhere, fences were torn down, fruit trees had died and everything had become hopeless. Once cultivated fields became filled with brush, making the land a fearsome place as lions, bears, hogs, and other animals ravishing the land. The Promised Land didn't look promising anymore.

But God moved into the picture. He gave the Israelites the promise of a new day in their land to which they would return. God told Ezekiel to let the people hear the news of the beginning of their restoration. The rich promises of Leviticus 26:1-13 would become a reality for them, as Ezekiel 36:8-15 underlines. The list of blessings that God gave to His people is proof of God's covenant love for them.

(1) The mountains would be blessed with fruitful trees: 36:8;
(2) The land would be plowed and planted again: 36:9; (Leviticus 26:9);
(3) Cities would be rebuilt and inhabited: v. 10;
(4) Not only would people multiply, but animals would be productive as well: v. 11;
(5) The inhabited places would be better than in the beginning: v. 11;
(6) The people would know that God is the LORD: v. 11;
(7) God's people would walk on the mountains and possess them as their heritage: v. 11;

(8) No more would Israel suffer the loss of their children. This may mean that the pestilence, wild beasts, famine, and sword would end. The reference could also point to the end of the years when many sacrificed their children to pagan deities: v. 12;

(9) The land would no longer devour their people. Again, the allusion could be to the dangers from enemy forces, as well as wild beasts. Also, this reference could possibly be linked to the early years when twelve spies of Israel went into the land and some came back, saying, "The land through which we have gone as spies is a land that devours its inhabitants, and all the people whom we saw in it are men of great stature" (Numbers 13:32). Whatever the dangers might have been, God said He would remove them: v. 14;

(10) The taunt-filled days would come to an end. The enemies of God's people "poked fun" at them and reproached them. God would not let His people hear criticisms against them anymore: v. 15;

(11) Finally, God said their "stumbling days" would be over. What a future God had for His ancient people! God's presence with His people would become their security.

III
A Land Defiled
(36:16-21)

Many people suffer losses through circumstances beyond their control. However, Ezekiel pointed to the evils that the Israelites committed that caused them to lose their inherited land. This fact of ruining and losing their country comes as a shock as we remember that we do everything possible to take care of our property. No person puts dirt, sticks, or rocks in the gasoline tank of his automobile. No rational person spits on the carpet in his or her home, scatters broken bottles over the floor, or writes all over the walls of the house. A secretary, teacher, or doctor likes to see his or her office kept reasonably clean and in order. But Israel, blessed by God through the centuries, dared to defile the land that had been given to them from the ancient days of Abraham. That prized possession, "flowing with milk and honey," became polluted through the evil acts of the people (Deuteronomy 31:20).

God knows what His people do, whether good or bad. Israel may have overlooked the fact that God knew all about her evil way. In case they forgot, the Lord gave the message to Ezekiel about the past deeds of the exiles before their deportation time. as well as the earlier captivity of the Northern Kingdom. The message was clear and to the point. The people had defiled or corrupted their land "by their own ways and deeds" (36:17). They could not blame the desecration on previous inhabitants or those who passed through the land in their own day. God's people caused their own country to be unclean. Daniel Block writes the following about the pollution of the land, "Given the prominence of the land in Ezekiel's oracles, it is remarkable that this is the only time he speaks of the land as defiled" (The Book of Ezekiel, v. 2, p. 345). Block states that Ezekiel speaks of defiling the temple, a neighbor's wife, or God's holy name (5:11; 18:6; 43:7-8, etc.). And yet this mention of defiling the land does reflect the heinous crimes of the people that caused suffering to them, the land, and the Lord. Look at two sins that Ezekiel specifically mentions that brought curses upon the land.

Murder is the first sin of God's people. They became guilty of taking the lives of their fellow countrymen. Interestingly, Ezekiel never uses the word "murder" in his book. He does, however, mention about ten times those who "shed blood," as well as those who are guilty of murder in other ways. In Ezekiel 9:9 the statement is given that the "land is full of bloodshed." Chapter 16:16 tells the horrible story of parents who passed their children through fire by giving them to abominable idols. Ezekiel 22:6 speaks of princes who used their political power to shed blood. The story of murder includes women who also became guilty (Ezekiel 16:38; 23:45). In a shocking note, Ezekiel's book mentions those who take bribes to shed blood (22:12).

Perhaps the most subtle murderer that the book of Ezekiel mentions is the one who slanders or gossips to cause bloodshed (22:9). Those who circulate rumors probably never intend to end the life of another, but tales or "smear tactics" can destroy others. Someone wrote, "Sticks and stones may break my bones, but words can never harm me." However, that little jingle is not true, because a person may harm another with words that insinuate guilt in that one's life or within a group. Indeed, murder may be done with the tongue, as well as with a gun, knife, or bomb. The ancient people of God as well as those in every generation may become guilty of murder.

Idolatry is the second sin that the book of Ezekiel mentions that polluted their land. God declared, "I poured out My fury on them for...their idols with which they had defiled it" (the land) (36:18). Will a little thing like an idol of wood or stone that can not speak, see, or hear pollute a person or the land where one lives? The answer to this rhetorical question from God is "Yes." A person with an idol gives his or devotion to that which is not God. The greatness of God is so awesome that anything that man makes is a bad representative of Him. The Lord from ancient times warned about the dangers of idolatry, saying "Leave them alone" (Exodus 20:4)!

God's fury scatters His people when they disobey His word. Because of their dual sins, God said, "I scattered them among the nations, and they were dispersed throughout the countries" (v. 19). The Assyrians carried into captivity many from the Northern Kingdom even as the Babylonians carried a large number from Jerusalem into captivity. God placed Ezekiel among those exiles in order that a prophet would be among them. On other occasions, some of the Israelites fled to Egypt, and some were captured by smaller nations surround their land. "Why the punishment?" we may ask? The nation reaped a harvest full of suffering and death because of their disobedience to God. They faced judgment according to their ways and deeds (v. 19). God said He would "purge the rebels from among you, and those who transgress against Me" (Ezekiel 20:38).

F.B. Huey writes for God "not to punish them (Israel) would have opened Him to the charge of being indifferent to sin...By His mighty acts of deliverance from their enemies, God would vindicate His holiness, and the pagan nations would have to acknowledge His existence and power" (Ezekiel, p. 85).

God's scattered people reap reproach and ridicule from those where they live. In the countries to which the enemy carried the Israelites, the people said, "These are the people of the Lord, and yet they have gone out of His land" (36:20). The implication seems to be that God didn't really care about His people, or He would not have allowed them to have been taken away. A second implication seems to be that perhaps the God of the Israelites is like pagan gods. They calculated that the Lord of the "sons of Jacob" probably didn't have the power to protect His people, and therefore, they were taken into captivity. Because of their thinking about the kind of Lord the Israelites had, God's name had become profaned (vs. 20, 21). The implication was: "Look! They serve a god who can't help them." Thus, God's name became profaned because of the sins of His people. His holy name had become common, but God was going to rescue His name.

An event that profaned God's name occurred as Lot was told to leave Sodom that was going to be destroyed because of the depravity of the people. He spoke to his three sons-in-law who thought of his words as a joke (Genesis 19:14). God's name had been profaned in Sodom, even as that glorious name is desecrated in many ways today.

IV
The Divine Motivation for the Restoration
(36:22-32)

God recovered the glory of His name. He declared that He would not bring His people back home for their sakes, but for the sake of His holy name (36:22). This statement is not man centered, but God centered. God comes first because He is LORD! The Scripture declares what God said about the return of the exiles, "I do not do this for your sake, O house of Israel, but for My holy name's sake, which you have profaned among the nations wherever you went. And I will sanctify My great name" (vs. 22, 23). God is jealous of His name that represents His character and all He is. He does not want anyone to tarnish His impeccable name. He said He would "sanctify" or make His name holy again (v. 23). As He rescues the glory of His name, the heathen, as well as the Israelites, would know that God is Lord (v. 23).

The restoration of Israel will involve an exchange of the heart of stone for one of flesh. Also a "new spirit" would be given God's people so they would obey His will. God will cleanse His restored people. Ezekiel 36:25 states, "Then I will sprinkle clean water on you, and you shall be clean; I will cleanse you from all your filthiness and from all your idols." These electrifying words bounce with divine power. God put "clean water" upon His people and cleansed them from all their transgressions. God stated that He would do the cleansing work.

To bring the symbol to our day, the "clean water" does not refer to baptism. This reference about sprinkling with clean water refers to ceremonial and ritual cleansing. The water of purification was the anti-type of the blood of Christ that gives cleansing. First John 1:7 states, "The blood of Jesus Christ, God's Son, cleanses us from all sin." The words of Titus 3:5 "through the water of rebirth and renewal of the Holy Spirit" as well as Hebrews 9:13-14 give emphasis to the work of removal of sin through the sacrifice that Jesus made on the cross. God would purify Israel from her sins and give that nation new life. When anyone is cleansed from sin, the Holy Spirit renews that one, removing the heart of stone, giving a new spiritual heart.

The old heart of "stone" could no longer function in the nation of Israel. They needed a "heart transplant." Even the heart that palpitates wears out and comes to an end. In a physical reference, God gives man a wonderful organ called the heart that is one of the greatest instruments known. It beats about thirty-seven million times a year, pushing six ounces of blood with each beat. Within a twenty-four hour period, the heart expends enough energy (systolic) to lift a ton weight forty feet into the air. The amount of blood that moves through the body within a year is equal to more than four thousand tons. By the time one reaches fifty years of age, the heart has moved the equal of more than two hundred thousand tons of blood. Praise the Lord for the spiritual heart that now, connected to God, lets one live eternally!

By the genius of His Spirit, God now lives within His people. God never will move back into a building made of stones, nor use the old sacrificial system that was used before the coming of Christ. The old covenant has decayed and vanished (Hebrews 8:13;

Jeremiah 31). The New Covenant through the blood of Jesus is the one that counts. Christ's priesthood supplants the Aaronic or Levitical priesthood that was weak and unprofitable (Hebrews 7:1-10, 18). The Levitical symbolized the eternal priesthood of Jesus that was to come (Hebrews 7:21, 24). Through the new covenant, God furnishes His people new hearts.

Because of the "new heart" empowered by the Spirit of God, the returning Israelites would walk in God's statutes and do them (36:27). The giving of His Spirit indicated the dawning of the Messianic age. Isaiah 42:1; 44:3; 59:21; and Joel 2:28-30 refer to the times of the Messiah (Luke 4:17-19). Ezekiel 37:14 and 39:29 gives further emphasis to the new age of the Spirit. Simon Peter quoted Joel's prophecy as he preached on the day of Pentecost, declaring that Spirit-empowerment was the fulfillment of God's message where He declared, "I will pour out of My Spirit on all flesh" (Acts 2:17).

God's promise of restoration would not fail. He would claim His people again, and He would be their Lord, as well as the Lord of all nations (36:23, 28). Even though God forgave the sins of the people, they would remember their past transgressions. The remembrance would cause them to "loathe themselves" (v. 31). That is, they repented, and had a change of attitude. Rules and regulations can not bring about conversion, but a divine operation changes God's people so they will walk in His way.

Conversion is God's work. We respond to God's Spirit, but He does the work. He changes us because spiritual transformation is for God's sake (36:32). He restores the glory of His name that has been tarnished. The benefits from God's work in the lives of His people are great. And yet, God emphasizes that the primary reason for His work is for His name's sake. We need to keep God's honor and glory in focus.

V
The Testimony of the Nations
(36:33-38)

God gave His people the promise of material blessings. The reference is to "the desolate land (that) shall be tilled...has become like the Garden of Eden" (vs. 34-35). The promise that the country would become like "Eden" possibly was/is as yet unfulfilled prophecy.

The dawning of a new day is an ongoing process. God works in the lives of those who respond to Him in the right way (36:38). God invites His people to decide and walk in His ways. The revolutionary truth that never becomes dull for those who respond to God is that we know that He is the Lord (36:38). The work of renewing and restoring God's people never signals the non-participation of His people. We must respond to what God is all about. We become willing participants who actively move along as God does His work. God restores, but each person must respond to God's call to repentance.

The testimony of the nations who see God doing His work of restoration is noteworthy. They declare that "This land that was desolate has become like the garden of Eden...Then the nations which are left all around you shall know that I, the LORD, have rebuilt the ruined places and planted what was left desolate" (vs. 35-36). What's the evidence for such a great day that will dawn? God answers, "I, the Lord, have spoken it, and I will do it" (v. 36). If God says it, that's enough, isn't it?

A man sat in a barber's chair one day. The barber began to tell the client that he was an atheist and thought that any idea of God was foolish. The barber continued to tell his client that if God was real, that He would not let the world get in such a mess. He also declared that if he could become God, he would not allow crimes, wars, and other disasters to continue. That nonsense talk continued until the barber finished his job.

After paying the barber, the client walked out of the barber shop. He saw a dirty, long-haired fellow walking down the street. The client walked back into the shop and said to the barber, "You are not really a barber. You don't care how people look. You only have a name of being a barber. If you were a barber, you would not let a long-haired, unshaven man, like the one that I just saw, walk down the street without giving him a shave and a haircut and helping him look decent." The barber replied, "Well, my friend, all he has to do is to come in and tell me he wants a hair cut, and I'll do the job for him." The client responded, "You are right. And that's the way it is with God. If people will go to God, He will restore them. God invites His people to share this message of reconciliation with everyone. Will we do it?

Chapter 22

The Valley of Dry Bones
Ezekiel 37:1-28

—ɷ—

The name of Dwight L. Moody has been indelibly inscribed in Christian history. His employer talked to the seventeen year-old shoe salesman one day about Jesus. Soon the heart and mind of the young man responded to the invitation to accept Jesus as Savior. After a few months, Moody found himself rounding up children in Chicago to hear God's Word. Three or four years later, the shoe salesman knew that God wanted him in full-time ministry, although he never became an ordained preacher.

Moody began preaching to crowds of people in Chicago, even though he had only a third grade education. His fame spread. Preaching missions took him from Chicago to New York, and eventually to the British Isles. One night as he preached, he noticed two ladies sitting near the front of the tent. They seemed to be praying during the entire service. He asked the two Methodist ladies what they were doing. They answered that they simply prayed that he would "get the power." At this time, Moody was preaching to large crowds and had a busy schedule. Did he need more power? One day as he walked down Wall Street in New York, he experienced God's presence in an unusual way. He rushed to a friend's house nearby, and asked if he might stay there for a time. The friend had a vacant upstairs room where Moody remained for two days. He said, "God's hand came upon me in such a powerful way that I had to ask the Lord to 'stay His hand' lest I die." Moody came away from that place with a fresh anointing or baptism of the Holy Spirit. He never spoke in tongues, nor ever changed his messages; but as he preached, he became aware of God's fullness. God had control of what he said and did.

Ezekiel introduces chapter 37 with the words, "The hand of the Lord came upon me." Six times in his book, the expression about God's hand being upon this prophet is stated (1:3, 3:14, 22; 8:1; 33:22 and 37:1). The expression indicates something of an ecstatic experience of God's presence came upon Ezekiel. He came under the powerful influence of the Spirit. The fast-moving encounter of the vision of the "Valley of Dry Bones" appears in this chapter. God reassures His people through this vision that He has the power to give life to the dead.

Let's look at chapter 37 and the "Vision of the Valley of Dry Bones" as a drama with three acts. The first act describes Ezekiel's preaching to the bones. The second act is an explanation or interpretation of the events of that time. The third act relates to the anticipation or realization of what God was and is doing. Let's see this picture from Ezekiel's perspective. We can learn the basic truth of Ezekiel's vision that God has power to restore His people. Look at the first act of this restoration drama.

I
Preaching to Dry Bones
(37:1-10)

Most everyone who is familiar with the book of Ezekiel has heard of "The Valley of Dry Bones." Ezekiel's experience in that valley or plain is unique. No other prophet or leader ever was set down in a place like that. The vision that God gave to Ezekiel about a valley full of dry bones relates to God's ancient people and their restoration. We can learn some great lessons from the situation in which Ezekiel found himself, even though the experience was visionary with him.

God's people need to be under His control. Ezekiel's statement in this chapter that the hand of the Lord was upon him is dramatic.

God's hand "came upon him" was not an imaginary event nor some hallucination, because God took control of Ezekiel's life (37:1). The time became indelible in his experience. God's control may not be so dramatic for us, but it can be real. As we yield self to God, He takes control.

God's people need to be in the right place. We may be in a busy part of the world. Like Ezekiel, we may be "brought out" to the place where God wants us to be. We may be away from home, and suffer from loneliness, just as that prophet did. Simply stated, the Spirit may bring us out and set us down in unusual places.

Ezekiel's place might not appeal to many today. He had an eerie experience. In vision, God's Spirit carried Ezekiel away from his home by the Chebar canal to a plain or valley, and sat him down in the midst of that place full of dry bones. The description seems to be that of the aftermath of a great battle, after the bodies of the dead have decayed and the sun has bleached their bones. God had Ezekiel where he needed to be.

Mother Teresa of Catholic Church fame found her place among the poor and the outcasts of Calcutta, India. Ezekiel's place was in a battlefield that had been converted into a frightful cemetery! Where is our place? If God is with us, any place is right!

God led the prophet around a valley full of bones, "dry bones." They were "very dry." God may show us "dry bones" in our personal lives, in family life, or church life. In fact, we may be in the middle of a "valley full of dead bones." People walk around in stores, drive across parking lots, and talk to one another on computers and telephones. Many people are like dried up bones. Death is all around. God opens our eyes so that we may see what is before us. Do we have "eyes to see, and see not?" Moses and Jesus told about people who had an optical problem as well as auditory problem of having eyes to see, but could not see, and ears to hear, but did not hear (Exodus 29:4; Matthew 13:14).

God had a message for Ezekiel. The question needed an answer. God asked, "Son of man, can these bones live" (37:3)? What would Ezekiel say? What would you and I say? Humanly speaking, we might say "No" to God's question. What do we say about an impossible situation? We need to answer as Ezekiel did, "O Lord God,

You know" (37:3). Ezekiel leaves the question open. However, since God has the power of creation, He can do anything. Jeremiah 32:27 asks the question, "Is there anything too hard for God?" The answer is that God has the power to do anything He wants done. He saved Israel from slavery; He saved Shadrach, Meshach, and Abed-Nego from the fiery furnace; He brought Jesus back from death after His crucifixion. God can do anything.

Dry bones can live because of God's promises. By His Spirit, God's promises can never fail. 2 Corinthians 1:20 states, "For all the promises of God in Him (Christ) are yes, and in Him Amen." God gave warnings that the Israelites would be taken into captivity, but He gave promises to bring them back from foreign lands (Deuteronomy 4:27-29; 30:1-3; 2 Chronicles 6:36-38; Isaiah 10:22; Hosea 3:5; Jeremiah 30:10, etc.).

Dry bones can live because of God's plan for His people. The fresh message to Ezekiel is that dry bones can live again, because God plans for them to live again. That which God will bring about may be delayed because of human rebellions, but God's plans cannot be destroyed. He has carried out His plans for His people throughout history, and He will do so in the unfolding future.

Dry bones can live because God has His people participating with Him in His kingdom enterprise. He wanted Israel to cooperate with Him and therefore said to Ezekiel, "I want you to speak to these bones." What would our reaction be with a similar assignment? We might say, "Who — me Lord? Please get someone else. Another person or another group can do the job, but not me, not us." Anyone may be tempted to say, "I can't do what you want me to do, Lord!" When God says, "Speak to these bones," we might say, "Lord, what shall I say?" God answers, "O dry bones, hear the word of the LORD!" (37:4). God says, "Just tell them what I tell you to say."

God gave Ezekiel a brief preview of "things to come." He said that He would give breath to the dry bones, He would put flesh upon them, and they would live. Ezekiel prophesied, and while he was speaking, God began His amazing work. As Ezekiel looked across the valley of dry bones, he heard a noise. He felt a "shaking," a light earthquake, perhaps, and bones rustled in the dim light of the vision. Bodies started coming together. All two hundred six bones of each body came into place. The toes connected to the feet and the knees came into place. The jawbone, backbone, and the hipbones aligned themselves. Every bone moved to its place. Then flesh, tendons, and skin came upon the bones. The whole valley became filled with human bodies. But one thing was lacking; everyone needed life because none had it. Ezekiel saw the valley filled with human bodies, but he didn't see life in them because they were dead. Actually, they were worse off. Now a valley was full of corpses! Ezekiel was surrounded by defiling things. Now what should Ezekiel do?

God said for Ezekiel to speak, saying, "Come from the four winds, O breath, and breathe upon these slain, that they may live" (37:9). As Ezekiel spoke, God's breath entered every corpse in that valley, and life came to every corpse. Then the dead stood on their feet, "an exceedingly great army" (37:10). God put life into dead bodies. Ezekiel saw what God did. Our situation is different from Ezekiel's. However, the same God rules, and we can trust Him.

II
An Explanation
(37:11-14)

If a person were to read the first ten verses of chapter 37 without knowing the background, he or she might wonder about the meaning of the "dry bones." In fact, both Ezekiel and the exiles seemed to need an explanation or interpretation of Ezekiel's vision. A few verses of explanation in this chapter clarify the vision.

The vision zeroed in on God's people of that day. God said, "These bones are the whole house of Israel" (37:11). All twelve tribes show up in the vision. The Lord said the "whole house" is included in this vision. Of course, many Israelites lived in Jerusalem and surrounding areas at the time. Those from the ten tribes in Samaria who had been carried captive into Assyria became a part of the picture. Some had escaped to Egypt during Nebuchadezzar's attacks on Jerusalem. Many lived in Babylon during the exile years. The "whole house of Israel" included all of God's people, no matter if they were in their own land or another place. The bones encompassed all Israel.

The Israelites had come to the "end of their road," and they made a three-pronged confession: "Our bones are dry, our hope is lost, and we ourselves are cut off" (37:11). No cover-up would suffice. They looked upon the bleached, dried, scattered bones and said, "That's us!" Not only did the people recognize that their bones were dry, but they declared, "Our hope is lost." They could no longer expect anything good to happen to them. Their own captivity had taught them that they were hopeless without God. Listen to the third dismal cry of the Israelites. They expressed words of despair: "We are cut off" (37:11). They had become separated from their roots. Their capital city lay in ruins and, their houses had been destroyed. The temple had been burned, and the treasures had been hauled away. Cities and villages had no walls, and the leadership had been slaughtered or carried into captivity. Their confession was simple: "We don't have any life or any future. Everything has come to an end!"

True to His word, God let His people return following their Babylonian captivity, but that does not end the story. The Israelite saga is ongoing. More lies beyond the return of some exiles, more is beyond the rebuilding of Zerubbabel's Temple and the city. God has more for His people beyond a mini-nation under foreign powers. God's work of grace extends beyond that which we sometimes have "boxed in" as His final act.

God still carries on His work of restoring His people. Paul wrote in Romans that God would continue a miraculous work with Israel, grafting them back into the "olive tree" (chapters 9-11). The Lord has not cast away Israel, and He continues to bring into His kingdom everyone who accepts Jesus as Savior, both Jew and Gentile. With God, there is no difference. We all must go the "restoration route" that springs from God's grace. The result of repentance is a changed life. Jesus is the way to restoration and life.

III
Two Sticks: One People
(37:15-28)

God unites His people. To illustrate His uniting work, God asked Ezekiel to take two sticks. He was told to write the name of "Judah" on one of the sticks. Judah's name represented the southern two tribes of Judah and Benjamin. God told His prophet to write the name of "Joseph" on the other one (v. 19). That stick with the name of Joseph on it represented the ten Northern Tribes called Israel with their capital in Samaria.

Ezekiel placed both sticks in his hands, and united them. This symbolized that God was going to unite the two nations of Judah and Israel. (The Mormon teaching that the sticks represent the Book of Mormon and the Bible being united is absurd). The Bible states that the symbol of the two sticks showed that God placed the two nations together, making them one nation (v. 22). That restoring of the Israelites in 539 B.C. (circa) was the beginning of God's work, not His final act with His people.

The complete picture of God's work is that the redeemed will be together in His future eternal kingdom. God told His people that they would become "one nation." The twelve tribes had been one kingdom under the reign of Saul, David, and Solomon. When Solomon died, the kingdom divided and became two rival nations.

First Kings 12 and 2 Chronicles 10 tell the story of the division of the kingdom. When Solomon died, Rehoboam began his reign over Israel, refusing the counsel of the older men who asked him not to impose heavier taxes. As a consequence of the action of Solomon's son, the ten Northern Tribes separated from the two Southern Tribes of Judah and Benjamin. From the time of Solomon's death in 931 B.C. until the Assyrian captivity, the once-united nation became two: Judah and Israel. Judah continued to exist as a nation until Babylonian forces destroyed them in 586.B.C. In 539, God made it possible for the exiles to return to their homeland, making the Israelites one nation again.

The Lord promised an eternal King for His people. Ezekiel 37:22, 24 states, "One king shall be king over them all... David my servant shall be king over them; and they shall all have one shepherd." The reference to David points beyond him to the "Son of David" who is Jesus, the Messiah. We rightly call Jesus "King" and "Shepherd." Jesus said in John 10:11, 14-16, "I am the good shepherd. The good shepherd gives his life for the sheep...I am the good shepherd; and I know my sheep, and am known by My own...And I lay down

My life for the sheep." The "other sheep" refers to Gentiles who would believe on Him. The term "shepherd" was a common term for "king" in the Near East. The king is the shepherd of his people.

In the time of Ezekiel, the Lord said Israel would dwell in their land forever with His "servant David" as their eternal prince (v. 25). Nathan spoke to David, saying, "Your house and your kingdom shall be established forever before you. Your throne shall be established forever" (2 Samuel 7:16). The servant title pointed to the future Messianic reign, not to David himself. When Jerusalem fell in 586 B.C., the Babylonians killed the sons of King Zedekiah, gouged out his eyes, and took him to their country where he later died (Jeremiah 52:8-11). That king's demise ended the Davidic line of kings. In the New Testament era, the Herod line of kings were Idumeans, descendants of Esau or Edom, not David (Matthew 2:1, etc.). Neither did Israel have a continuing kingdom after the destruction of their city and temple in 70 A.D. and their disastrous defeat by the Romans in 135 A.D. What then can be said in defense of David's throne? John B. Taylor states that the phrases "for ever, for evermore" in verses 25, 26, and 28 of Ezekiel 37 are "a strong indication that Ezekiel is thinking...of a supernatural kingly being in whom would be concentrated all the qualities of wisdom, enduement with the Spirit, righteousness and peace that were expected of God's anointed ruler" (Ezekiel, pp. 240-241). Clearly, the prophecy goes beyond David to Jesus.

During the engagement of Joseph and Mary, an angel announced to her that she would give birth to a son, and His name would be Jesus. The angel also said, "He will be great, and will be called the Son of the Highest; and the Lord God will give Him the throne of His father David. And He will reign over the house of Jacob forever, and of His kingdom there will be no end" (Luke 1:32-33). The New Testament gives emphasis to Christ's eternal kingdom, not one that will be restored to Israel again.

The "land issue" is one that's thorny. Since the founding of the State of Israel in 1948, the "Land" issue has become a "hot topic" for many Bible enthusiasts. The "Land Promise" that God gave to Abraham is recorded in Genesis 17, and states four basic facts:

1. The "land" would be the everlasting possession for Abraham and his descendants.
2. Abraham's descendants would multiply in multitude as the stars in the sky.
3. God promised Abraham an everlasting covenant.
4. Finally, the Lord said that He would bless all who blessed that "chosen race" and that the world would be blessed through them. (See Chapman, pp. 114, 119).

In the time of Moses, God said the land belonged to Him, and that the Israelites were only "aliens and tenants" on the land (Leviticus 25:23). The Lord said that if they defiled the land that He would cast them out and scatter them (Lev. 18:24-29). Emphasis to the real land ownership is given by Moses as he spoke to Pharaoh, saying that the hail would be stopped so "you may know that the earth is the Lord's" (Exodus 9:29). He wrote in Deuteronomy 10:14, "Indeed heaven and the highest heavens belong to the Lord your God, also the earth with all that is in it." Psalm 24:1 echoes the same truth.

Interestingly, Jesus never spoke of "The Land" as belonging to Israel. His focus centered upon the coming kingdom of God that encompassed all creation, not a "real estate restitution." Jesus bypassed the question of the Apostles about "restoring the kingdom" to one of evangelism without frontiers (Acts 1:6-8). He never implied a geophysical nation or state in those final words to the disciples.

The restitution mentioned by Simon Peter on the day of Pentecost does not mention anything about the land of Israel. Rather, that "restitution of all things" has fulfillment in the incarnation of Jesus and His reconciling work by His death and resurrection (Acts 3:21). Later, Peter wrote about an "eternal inheritance" reserved in heaven for God's people (1 Peter 1:3-5). He connected Exodus 19:6 about Israel's priesthood with the priesthood of all believers who share the good news of Jesus (1 Peter 2:9).

The apostle Paul never mentioned the "land issue" as he wrote about faith in Christ (Romans 4:13; 9:15; 11). All believers in Christ, now and in the future, are "one in Christ," because the wall that separates Jew and Gentile has been broken down through the death-resurrection of Jesus (Ephesians 2:14; Galatians 3:26-29). That wall is never to be reconstructed because it came "tumbling down" once and for all at Calvary. Charts and diagrams that are constantly being revised can never separate Jew and Gentile again. For our encouragement and edification, Paul wrote mind-boggling words in 1 Corinthians 3:21-23, stating that God's redeemed people now come into possession of all things! Even Abraham never felt satisfied with a "land promise," because "he waited for a city which has foundations, whose builder and maker is God" (Hebrews 11:10).

Colin Chapman quotes N.T. Wright who wrote, "Through the Messiah and the preaching that heralds him, Israel is transformed from being an ethnic people into a worldwide family" (p. 223). The Church, therefore, is the renewed and restored Israel, but not ethnic Israel. Early Christians regarded themselves as a new family that descended from Israel, but transformed. They are not to be thought of as people who have replaced Israel, but rather as the new people of God (Wright). Jesus is the perfect fulfillment of the hopes and longings of all people, both Jew and Gentile. Haggai 2:7 describes the Messiah who would come as, "The Desire of all nations."

In his paper entitled, "The Land of Israel in the Bible," Marvin E. Tate states that "The Land has become the world, and holy ground may be present in any geographical location" (p. 10). On page 11, he writes, "The Land ideology is not lost in the New Testament, but is transformed and extended to encompass the whole earth, which is full of the Glory of YHWH-God." Then he asks the question about the meaning of the Land for today's Christians. On pages 11-12, Tate writes:

1. The theological legitimacy of the Jewish desire to live in the Land of Israel, with indeterminate borders, should be acknowledged and accepted. They are the chosen people of YHWH-God and we who are Gentiles have been privileged to become part of the enterprise of salvation brought into the world through them. They should be allowed living rights in the Land historically given to them for that purpose.
2. The modern state of Israel does not merit the status of theological imperative. Politically, it is legitimate, and deserves our support as a democracy of free people. The policies of the Israeli

government, however, do not justify automatic support, as some Christians are prone to do...Of course, the people of Palestine who are not Jewish have no divine right to the Land that refuses a Jewish presence in the Land of Israel. A homeland in Palestine should be respected and supported for both Jews and Palestinians. Palestine belongs to the world, and no national interest, such as a Jewish, Muslim, or Christian state, should seek to drive other groups from the Land – especially not by using religious justification for their efforts.

God makes His people pure. Verse 23 declared an end to Hebrew idolatry. After the Babylonian captivity, the exiles should have stopped all their idolatry, because God purged them from those vile things. God is still in the business of purging His people from their transgressions, and He equips them to walk in His statutes (v. 24).

Also, God gives His people a "covenant of peace." This covenant is mentioned seventeen times in chapters 16, 17, 20, 34, 37, and 44 in Ezekiel. Man lost spiritual life through his "Fall" in Eden. The restoration of peace comes through God's grace expressed in the "second David," who is Christ. God's covenant of peace or "shalom" means one's total health and well-being which is for everyone who returns to the Lord. Old Testament promises of peace are numerous. Interestingly, God's princely prophet wrote in Isaiah 26:3 that the Lord would keep everyone who continue to think on Him in perfect peace. Isaiah 53:5 states, "The chastisement for our peace was upon Him (the Messiah, Jesus the Christ)." Isaiah 54:10 states that God's covenant of peace would last forever, never to be removed! Jesus said in John 14:27 that His peace was different from the fragmentary peace of the world. The Apostle Paul gave emphasis to that divine peace that comes through "the blood of the cross" (Colossians 1:20). Jesus reprimanded two who walked the seven miles from Jerusalem to Emmaus on the day of His resurrection because they failed to understand that He came to die and be raised again, according to all that the Old Testament said of Him from Moses to Malachi (Luke 24:13-27). God's promise of peace finds its fulfillment in Jesus.

God promised His presence with His people. Ezekiel spoke about "the sanctuary in the midst of God's people for evermore"

(37:26). Jesus came as God in human flesh — the incarnation. He "tabernacled" upon this earth for 33 years (John 1:14). The Holy Spirit came to dwell within God's people at Pentecost. Paul wrote of the Spirit living in God's people (1 Corinthians 3:16; 6:19). God never will live again in "temples made with hands" (Acts 17:24). Ezekiel 48:35 and Revelation 21:3 state that God will live with the redeemed. The Lord restores His people and causes the present and the future to sparkle with glory because He indeed lives with His people forever.

Chapter 23

Gog of Magog: The Age-old Rogue
Ezekiel 38:1-39:29

—ᵐ—

Most everyone looks into a mirror several times a day because we want to know how we look. The Bible is a mirror that tells about God and the way He works in the world. We discover a great many facts about the past, present, and future from God's Word. And yet, we will never be certain about everything in God's Book. Paul wrote in First Corinthians 13:12: "For now we see in a mirror, dimly, ("darkly") but then face to face." After the crucifixion and resurrection of Jesus and before His return to heaven, Jesus answered the apostles' question about restoring God's kingdom saying, "It is not for you to know times or seasons which the Father has put in His own authority" (Acts 1:7).

We don't know everything about God's plans for the future. Some may preach and teach volumes about the future. A person may memorize hundreds of verses about eschatology. Some preachers hop back and forth over platforms that are half as long as a basketball court, declaring their views on the "end times." And yet, we don't know exactly how God is going to close history, except that He is going to be the Victor.

We may find one, two, or a half-dozen ways to interpret some Scriptures. We need to exercise caution in declaring that "My way is right, and everyone else is wrong." For instance, spiritual giants across the years have looked at the return of Christ with different interpretations. but not all agree on the "how and when." For instance, B.H. Carroll, the founder of Southwestern Baptist Theological Seminary of Fort Worth, Texas, held to the postmillennial. Some interpret the Bible to say that the millennium is a symbol of God's eternal rule. Augustine, John Calvin, Martin Luther, and others fall into this camp. Premillennial views break up into "pre-trib," "mid-trib," and "post-trib" groups. They believe that Christ will return, but their interpretations of this event vary, and some from each group preach endlessly to prove their argument. (The "pre-trib" rapture view was unknown until 1830 when Margaret MacDonald of Scotland had her "visions." See The Incredible Cover-Up, Dave MacPherson, Omega Publications, Medford, Oregon, 1991).

Chapters 38 and 39 of Ezekiel have many interpretations. Are these two chapters literal, symbolic, or both? God's overthrow of Gog and his evil forces has a litany of interpretations. That slice of history did not have total fulfillment in Ezekiel's day. The Apostle John retells the event in Revelation 20:8 as future. He wrote of "Gog and Magog" not "Gog of Magog" as Ezekiel did. Here is one attempt to understand this evil, godless Gog in a few fast-moving scenes.

I
The Plot of Gog
(38:1-13)

The first encounter with the name of Magog appears in Genesis 10:2. Noah had three sons: Shem, Ham, and Japheth. Magog was the second son of Japheth, and some of Noah's grandsons through this line were Magog, Gomer, Mada, Tubal, Meshech, Togarmah, and others. Gog's name along with these names appear in Ezekiel as countries named for Japheth's (and Noah's) descendants (38:2-3, 14, 16, 18; 39:1, 6, 11). Other references to these names appear in 1 Chronicles 1:5 and Revelation 20:8.

Gog's identity is obscure. We may conclude that the word is a title, such as the Prime Minister of England, the President of Mexico, the Shah of Iran, or the Pharaoh of Egypt. In the time of Ezekiel, Gog might have been a ruler. Gog's name appears eleven times in the Bible (See 1 Chronicles 5:4; Ezekiel 38:2, 3, 14, 16, 18;

Ezekiel 39: 1, 11 and Revelation 20:8). In Ezekiel's writing, Gog's name seemed to be connected to the people of barbaric areas on the borders of Armenia and Cappadocia (Glaze, p. 172).

Others say Gog's name comes from Gyges, King of Lydia. The Sumerian term, "Gug," means "darkness." We may conclude that Gog is a symbolic term that represents eschatological powers of evil in history. We do not find proof to link the name to modern-day nations. Rather, Gog seems to be connected to a worldwide anti-God coalition of forces that attack God's people. Satan is not limited to one area because his terrain is planet earth!

Gog's ideas are evil. His arrival in the restored land presents Gog attacking unwalled villages and mountains of Israel, but not Jerusalem. He is pictured as coming from the north, because in ancient times forces that attacked Israel came from that direction and not directly across the desert. They moved toward Asia Minor, then turned south to make their attacks. Ezekiel states that the evil forces will come against God's people "in the latter years" or "after many days." John mentions satanic attacks upon God's people coming from the "four quarters of the earth" (Rev. 20:8). The last times began with the first coming of Jesus, which means that the final "Gog-Magog" attacks should not be pinpointed by anyone. (Acts 1:6; 1 Peter 1:20; 4:7; Romans 13:12; Hebrews 1:2).

God involves Himself within the scope of Gog's activities. As a preview to what will happen to Gog, Ezekiel wrote in Chapter 38:4 that God would put "hooks into the jaws" of Gog and turn him back from his final attack upon Israel. Gog and his coalition forces can never be a match for the all-powerful God. More than a century before Ezekiel's time, Sennacherib of Assyria came against Jerusalem. God sent a blast upon Sennacherib, putting "hooks in his nose," sending him back home, and leaving his army of one hundred eighty-five thousand dead outside the city walls (2 Kings 19:28; Isaiah 37:7, 29). All who oppose the LORD will go down in defeat.

Gog intends to destroy Israel in her unwalled villages, descending upon them "like a storm, covering the land like a cloud" (38:9). Storm clouds threaten destruction whenever they appear. Thoughts arise in the mind of Gog, and he will make an "evil plan" against the unwalled villages who seemingly are without protection as they enjoy peaceful, prosperous lives (38:8-13).

The age-old strategy of the devil is to devour the people of God (1 Peter 5:8). Satan, in the form of a serpent, moved with all his vigor against Adam and Eve in the Garden of Eden. He spent his energy against Job, trying to make him turn away from God. When Jesus came as God incarnate, the devil tried to destroy Him through King Herod. The devil spent his energy against Christ as he strategized the crucifixion of the Son of God. The devil and Gog don't slow up as the end approaches, because their plans are brutal.

Godless forces come from six nations that Ezekiel mentions in chapter 38. Mention also is made of Sheba, Dedan, and the merchants of Tarshish, and all their young lions (38:13). Lesser-known evil leaders join the big parade of evil giants, thinking that they will share in their spoils of victory. Gog always has a list of those who are ready to join him in his plans to annihilate the people of God.

II
God's Response to Gog's Plans
(38:14-23)

The Lord God knows what is going on in His world. "The Lord knows the thoughts of man, that they are futile" (Psalms 94:11). The plans of Gog of whatever date are all known by the omniscient Lord. Ezekiel 38:14-16 states that God knew that Gog and his forces would come from the north, the usual route of Israel's invaders. They would come "riding upon horses, a great company, and a mighty army" (v 15). God has a precise understanding of what evil forces plan and attempt. In fact, God knows about Gog's movements because the Lord Himself says in 38:16, "I will bring you against My land!"

Notice this strong hand of the Lord again that's involved with Gog's movements. Ezekiel 38:16-17 states that the enemy would come upon "God's land," but they would be brought there by the LORD. The purpose in giving Gog and his coalition forces the opportunity to attack Israel was to display the Lord's holiness before them. The LORD declared, "I shall be hallowed in you, O Gog, before their eyes" (38:16). All nations would see that God, and not

Gog, has the final word. The prophets from ancient years had made these prophecies (38:17).

God punishes those who try to stop Him and His righteous plans. Ezekiel 38:18 states that God's fury would come to those who reject Him. The "fire of God's wrath" would center upon Gog. Three illustrations show God's operation against evil forces. No one can fight against God and win.

God would produce a "great earthquake in the land" (v. 19). These words are again reflected in John's writing in the book of Revelation (20:7-9). God wars against His enemies, causing all life in the air, sea and on land to tremble because of His response to man's evil. The fish of the sea, the birds of the air, the beasts of the field, creeping things upon the earth, and man himself quakes because of God's presence. When God appears on the scene, all creation shuts its mouth! Romans 3:19 states that "every mouth may be stopped" as the world becomes guilty before God. God is going to "shake the world" again, one day. Judgment time is on its way.

God puts evil forces on the route to self-destruction. When Gog and his coalition forces of evil fight God, He puts them in a confused state. Ezekiel 38:21 states that God will send a sword throughout the land, and "Every man's sword will be against his brother." The temporarily united forces of evil will turn upon one another. Once when the Midianites and Amalekites came against Israel "like grasshoppers in multitude," God answered them with a strategy through Gideon (Judges 7:1-22). The Lord sent Gideon and his 300 men at night near the camp of the enemy. They had trumpets which they blew, lamps in pitchers which they suddenly exposed, and then shouted, "The sword of the Lord, and of Gideon" (Judges 7:16-20). The enemy forces awakened, and in their confusion, they began to slaughter one another. God won the victory that night, even as He will against Gog in "the latter days."

God will bring about a threefold attack against Gog. He will bring Exodus-like plagues upon the enemy. Pestilence, blood, rain, hailstones, fire, and brimstone are still in the Lord's arsenal. If the enemy imagines that he can escape the first two divinely-ordained strategies for defeating God, he had best reconsider. Just as Pharaoh could not win against God in the day of Moses, neither can Gog win against God in the time of Ezekiel, John the Apostle, or in any future age.

God's purpose in allowing the forces of evil to operate in the world is for His glory.

The Bible is replete with the stories of people as well as heavenly hosts praising God following a time of trials and tribulations. When the Hebrews returned from exile and Ezra preached to multitudes in the street (without a microphone), "All the people answered, Amen, Amen! while lifting up their hands. And they bowed their heads and worshiped the Lord with their faces to the ground" (Nehemiah 8:6). A few centuries earlier, David wrote, "Let heaven and earth praise Him" (Psalm 69:34). When Jesus was born in Bethlehem, shepherds returned to their flocks, praising the Lord (Luke 2:13, 20). Not too far from the exiles along the Chebar canal, Daniel heard Nebuchadnezzar giving praise to the Lord (4:37). God will even cause Gog one day to recognize Him and bow at His feet. The "strong arm" of God reminds everyone that He will be sanctified among all people so that everyone may know that He is the Lord. One day, "At the name of Jesus every knee shall bow... and every tongue should confess that Jesus Christ is Lord, to the glory of God the Father" (Isaiah 45:23; Philippians 2:8-11).

III
The Fight to the Finish
(39:1-10)

Sept. 11

At the beginning of chapter 39, God instructed Ezekiel to speak another word against Gog, the chief prince of Magog. Gog will be turned back to face the six plagues of pestilence, blood, overflowing rain, hailstones, fire, and brimstone that came as headline news in 38:22. Ezekiel 38:4 warned that God would draw Gog back with hooks in his jaws. Those hooks most likely refer to the six plagues that Gog would face. The godless enemy would meet his fate "upon the mountains of Israel" (39:2).

God will disarm His foe. In ancient times a warrior knew that if he lost his bow and arrows in a struggle, he would lose. God stated that He would yank the bow from Gog's left hand, and all his arrows would fall to the ground, leaving him in defeat. A bank robber without his weapons is helpless. A soldier without guns and bombs can't attack or defend himself. When God strips Gog of his weapons, he falls in defeat. As Julian the Apostate fell mortally wounded on a battlefield in 313 A.D., he cried, "Thou hast conquered, O Galilean!" One day Gog will gurgle his cry of defeat.

God will destroy His enemies. He leads them to defeat "upon the mountains of Israel" (v. 4). Gog and all his forces fall "upon an open field." The Lord of the universe liquidates them (v. 7). The disaster for God takes place as the enemy gets in the ring with God. But this time, Jehovah wins the world heavyweight fight. The enemy never gets up again; he's gone. God sends fire on Magog, and the end comes to the enemy (39:6). Revelation 20:11-15 gives fulfillment of that victory.

God will display His honor in victory (39:9). The truth of God's victory echoes repeatedly in Ezekiel's book. The last book in the Bible also gives emphasis to God's eternal victory (Revelation 19:1, 6). People celebrate with God as He displays His honor, or they go down in an agonizing TKO with Gog. What plans do you have?

God devises a new purpose for the weapons of the enemy. They will be used for the benefit of God's people. Ezekiel 39:9-11 states that the wooden weapons are going to be used for firewood. The shields made of wood, the bucklers, bows, arrows, hand staves, and spears shall be used as fuel for fires for seven years, perhaps a symbolical number (39:9). People will not need to go to forests to cut wood for their homes because enemy weapons will serve this need.

Farming people in years gone by would cut trees to be used in the fireplace and kitchen stove. Normally, oak trees served for the living room fireplace, and pine trees furnished the wood for the kitchen stove. Hardly anyone ever had a supply of wood piled up for use for future years, especially for seven! The story in Ezekiel, however, states those who live in the cities of Israel will burn the weapons of their enemies for seven years (39:9). The enemy and his weapons vanish when God steps into the picture. God's people pillage and spoil their enemies (39:10).

IV
Burial of the Dead
(39:11-16)

Some people may know about funeral homes that close because of a lack of business. Competition stays strong for some, and sometimes people live too long for this kind of business to prosper!

Gog's place of burial booms! The cemetery has the name, "Hamon-Gog." The trans-historical town refers to a place where "multitudes" are to be buried. We may ask, "How large will this funeral be?" The answer comes back that the most extensive funeral arrangements in the history of the human race have been mapped out by the Lord. The world's obituary column includes Gog and his entire multitude (39:11). All the evil coalition forces meet the same fate: death in "Hamon-Gog."

The time taken for burial indicates a booming business related to Gog and company. Seven months for an extended burial is a long time. Again, seven is a cryptic or symbolic number, indicating total ruin of the enemies of God. When man reviews the rise and fall of nations, he should know that God has final control over death and every cemetery of the world. God has reserved cemetery plots for all those who oppose Him!

The people involved in the burial indicate something of the booming business. For

seven months the house of Israel will be burying them, in order to cleanse the land. Indeed, everyone will be helping in the burial enterprise (39:12-13). The utilization of all the living to bury all the dead is a graphic way of stating that annihilation will come to God's opponents. The truth is clear that God's enemies can't stand up against Him, even though the parabolic language needs to be understood. The strangers who pass through the land will be conscripted to help in the disposing of the dead (v. 14).

The non-residents who "pass through the land" help after the seven months of burial (39:15). These people start looking for the bones of the dead that didn't get buried during the first burial rites. The search party places a marker by every bone they see in order that the gravediggers might do a final job of cleansing the land

(39:15). Thus, "Hamon-Gog" (multitudes) is named "Hamonah," or "Multitude of Gog" (39:16). The burial is on the east side of the Dead Sea, eliminating all contamination of the Holy Land.

V
Sept. 18 A Banquet for Birds and Beasts
(39:17-20)

One day a friend sent me an e-mail note, asking, "What are you having for your evening meal?" I answered, "I'm having a banquet of chicken soup." Every day, Solomon's table was like a lavish banquet (1 Kings 4:22-23). King Solomon should have known something about the size of the dining hall he would need when he brought in 700 wives and 300 concubines! Belshazzar's feast was a banquet with a thousand "lords and ladies" present (Daniel 5:1). Some go to convention or school banquets that are elaborate. However, no person has ever seen a banquet like the one Ezekiel described in chapter 39.

The banquet guest list is all-inclusive. The invitation is given to all "feathered fowl." Name them: buzzards, hawks, and all birds that eat flesh. Every bird has a welcome to the banquet. Every beast of the field has an open invitation to be a celebrant at the event. Big beasts, hungry beasts, small beasts, mean beasts, and flea-filled beasts. Not one is excluded — perhaps even alligators may come!

The banquet table is a large one. The "mountains of Israel" serve as the table. No one has ever seen such a table that covers thousands of acres. Now we understand a little more of the symbolism in this picture, hopefully.

The banquet menu is one that "birds and beasts" applaud. The flesh of the mighty...the princes of the earth...horses...mighty men...men of war (39:18-20). The menu includes Gog and his forces that oppose God and His Messiah. The vast hordes become the menu for the "banquet for birds and beasts." They drink the blood and eat the flesh of the fallen (39:19-20). The sacrifice that God provides satisfies their hunger and lust for flesh and blood. The banquet exhibits the magnitude of Gog's defeat as well as God's victory. This section in chapter 39 gives emphasis to Gog and his defeat. The eschatological end of Gog has come, but until that future time, the battle goes on. The final victory of God must overcome a big threat that comes unexpectedly (M. Tate).

VI
A Display of God's Glory
(39:21-29)

God displays His glory by showing that when His people disobey Him that He still maintains control of everything, even when His own people seem to be falling apart. The Lord explained His actions to both Israel and the world of nations. As Israel faced her judgment, all nations would see that God chastens His people because of their transgressions. The punishment of the exiles came as a reflection of God's power over His people. From that time forward, the Gentiles would know that Israel faced captivity because of their sins. Also, "the house of Israel" learns through exile that the Lord is their God (vs. 21-23). Israel's sin led to the departure of God's glory. God "hides His face" from His sinning people, and yet God never fails in His promises (vs. 23-24).

God displayed His glory by showing mercy to His people, giving them the opportunity to repent and begin again. After they "bore their sin and shame," God accepted them (vs. 25-26). Despite the rebellion of God's people and their punishment, the restoration which the prophets foresaw must be kept as headline news. The overall message of the prophets is God's intention to complete the work of salvation in His people. The alien forces that oppose God will lose in this titanic struggle as unrelenting judgment is brought against them. Because of God's mercy, His people will prevail.

God displayed His glory by sanctifying Himself in the sight of His restored people (v. 27). He brings them back to their land. God said He would "restore their fortunes." These statements have great eschatological overtones and also had partial fulfillment in the time of Ezekiel. If not, why did Ezekiel give the message to the exiles in Babylon where he also lived (v. 28)?

The theme of God magnifying Himself appears again before this chapter closes. He displayed His glory by pouring out His Spirit "on the house of Israel" (v. 29). The passage from Joel chapter 2 found non-exhaustive fulfillment on the day of Pentecost (Acts 2). The Lord gives His people the opportunity to drink from the flowing river of the Holy Spirit that Jesus promised (John 7:37-39).

Where do you and I stand in relation to "Gog, the rogue?" What about our relationship with the Lord who wins the victory over Gog? Many times we need to step back and allow God to show His strength and win the victory for us. Soon after David had been anointed king, Philistine enemy forces came against him. David inquired of the Lord what should be done. The answer came that he should repel them, and God gave victory over that marauding group. The enemy made another attack on David's forces. He inquired of the Lord again, and God told him to wait until he heard the "sound of marching in the tops of mulberry trees," and then repel the enemy. Meanwhile, God moved among the enemy forces, putting them in disarray, equipping David to defeat the Philistines (1 Chronicles 14:8-17). God's people have victory when they wait on Him.

When the Israelites left Egypt, they celebrated with songs of victory because God worked on their behalf. Miriam, led the women with timbrels and dances. The words of that prophetess sparkle in Exodus 15:21, "Sing to the Lord, For He has triumphed gloriously!" The Lord gave His people victory by destroying Pharaoh's power.

Paul wrote in 2 Corinthians 2:14, "Now thanks be to God who always leads us in triumph in Christ." The enemy wants to decimate God's people, but "He who is in you is greater than he who is in the world" (1 John 4:4). Through Christ, God's people can celebrate victory over "Gog," whether we refer to the "Israelites in the flesh" or the "Israelites of faith who are the sons of Abraham" (Galatians 3:9). Are you in the camp of Gog or in God's camp? Each person makes his or her own decision to be against the Lord or to join with Him and His people in the eternal march to victory.

Chapter 24

A Vision of God's Temple
Ezekiel 40:1-48:35

—ɯ—

Jewish leaders tell their people not to read the book of Ezekiel until they are thirty years of age. They say the book is too difficult to understand by young people and most everyone else. The rabbis say when Elijah comes that he will explain the book to them.

Many commentaries have the story of a first-century rabbi, Rabbi Hanina ben Hezekiah, and the book of Ezekiel. Reportedly, he had recourse to three hundred jars of oil for his night lamps as he studied the book. He labored long and hard over the pages of Ezekiel in preparation for his defense of keeping the book in the Old Testament canon. The world has been "blessed and bruised" because of this writing. The first chapter of Ezekiel, as well as a few other chapters, gives the reader difficulties in understanding the writing. Especially hard to understand are the closing nine chapters of the book, 40 - 48.

One reason Ezekiel is hard to interpret is that much of the book is given to visions. This writing begins and closes with a vision. Also, the symbols, allegories, and parables move the writing away from what might be called the "purely literal." The truths are couched in a different literary form than the narrative style, because the prophet speaks in first person. A second cause of difficulty in understanding the book is its length. By the time a reader gets through the chariot scene in chapter one, he feels that an endless jungle is before him.

The length of the writing discourages the reader almost from the start. A third problem in understanding Ezekiel is the closing vision of the temple scene with all the complex details in chapters 40-48.

In his book on Ezekiel in the <u>Tyndale Old Testament Commentaries</u>, John B. Taylor keeps a balanced interpretation of this book. He gives four main approaches on the interpretation of this section, and the following is a paraphrase of his discussion.

The first approach to interpreting this vision is called the "literal prophetic" in which the temple would be rebuilt according to the specifications given in the vision. Although many exiles would return from Persia by the decree of Cyrus in 539, and although they would rebuild a temple, the prophet may not have thought of their temple as he saw in the vision. Taylor states that the ground plans and other details leave too much to the imagination for the building of a literal temple. The vision was given to a prophet, not an architect. However, Ezekiel 43:10-11 states that if the people were ashamed of their sins and repented that Ezekiel would give them the plans for the temple. Indeed, they should have been ashamed of their idolatry and immorality that stunk! Ezekiel's description and measurement of the temple was to show the people God's holiness and let them see how they had polluted God's house (v. 12). The prophet excludes those from the Lord's temple who desecrate it.

The returning exiles and their leaders did build another temple. Ezekiel wrote that the priests of *his day* were to serve in the temple, which negates any idea of a temple being rebuilt centuries later (40:6; 43:19; 44:15-16). Ezekiel saw himself involved in that temple worship if that "ideal temple" had been realized (43:18-25).

The second interpretation sees the Christian Church symbolically fulfilling the vision. This approach breaks down because this interpretation takes the message away from Israel in that time. The vision had to relate originally to the Israelites in exile and in Jerusalem, otherwise the vision would have been useless for them.

The third interpretation is dispensational. This view became popular in the 1800's and spread like "wild fire" during the twentieth century across most of the world . The dispensational view has the Old Testament rites and rituals, including sacrifices, being repeated in the future, including a rebuilt temple. This view misinterprets Christ's once-for-all sacrifice on the cross, plus other problems of interpretation.

The fourth view interprets these chapters as apocalyptic, not prophetic. Ezekiel's vision related to the "then and there," but it also relates to the Messianic age with its symbols, symmetric dimensions, etc. John B. Taylor summarizes chapters 40-48 in the following ways listed below. Keep in mind that God's people, and many in scholarly circles, continue to interpret these chapters in differing ways. It is possible to be scholarly and spiritual at the same time, or we would have to reject Ezekiel himself. Taylor's summary of Ezekiel 40-48 is the following:

(a) the perfection of God's plan for His restored people, symbolically expressed in the immaculate symmetry of the temple building;

(b) the centrality of worship in the new age, its importance being expressed in the scrupulous concern for detail in the observance of its rites;

(c) the abiding presence of the LORD in the midst of His people;

(d) the blessings that will flow from God's presence to the barren places of the earth (the river of life);

(e) the orderly allocation of duties and privileges to all God's people, as shown both in the temple duties and in the apportionment of the land (Taylor, John B., Ezekiel, pp. 253-254).

Despite the difficulties we encounter in understanding this long vision in Ezekiel, an overview of some major ideas in these chapters can give us refreshing insights. One arresting truth needs to be noted. Ezekiel never called the temple a "millennial temple." In other words, the vision that Ezekiel had of the temple was one for his day, and probably not an "eschatological temple." Ezekiel's experience with "God's hand" upon him is given at the beginning of chapter 40, taking him to a very high mountain in Israel where he saw a heavenly being with a measuring rod in his hand. That heavenly being began to measure the temple because it was already there in vision as an ideal house of the Lord, and it might have been built if the people of God had become ashamed of their iniquities (40:4;

43:10-11). Since they did not repent, the "visualized temple" never became a reality. Let us consider some major ideas in this vision of chapters 40-48.

I
God is the Central Focus of the Book

Before considering anything else in Ezekiel, before considering the author of the book, before thinking of the nation of Israel, or even their captivity in Babylon, let's remember that God is the central person in the book. What do we learn about God from Ezekiel?

God is sovereign. He is in control at the beginning, middle, and end of the book, as well as throughout history. God is owner of everything, and whether we recognize the truth or not, He has control of the small and large events of human history. Think for a moment of a Texas-size ranch. The rancher may have a thousand cows on his land. He may have well-trained horses, or mavericks by the dozens. The cattle and horses have free range to a certain extent on the ranch. They enjoy the grass in the pasture, the streams that may flow through a part of the land, and the hay that may be tossed out to them. The animals may roam all over the land, but when the rancher gets ready to sell his cattle, he can round them up in a corral, or in any place he wants them to be. Although the animals have freedom in large measure, they still belong to the rancher and are under his control. Likewise, God gives His people a lot of freedom in the world. And yet, He owns the earth, and is able to round up His property any time He chooses. God is in charge, even though He allows human freedom.

God is holy. He is free from all defilement because He is sacred, ethical, pure, sinless, and separated from all wrong. He is just and honest, with never a blemish upon His character. Ezekiel speaks of "holy" several times in his book (20:39, 40; 22:26; 36:22, 38; 39:7; 42:3, 13; 45:4; 48:20, etc.). He mentions God's holy name, holy mountain, holy flock, holy offerings, etc. More than a century earlier, Isaiah had a vision and heard seraphim saying, "Holy, holy, holy is the Lord of hosts" (Is. 6:3). The basic thesis of the book of Leviticus is, "You shall therefore be holy, for I am holy" (11:45).

God is glorious. Glory or glorious refers to the splendor, excellence, honor, majesty, and transcendence of God (1:28; 3:23; 10:4; 44:4, etc). The revelation of God's splendor causes Ezekiel to "fall on his face." Also, Ezekiel gazes on the revelation of God's glory as that glory departs from the temple (Chapter 10). He witnesses the return of divine glory in the temple vision in chapter 43. Those visions of the Lord's glory both overwhelm and empower Ezekiel. The wonderful truth of God's sovereignty, holiness, and glory needs to become real in our lives. Some words from one of today's contemporary songs by David Billington should cause us to become awestruck with God's presence as Ezekiel felt six centuries BCE.

> You are awesome in this place, Mighty God.
> You are awesome in this place, Abba, Father.
> You are worthy of all praise,
> To you our song we raise,
> You are awesome in this place, Mighty God.

II
God Has Work for His People

In Ezekiel 40:3 a reference is made to "a man, whose appearance was like the appearance of bronze." The heavenly visitor had a job to do, measuring the various parts of the temple, the Holy Land, and other details in the vision. (John sees an angel measuring the city, but not the temple, because there is no temple in the future Jerusalem: Revelation 21:15-22). God called Ezekiel to do a special work in Babylon, keeping alive the hopes of the exiles who lived away from their homeland. His ministry from his call to be a prophet in 593 until 573 B.C. (40:1), indicates that God had a monumental work for him.

In Ezekiel's vision of the temple, he tells about priests, princes, Levites, and singers who had work to do. Everyone related to God and His house had responsibilities (40:44; 43:13, 19; 44:15; 45:17, etc). In fact, God's work involved all his people as they took care of their families, worked in the temple area, worked on their farms and their businesses, and prepared for a return to their homeland following their exile.

The ministry opportunities are unlimited for all of God's people. We may help in visitation work, speak encouraging words to children and anyone else who may be lonely, visit those who are ill or in prison, help clothe the migrants, pray for the military, go on mission trips, pray for people in war-ravaged lands as well as the poverty-stricken, take care of our families, pray for leaders in government, or serve in other ways. The Bible states that we are to do everything for the glory of the LORD (1 Corinthians 10:31). Invitations to invest life in God's service pop up throughout the Bible, such as is found in the story of a man who owned a vineyard: He "went out early in the morning to hire laborers for his vineyard" (Matthew 20:1-2). God always can use workers in His cause. Are we ready to become a part of His work force? The truth of being one of God's helpers may be discovered in Ezekiel's vision. Are we responding to God's voice?

III
The Details of the Temple Vision Attract and Repel

Of course, Ezekiel felt "caught up to glory" with the incredible temple scenes. He had prepared for the priesthood until the Babylonians carried him away. With his early priesthood studies and familiarity with the temple, the vision of the temple became without doubt a never-to-be-forgotten experience for him. Ezekiel must have loved the vision with the details of the temple, the temple grounds, the priests and musicians, the sacrifices, and the ever-enlarging sacred territory of the twelve tribes.

The exiles in Babylon who heard about Ezekiel's vision of the temple must also have become excited about the prospects of their return. They knew about Solomon's temple, and now their hopes revived about their new place of worship. They surely loved every word they heard about the new temple. Ezekiel 43:10-12 seems to be a kind of "thematic summary" (Marvin Tate) of the vision:

'Son of man, describe the temple to the house of Israel, that they may be ashamed of their iniquities; and let them measure the pattern. And if they are ashamed of all that they have done, make known to them the design of the temple and its arrangement, its exits and its entrances, its entire design and all its ordinances, all its forms and all its laws. Write it down in their sight, so that they may keep its whole design and all its ordinances, and perform them. This is the law of the temple. The whole area surrounding the mountaintop is most holy. Behold, this is the law of the temple."

These verses became the wake-up call for God's people to repent and renew their commitment to Him. The above-cited verses seem to be limited to the Israelites of Ezekiel's day. They had the call to be ashamed of their iniquities, and if they would repent, they would hear the design of the temple, and the charge to keep the ordinances that God laid out for them to observe. The further elaboration about their defiling God's house by bringing in foreigners and "uncircumcised of heart" seems to be speaking directly to Ezekiel's day, not to some far-off event (44:6-9).

Those with or without a biblical orientation will find the details in the vision of the temple hard to understand. As we wade into chapters 40-48, a feeling of confusion may overwhelm us. And yet, a simple analogy may help explain the jungle of minute details that relate to the temple. Apply the design of a modern-day church to the descriptions of the temple, courtyards, rooms for sacrifices, regulations about worship, and special days of the year, and one can begin to understand what seems complex about Ezekiel's vision.

Think about a church with several staff members plus all the church property. Parking lots and garages occupy a lot of space. Take a look at the worship center with its vestibule, large auditorium, balcony, platform and pulpit, choir loft, and baptistry. Walk through the offices of the church secretaries, senior pastor, and other staff personnel — minister of education, music, youth, and children.

Stand in awe before a three- or four-story educational building for Sunday School, Bible study, or other uses. The description of the church facilities becomes more complex by mentioning the Family Life Center, rooms for choir and baptismal robes, and custodial rooms. If measurements are given of the worship center, hallways, gymnasium, parking lots, and restroom facilities, the details become complex. And yet, as people walk through the buildings, they have a sense of understanding the layout.

The Israelites in Babylon and Jerusalem would have had no difficulty in understanding Ezekiel's vision of the "ideal temple." They would relish the vision story that God told the prophet to give them. They would eventually have their temple, land divisions among the tribes, Zadok and Levitical priests, and regulations about worship, even though they would not see the vision fulfilled to perfection.

Jeremiah and Ezekiel spoke of a future time for the Israelites when they would have a "new covenant" that would replace the old one (Jeremiah 31:31-33; Ezekiel 16:60; 34:25-26; 37:26). By His sacrificial death and resurrection, Jesus ended the old covenant. His words in Matthew 26:26-30 about the "new covenant" through His blood expressed a "thank you" and "farewell" to the old religious system. When God's Messiah came, He fulfilled the "types and shadows" and brought an end to the animal sacrifices and other rituals of the ancient Jewish religion (Hebrews: chapters 8-10).

An additional word may be given about an end to all Old Testament sacrifices. That is, Jesus came from Judah's tribe, not from Levi's line. He ended the old priesthood of Aaron, Zadokite and Aaron, giving all believers the right of approach to God for themselves. Christ made an eternal sacrifice, putting an end to the need for another one *forever*. There will never be another temple established for animal sacrifices, with restored rituals and other "reruns" of the already fulfilled ancient practices.

Of course, the vision of the return of God's glory was a message to the exiles that God would again be with His people in the temple that Zerrubbael would build. The Israelites understood that message, and all those who returned after the decree of Cyrus in 539 B.C (or 536). anticipated with excitement their new start in the old homeland.

An interpretation of the land division among the twelve tribes of Israel comes as a nightmare to most readers (chapter 45:7, etc). Interestingly, however, the book of Revelation gives no interest in the land division in Jerusalem and elsewhere. Neither Jesus nor the apostles mentioned a geophysical riddle of land division. Jesus said that God has His own agenda, and the Christian's business is to proclaim the message of salvation in Christ to people everywhere (Acts 1:6-7).

Abraham looked beyond an earthly inheritance, because "he waited for the city which has foundations, whose builder and maker is God" (Hebrews 11:10). One difficulty in a literal land division in the future would be that of space. If David, for instance, is to rule over the Israelites in Palestine, would all of them from Abraham to some future date have space enough to stand? Such a plan with David ruling over the Israelites misses the whole point of who the Messiah is, plus His eternal reign over all creation. God and His Lamb rule forever, according to the book of Revelation.

Paul wrote to his converts in Corinth, "...All things are yours: whether...the world or life or death, or things present or things to come — all are yours. And you are Christ's, and Christ is God's" (2 Corinthians 3:21-23). He emphasized in 2 Corinthians 3:18 that his mission was to preach "the message of the cross" (v. 18). The confession is made that some Scripture is hard to interpret. Perhaps we can wait for Elijah to explain the land issue, too! The part of Ezekiel's vision that is abiding and permanent is the "spiritual river" that flows from God's throne, and His promise to dwell with all the redeemed in the eternal city — His people (Revelation 21:12-14).

IV
The Spiritual River

Chapter 47:1-12 of Ezekiel has incalculable meaning. Ezekiel's river in his vision flows from the temple and gives life to the land from Jerusalem to the Dead Sea. Revelation 22:1-3 presents the symbolic river flowing from the throne of God and the Lamb, giving nourishment and healing to all. The symbols in Revelation are based on Ezekiel and follow that prophet's outline step by step, but the visions of God in Revelation transcend all that Ezekiel saw. (See: J. J. Roberts' paper, "A Christian Perspective on Prophetic Prediction," John Hopkins University, 1979, Interpretation. Roberts gives a nine point comparative study of Ezekiel 37-48 and Revelation 20:4-22-5).

Daniel Block lists five noteworthy theological implications about this river that flows from God's throne (pp. 701-702). He states the following: (1) The restoring of the relationship between God and His people is a prerequisite to the renewal of the environment. Block says the stream which flows by the altar to renew the land symbolizes God's desire to receive sinful humanity, and it also shows His delight in their worship. (2) The environment's renewal represents spiritual renewal because they go hand in hand with lifting the curse on the land from the fall. He points out that Revelation 22:3 signals "the curse removed." (3) The entire renewal, physical and spiritual, comes through the miracle of God's grace, and it originates in the house of God. (4) God's concern for His holiness is matched by His desire to bless His people. The well-being of the earth reflects God's concern as He lets the stream flow across the barren wastelands. (5) Finally, the abundant life becomes available to everyone who worships the Lord in spirit and in truth. Rivers of living water will overflow in the lives all who believe (John 7:38). The words of Ezekiel parallel Zechariah 14:8 which describes living waters flowing from Jerusalem, and Joel 3:18 that has mountains and hills flowing with wine and milk.

As earlier noted, the Lord's glory returned, never to leave again (43:1-5). God's throne expresses the ever-enduring glory of the consummation. Jesus addressed the theme of "living water" when he talked to a Samaritan woman (John 4). He promised that believers would have "rivers of living water" flowing from within (John 7:38-39).

Block states (from my understanding) that it would be inconceivable for Ezekiel to envision a full restoration of the Israelites without a literal fulfillment of the return of the twelve tribes, the Davidic dynasty restored, and God's covenant of peace renewed. And yet, Block states that it seems best to interpret Ezekiel 40-48 "ideationally." (Webster's dictionary defines "ideational" as "consisting of or referring to ideas or thoughts of objects not immediately present to the sense; to form an idea"). However, Block says the issue for the prophet is spiritual realities, not physical geography. He states that Ezekiel's vision presents a lofty spiritual idea: Where God is, there is Zion (pp. 505-506).

In his book entitled Explore the Book, J. Sidlow Baxter writes that the symbols of the visionary temple teach great lessons for today. He concludes that the dimensions of the temple reflect the transcendent greatness of the temple and city. The cube measurements symbolize the perfection of the temple while the sacrificial rituals reveal the absolute purity of worship.

F. B. Huey gives some practical lessons from the picture of the life-giving water that flows from the visionary temple. He states, "(1) It reminds us that God is the one who can turn death into life. (2) Sometimes God begins His work in small and ordinary ways. (3) God is the source of all blessings. (4) God's blessings flow from Him to all parts of the world and are abundant and unending. (5) The power of God can transform everything it touches. Revelation 22:1-2 evidently builds on the description of the river that Ezekiel saw and calls 'the river of water of life'." (Ezekiel, pp. 114-115). It seems to me that we can comfortably accept the river's meaning in the following paragraphs and be on the safe side of interpretation.

Life-giving water from God's throne is available for the whole world. We may all drink from that fountain that never shall run dry! Revelation 22:1 reflects the same message about the river and the "water of life." Everyone who has spiritual thirst finds an answer in the perennial stream that flows from God's throne.

Spiritual health and healing are provisions from God. We recognize these terms as ideal. This is an ongoing event, and the transformation continues wherever and whenever God enters life. Sustenance is another benefit from the river that flows from God's throne. Fruit trees grow on both banks of the river in an Eden-like atmosphere. This is the picture in the two closing chapters of Revelation that John described.

Worldwide blessings come from God's river. The salty water of the Dead Sea comes to life with the influx of water from God's throne. Fish swim in the once-salty water, and fishermen cast their nets into that body of water that is fifty miles long and fifteen miles wide. I think these terms are symbols of great spiritual blessings to all the world, not the story of smelly fish being brought in by fishermen.

God's river goes out to change the world. Again, we understand something of the symbolic picture that Ezekiel gave in Chapter 47. God's spiritual river gives a transformation to everything that it touches. Step into that river where it is ankle deep or where it is deep enough for swimming, and life changes forever.

An overall view of the book of Ezekiel begins with the prophet sitting among the Israelite captives by the stale waters of the man-made Chebar canal, and as the heavens open, he sees "visions of God" (1:1). An awesome storm cloud appeared in the vision, symbolizing God's fast-paced judgment; however, above that cloud, God sits upon His throne. Ezekiel had another vision of God's glory moving away from the temple, indicating that the nation soon would lie in ashes (10:18-19). After judgment, God gave His people new hope as His glory returned (43:1-5). The climactic moment came as God promised to dwell with His people forever. Ezekiel's exiles and all of God's redeemed are marching toward that consummation day.

A few pastors were traveling to a meeting in an automobile, and one lady was with them. For several minutes the men talked about heaven and eternity. After listening to the discussion for a while, the lady said, "Well, I don't know what heaven is going to be like, but I'm sure of one thing, and that is, I'm going to like it!"

When we step into eternity, we will not be frustrated about understanding the visions in Ezekiel's book or a dozen other questions. We will praise the Lord and live with Him and the redeemed forever. God's prophet closes his writing stating eloquently, "THE LORD IS THERE" (48:35). Aren't you glad that Ezekiel is a part of God's authoritative, eternal Word?

Review Questions
(Study Guide)

—⁓—

Open Bible test. You do not have to write any answers to the questions, unless you prefer to do so. You may review the questions alone, or have a general discussion with a group or another person and let this time be pleasant for everyone.

Introductory Chapter

1. How many chapters are in the book of Ezekiel? Do you have a few friends who can review the questions in this Study Guide once a week with you? Would your church like to use these questions perhaps each Wednesday or Sunday night for study?

2. What is the meaning of Ezekiel's name? In what approximate year BC was he born?

3. What three broad facts may help a person know Ezekiel in a better way?

4. Name two friends of Ezekiel who were prophets: before and after Ezekiel's book.

5. Who did God call to leave Babylon who became the "father of the Hebrews?"

6. When did Babylon conquer Assyria, making Babylon the leading world empire? *612 B.C,*

7. When was Daniel taken into Babylonian Captivity? *606 BC,*

8. When did the Babylonians take Ezekiel into captivity? *597 BC,*

9. About how many Israelites did Nebuchadnezzar take into captivity along with Ezekiel in 597 B.C? (2 Kings 24:14) *10,000*

10. Name three or four influences in the life of Ezekiel. Name a few influences in your life. What about the family? The church? School friends, etc.
11. Name a few contributions that Ezekiel made. What contributions can we make? How can we help our family? Our church? Our community? The mission cause?
12. Look for the references about the "son of man" in Ezekiel's book. Why did God call the prophet that name?
13. What did Ezekiel prepare to do in life? What did God call him to be? (1:3). Does God still change the direction in the life of His people? When? How? With whom?
14. Read about the revival under King Josiah that influenced Ezekiel. (2 Kings 22:3-13). Name one or two spiritual experiences that have been turning points in your life?

Ezekiel Chapter 1
1. The first chapter begins with a statement about the "thirtieth year," which has several technical interpretations (no one knows for sure). Also, this date possibly referred to Ezekiel's age when God called him to be a prophet. (1:1).
2. Who were the "captives?" Where and what was the river "Chebar?" (1:1).
3. What do the words "visions of God" mean? Who initiated the vision? (1:1).
4. Name two or three truths about Ezekiel which may be learned from him (1:3).
5. Try to describe the whirlwind or storm vision that Ezekiel saw. Why did it come from the north? (1:4).
6. A hard-to-understand part of Ezekiel's vision is found in Ezekiel 1:5-11. Try to give your interpretation of these verses. (Don't give up if this seems hard to you!).
7. What is the meaning of the wings, hands, and feet of the cherubim? 1:7-9).
8. What does the face of a man, ox, lion, and eagle mean (mole)? (v. 10).
9. When did the cherubim or "living creatures" move forward? (1:12). What lesson can we learn from this verse?

10. Read Ezekiel 1:13-14 and explain this part of the vision.
11. What seems unusual about the wheels in this vision? (1:15-16).
12. What do the eyes on the rims mean? Does God also see us today? (1:17-18).
13. When did the wheels move? What lesson can we learn from the wheels? (1:19-21).
14. Describe the firmament or "platform." (1:22-23).
15. What three kinds of sounds came from the wings? (1:24).
16. What did the cherubim do when they heard a voice? Should we listen for God's voice today? How does He speak to us? (1:25).
17. What appeared above the "firmament" or "platform? (1:26).
18. Describe the throne and the "man on the throne" in verses 26-27.
19. What was around the throne? 1:28. Read Genesis 9:13
20. What was Ezekiel's reaction when he heard a voice? 1:28

Ezekiel Chapter 2
1. What did the voice tell Ezekiel to do? Does God tell us to "get up?" (2:1)
2. What kind of audience did Ezekiel have? Do these verses apply to us? (2:3-5)
3. Read another description of the Israelites. How do we fit into this scene? (2:6-7).
4. Describe the scroll that the prophet saw. (2:9-10).

Ezekiel Chapter 3
1. What is a scroll? What was the normal size of ancient writing scrolls? (3:1).
2. What did Ezekiel do with the scroll? Did he literally eat it? (3:2).
3. Why did the scroll become "sweet like honey" to Ezekiel? (3:3).
4. What commission or mission did God give Ezekiel? What about us? (3:4).
5. Read again a description of God's people. What do you think about God's people in years gone by compared to God's people today? (3:4-7).

6. What did Ezekiel need to do when he met the Israelites? (3:9-10).

7. What gave Ezekiel courage to do his work? Are we courageous? Why or why not? How do you fit into this picture when it comes to doing what God's mission is for you and your friends or family members? (3:12, 14).

8. Tell about Ezekiel's visit with his fellow exiles. Why was he astonished at them? Remember that they had been "yanked" out of their country in 597, leaving behind their possessions and many relatives. How would we have felt? (3:15).

9. Describe a watchman's job. Do you think Ezekiel lived up to being a good watchman? Do you think the average church members thinks of herself or himself as being a watchman or "caretaker" of others? Why? Why not? How? (3:17-19).

10. Again, how was Ezekiel encouraged? Do you believe God wants to encourage us? How does He do it? (3:22).

11. What did Ezekiel see by the river Chebar? (3:23).

12. Describe an unusual time in Ezekiel's life (3:24-27). Remember, however, that Ezekiel had "elders" coming to visit him for seven years (8:1; 14:1; 20:1). God did not let him proclaim publicly His word during those years, because he was "dumb" — that is, not free to speak part of the time. (3:26; 24:27; 33:22; also Daniel 10:15).

13. What do you think of Ezekiel up to this time in his writing? Can you summarize a part of his life and ministry?

Ezekiel Chapter 4

1. In Ezekiel 4:1, God gave Ezekiel the "son of man" title. What does this title teach about Ezekiel, as well as about ourselves?

2. What symbol did Ezekiel use to show Jerusalem's soon-to-be destruction? (4:1).

3. What kind of attacks did Ezekiel make on the tile with the diagram of the city? (4:2).

4. What was another symbol of Jerusalem's destruction? Explain it (4:3).

5. Explain the meaning of the prophet lying on his left and right side. (4:4-6).

6. What meaning may be given to Ezekiel's "uncovering his arm?" (4:7).
7. Ezekiel 4:8 seems to indicate the immobility of the prophet. What does the verse mean, considering his other daily activities?
8. What do you think about the food that Ezekiel was told to eat for several months? What about his limited intake of water? (4:9-16). How would you have felt if you had been in Ezekiel's place?

Ezekiel Chapter 5
1. Who gave Ezekiel a shave and a haircut? (5:1).
2. What did Ezekiel do with his hair? Explain the symbolism. (5:2-4).
3. Why did God punish Jerusalem? Is God fair? Why? (5:5-9).
4. How bad would the famine become in Jerusalem? (5:10).
5. What had God's people done that brought divine wrath upon them? Is judgment possible for God's people today? (5:11).
6. How where the Hebrews punished as the Babylonians destroyed Jerusalem in 587-86 B.C? (5:12).
7. What lesson would the surviving people learn? Do we learn easily? (5:13).
8. When God judged Jerusalem, what would heathen nations think of the suffering Israelites? (5:14-15).
9. Who had control of the judgment that befell Jerusalem? Does God have control of nations and individuals today? (5:16-17).
10. Who said that judgment would come to Jerusalem? (5:17).

Ezekiel Chapter 6
1. God told Ezekiel to prophesy against the mountains of Israel. What did those words mean about God's created world or the mountains? (6:1-2).
2. Describe the judgment that Israel had to face. (6:3-7).
3. What group would escape death by the sword? Where would they be? (6:8).
4. How would the survivors of judgment feel about themselves? (6:9).

5. How did their sins effect God? How do you think God feels about our transgressions? Do those who do wrong ever think of God's feelings? (6:9).
6. What two great lessons did the survivors from the judgment learn? (6:10).
7. How was Ezekiel told to react to the abominations of God's people? How do we react or feel "deep within" when Christians sin? (6:11).
8. In what three ways would judgment come to the Israelites? (6:11-12).
9. What do you think God's "fury" means? (6:12)?
10. Where would the idol worshipers be found who had been killed? (6:13).
11. What would God's judgment teach His people? Do you think we have learned this truth that the Lord is God? (6:14).
12. When God "stretches out His hand" in judgment, what happens? (6:14).

Ezekiel Chapter 7
1. God said to Ezekiel that "the end" had come to what country? (7:1-2).
2. What is the meaning of "the four corners of the land?" (7:2).
3. How many times in chapter 7 do the words "the end is come" appear?
4. In what ways did God say He would judge Israel? (7:3).
5. What lessons would the Israelites learn as God punished them for their abominable ways? Are we learning any lessons when God chastens His people? (7:4).
6. How does Ezekiel describe three expressions of immediate judgment? (7:5-6).
7. How seriously does God judge His people who do wrong? (7:7-9).
8. The expression about "the rod has blossomed" refers to what nation? (7:10).
9. Did God say that He would feel sympathy for His wicked people? (7:11).

10. Give your interpretation of those who "bought and sold" as destruction was coming to Jerusalem. What lessons can we learn about material possessions? (7:12-13).
11. What response did God's people make as they heard the trumpet? (7:14).
12. In what three ways were the people going to die? (7:15).
13. During the attack upon Jerusalem, what would a few people do? (7:16).
14. Describe another reaction of the people during Nebuchadnezzar's attack upon Jerusalem in 587-86 B.C. (7:17-18).
15. What would the people do with their silver and gold? What does that example teach us today? (7:19).
16. What would happen to the idols that the Israelites had made? (7:20-21).
17. What would God do at that time? (7:22).
18. What is the meaning of "the chain" in Ezekiel 7:23?
19. What two sins of Israel are listed? How do these words describe us today? (7:23).
20. How did God say He would punish His people? (7:24).
21. What happens when destruction comes? (7:25-26).
22. Describe the religious leaders in the time of Ezekiel. (7:26).
23. What three groups of Israelites faced judgment? (7:27).
24. What refrain appears in Ezekiel 7:27?
25. You might need to remember that the outside world usually referred to the Israelites as Hebrews. However, they nearly always referred to themselves as Israelites.

Ezekiel chapter 8
1. Where was Ezekiel in the "sixth year," after his having been carried away into captivity? This date of writing was 591 B.C. (8:1).
2. Who visited Ezekiel? What kind of spiritual experience did Ezekiel have? (8:1).
3. Describe the "likeness" of the person who revealed himself. (8:2).
4. In this vision, what did the heavenly visitor do with Ezekiel symbolically? (8:3).

5. The Israelites worshiped Ashtaroth or Ashera, the goddess of the Babylonians. The male counterpart of this goddess that they worshipped was Baal.

6. What was the "image of jealousy?" Where was it? (8:3, 5) What are some idols of today's world? Are you guilty of idolatry?

7. Describe the departure of God's glory. What caused His glory to depart? Do you think that we can "drive" God's glory from us today? How? (8:6).

8. Ezekiel had a vision of the temple and courtyard. He also saw a "hole in the wall." What did Ezekiel see when he climbed in vision through that hole? (8:7-10).

9. Who were the "elders," and how many did Ezekiel see? What were they doing? Did they practice their pagan rites in God's house in view of everyone? (8:11).

10. What man stood among the elders? Who was he? (8:11).

11. The elders were not priests, but what did they offer to creeping things and beasts? What was evil in their actions? (8:11).

12. What two false views did the elders have about God? Do people think about God today as the Israelites did? (8:12).

13. What did Ezekiel see at the gate of the temple? Who was Tammuz? (8:13-14).

14. What greater abominable acts were the 25 men doing? (8:15-16).

15. What sins of the Israelites are listed in this passage? (8:17).

16. What is the meaning of "putting a branch to the nose?" (8:17).

17. What did God do when His people turned away from Him? Describe fully (8:18).

Ezekiel chapter 9

1. What did those who had "charge of Jerusalem" have in their hands? (9:1).

2. How many angels of judgment did Ezekiel see in the vision? (9:2).

3. What did the person clothed in linen have by his side? What did that mean? (9:2).

4. What happened to "the glory of God?" (9:3).

5. Tell something about the supernatural being that Ezekiel saw (9:3).

6. What was placed on the foreheads of the people who felt heart-broken over the sins of the Israelites in Jerusalem? Can God's people be identified publicly today? How? By whom? (9:4).
7. In what city did the angelic beings do their work? The judgment scene was a symbol of what forthcoming event? (9:4-5).
8. How severe was the judgment against the people of God? (9:5-6).
9. Where did the work begin of putting a mark on the people's foreheads? What did that mean? Is there an application to this truth today? (9:6; 1 Peter 4:17).
10. What happened in the temple and courts? (9:7).
11. Describe Ezekiel's reaction to the scenes of slaughter. How do we feel about those who are evil and have no hope of life? (9:8).
12. What did the sinful people do? How did they try to justify their evil deeds? (9:9).
13. What did God say He would do? (9:10).
14. What report did "the man clothed in linen" give? Should we be obedient? (9:11).

Ezekiel chapter 10
1. What did Ezekiel see above the cherubim? Cherubim is a plural word for two or more heavenly beings (not definitely said to be angels). A cherub is one (10:1).
2. What did God tell the man clothed with linen to do? (10:2).
3. What filled the inner court of the temple? What was that "cloud?" Explain. (10:3).
4. Describe God's glory in the temple. (10:4).
5. What kind of sound did the wings of the cherubim make? What are cherubim? What is a cherub? (10:5).
6. What did an angel do with the fire he picked up near the cherubim and the chariot wheels? (10:6-7).
7. In this vision what did Ezekiel see beneath the cherubim's wings? (10:8).
8. How many wheels did Ezekiel see? (10:9).
9. What seemed to be different about the wheels in this vision? Describe them (10:10).

10. In which direction did the wheels move? (10:11).
11. The vision showed the cherubim with many eyes. What did this mean? (10:12).
12. What do you think the word "wheel" meant? (10:13).
13. How many faces did the cherubim have? What were the faces like? (10:14).
14. Where and when had Ezekiel seen this vision previously? (l:1; 10:15).
15. What seems important about the wheels and wings of the cherubim? (10:16-17).
16. What did the cherubim and the Lord's glory do? (10:18-19).
17. Where did Ezekiel see the living creatures? (10:20).
18. How many faces and wings did the cherubim have? Explain. (10:21).
19. In which direction did the cherubim go? (10:22).

Ezekiel chapter 11
1. In this vision, what did God's Spirit do with Ezekiel? (11:1).
2. How many men did Ezekiel see? Who were two among them? (11:1).
3. What evil counsel did the leaders give? Can leaders still give bad counsel? (11:2-3).
4. What was Ezekiel's mission? What is your mission and mine? (11:4-6).
5. What did God say would happen to those leaders, and to others? (11:7-10).
6. Where were many of God's people going to be judged and what would they learn through that experience of judgment? (11:10-12).
7. What lifestyle did the Israelites have? Do God's people still do wrong? (11:12).
8. What leader died, and how did Ezekiel feel about that? How do we feel about the wrong of anyone who should be living for the honor of God? (11:13).
9. How did the people who escaped and were not taken into captivity to Babylon feel about themselves? (11:14-15).

10. What did God become for His people in their Babylonian exile? What message can we learn from their experience? (11:16).
11. What did Ezekiel say to his fellow Hebrews or Israelites in exile? (11:17).
12. Did God promise that He would regather His scattered people in the future? What else did He promise to do for them? (11:17).
13. What two sins did the Israelites stop practicing? (11:18).
14. What two "body organs" took the place of their idols? (11:19).
15. What would the people start doing? What else took place in their lives? (11:20).
16. What would happen to those who wanted to keep on in their sins? What happens to God's people today who persist in evil pursuits? (11:21).
17. What happened to God's glory? (11:22-23).
18. Where did God's Spirit take Ezekiel again? (11:24).
19. What did Ezekiel tell his fellow exiles? (11:25).

Ezekiel chapter 12
1. What kind of people did God's people become? What two problems did they have? What about our problems today? (12:1-2).
2. What symbolic act did Ezekiel do as the people watched? Describe. (12:3-7).
3. What did Ezekiel's fellow exiles say to him? (12:8-9).
4. To whom was God's message directed? (12:10).
5. In this vision, how was Ezekiel a sign to God's people when he dug through the city walls? (12:11-12).
6. What was going to happen to King Zedekiah (the prince)? Why wouldn't the king see the land of Babylon, even though he would be there? (12:12-13).
7. As God scattered His people, what would happen to some of them? And what to others? What would they learn? (12:14-15).
8. What would happen to the remnant? What would they do and learn? (12:16).
9. How did Ezekiel act during mealtime? What message did his activity say about the Israelites in Jerusalem? (12:17-19).
10. What would happen to "the land?" (12:20).

11. What did evil Israelite prophets say to the nervous people in Jerusalem? (12:21-22).
12. Whose word came to Ezekiel? God had a message for the wicked prophets. What was it? (12:23-25).
13. What repeated response did God make to the false prophets who kept saying that judgment would be postponed? (12:26-28).

Ezekiel chapter 13
1. What does God call those who speak in God's name, and yet they have no word from the Lord? (13:1-3).
2. Ezekiel compared false prophets to what animal? (Jackals). (13:4).
3. How do false (foolish) prophets fail? Explain. (13:5-7).
4. What is God's attitude toward false prophets? (13:8-9).
5. What did the foolish prophets do for God's people? How were they guilty of lying? (13:10).
6. What will God do to the work of false prophets as well as to them? (13:11-14).
7. What lesson is repeated about God? (13:14).
8. What else would happen to prophets who do not speak the truth? (13:15-16).
9. Describe the false women prophets or prophetesses. What were they doing to God's people and to God's name? (13:17-22).
10. What emphasis comes again in Ezekiel 13:23?
11. Does Ezekiel teach or imply that evil teachers were deceiving righteous people? Do you think evil prophets continue today? Why or why not? (13:17-23).

Ezekiel chapter 14
1. What group came to visit Ezekiel? Who were the "elders?" (14:1).
2. What message did Ezekiel have for the group? Where were their idols? (14:2-3).
3. What hindrances do idols bring? How many idols did the Israelites have? (14:4-5).
4. What does God tell His people who are guilty of idolatry? (14:6).

5. What does God say to those who "turn their backs" on Him? What judgment do such people face? Read carefully these two verses. (14:7-8).
6. How do you interpret God's dealing with false prophets? (14:9-11).
7. What three O.T. people did Ezekiel mention? How effective would their prayers be for the rebellious people? (14:12-20).
8. What four judgments did God send upon the people in Jerusalem? (14:21).
9. Who would be left after judgment time? (14:22-23).

Ezekiel chapter 15

1. Ezekiel compares God's people to what? (15:1-2).
2. How fruitful and useful do you think God's people had been at the time of Ezekiel as well as in former times? What about us?
3. What happens to a useless vine? Why? (15:3-5).
4. Who supplanted the useless vine and has become the 'True Vine?" (John 15).
5. What happened to Jerusalem's people? (15:6-7; 2 Kings 25:9).
6. What did the people learn from the experience of judgment? (15:7).
7. What took place in Jerusalem in 586 B.C.? (15:8).
8. Study carefully John chapter 15. What do you think about the "true vine and the branches?" Who are the branches?

Ezekiel chapter 16

1. Do people always recognize their sinful ways? Why? Why not? (16:1-2).
2. What heritage did the Israelites of Jerusalem have? Did such a background give them room for boasting? What lessons can we learn from them? (16:3).
3. God's description of newborn babies should teach what kind of lesson? (16:4-5).
4. How does spiritual life take place? (16:6).
5. How did God bless His people? Read slowly through this section, and carefully list six or seven ways that God enhances the life of His people. (16:7-14).

6. How did Israel trifle with God and His blessings? Read and list the prodigal actions of the Hebrews who forgot God's goodness. What about us? (16:15-26).

7. What strong word of warning did God give the Israelites? (16:23).

8. Who did God say He let ravage His people? Does God punish rebellious people today? Why or why not? (16:27).

9. What nation with pagan gods did Israel emulate? Does a person find satisfaction with the gods of this world? Why or why not? (16:28-29).

10. The Israelites had a "weak heart?" Why? What happens to weak people? (16:30-31).

11. People who forsake God go to the depths of shame and disgrace. Why? (16:32-34).

12. God gave a warning to the Israelites about their failure to keep their covenant or promise with another nation and to God. What happens then? (16:35-42).

13. What do you think about God's judgment? (16:42-43).

14. Read carefully Ezekiel 16:44-59. Remember that Samaria was the capital of Israel or the ten Northern Tribes. Genesis 19 gives the story of Sodom. God gave a shocking message to Jerusalem about being more wicked than those two cities. Write a paragraph about their spiritual condition. (16:44-59).

15. Is God faithful to His unfaithful people? Explain. (16:60; 1 Timothy 2:13).

16. What is God's "everlasting covenant?" (16:60; Hebrews 8:8-12).

17. When God's people remember their failures, how do they feel? (16:61).

18. What lessons should God's sinful people learn? (16:61-63).

19. What does God provide for His people? (61:63).

Ezekiel chapter 17

1. God spoke a riddle or parable to Israel. The story compares two eagles with what two nations? (17: 12, 15).

2. Explain the symbolism of Babylon being like an eagle. (17:3, 12).

3. Who were the "young twigs" that the first eagle broke off from the tops of the trees? Where did he carry those "young twigs?" (17:4, 12).
4. Babylon's King Nebuchadnezzar made Zedekiah King in Jerusalem in 597 B.C. What kind of place was Palestine during Zedekiah's reign or rule? (17:5).
5. Describe the land and king at that particular moment. (17:6, 13-14).
6. Who did the second eagle represent in this parable? Describe the relationship between the second eagle and Jerusalem. (17:7).
7. What did Zedekiah do about the covenant he made with Babylon? (17:7, 15).
8. What happened to Jerusalem or Judah as she broke the covenant (agreement or promise) that she made with Babylon? (17:8-10, 15).
9. What happened to King Zedekiah? (17:16).
10. Would Egypt help Judah when Babylon's forces came? Why not? (17:17-18).
11. What happened to Zedekiah and his people? (17:19-21).
12. Ezekiel 17:22-24 is a "messianic prophecy." Read Isaiah 53:2; Matthew 1:1; and Luke 1:52 as a commentary on these verses.

Ezekiel chapter 18
1. What proverb did the exiles in Babylon use? What do those words mean? Why and how do we sometimes refuse to accept responsibility for our failures? (18:1-3).
2. Who owns everyone and everything? Is each person responsible for his or her own life? (18:4).
3. List three or four activities of a just or righteous person. (18:5-9).
4. What happens to the son of a righteous man if that child (son or daughter) lives an evil life? (18:10-13).
5. If the son of an evil father does not live as his father lives, but lives righteously, what happens to him? (18:14-18).
6. Is a son responsible for his father's life, or the father for the son? What about responsibility in marriage? Who must give account to God? (18:19-20).

7. If a wicked person repents, what happens to him or her? How does God feel about the one who changes from evil ways to God's ways? (18:21-23).

8. If a just or righteous person turns from an upright way and becomes evil, what happens to him? Does this one forfeit eternal life? (18:24).

9. Read carefully the scenario of chapter 18:25-30. Is God fair? Why or why not?

10. What command does the Lord give His people? What two gifts does a repentant person receive? (18:31).

11. What attitude does God have toward sinful people? What is God's desire for everyone? What command does God give to everyone? (18:32).

Ezekiel chapter 19

1. God judged king Jehoahaz who had done evil. His "lioness" mother (Israel) nourished him, but God punished him in what way? (19:1-4; 2 Kings 23:33).

2. The second "young lion" was King Zedekiah. Nebuchadnezzar took him to Babylon in 586 because of his rebellion. What lessons can we learn from these two kings? (19:5-9; 2 Chronicles 36:6).

3. What happened to the nation of Judah? Interpret the parable. (19:10-14).

Ezekiel chapter 20

1. Why do you think the elders or older leaders of Israel visited Ezekiel? (20:1).

2. Why was God not pleased with the leaders? (20:2-4).

3. When God gave His command for His people to remain loyal to Him, what did they do? How do people disobey God today? (20:5-8).

4. God saved the Israelites from what slavery? How do people become enslaved in wrong habits today? (20:9-10).

5. What did the "sons of Israel" do during their 40 years in the wilderness after God brought them out of Egypt? (20:11-14).

6. What penalty did God's people face because of their disobedience? Is unfaithfulness to God costly? How? (20:15-16).
7. Did God destroy all His people in the wilderness? What did He tell them to do? (20:17-20).
8. What happened to the people who rebelled? What did they learn? (20:21-26).
9. Why did God refuse to hear the prayers of His people? (20:27-32).
10. What did God say He would do with the exiles when He brought them back from Babylon? (20:33-38).
11. What happens to God's holy name when His people serve idols and do not do what God says? (20:39).
12. In what way did Israel please God when He brought them back from Babylonian captivity? (20:40-41).
13. What did the exiles learn and how did they feel about themselves when God brought them back from captivity? (20:42-44).
14. What kind of judgment did God bring against His people? Do you think God is harsh and unfair in His judgments? Why or why not? (20:45-49).

Ezekiel chapter 21
1. Who in reality had control of the army that destroyed Jerusalem in 586 B.C.? Do we struggle in allowing God to control us? (21:1-5).
2. What response did the people make as the army of Nebuchadnezzar invaded Jerusalem? (21:6-7).
3. Describe the "sword scene" that was to come upon Jerusalem. (21:8-16).
4. When God judged Jerusalem, how did He do it? (21:17).
5. What do you think of God's actions at that time? (21:17).
6. What two ways to go did the king of Babylon see? (21:18-20).
7. Name three symbols that helped Nebuchadnezzar decide his route. (21:21).
8. What would the Babylonian soldiers do in Jerusalem? (21:22).
9. What did Israel's iniquities and transgressions bring about? (21:23-24).
10. What happened to King Zedekiah and his crown? (21:25-27).

11. Who would be given the "king's crown?" (21:27).
12. The Ammonites on the east side of the Jordan River took what kind of action when Jerusalem fell to Babylon? (21:28-32).

Ezekiel chapter 22

1. What was the source of Ezekiel's messages? (22:1).
2. Jerusalem received the title of the "bloody city." Why? (22:2-3).
3. How did pagan nations view Jerusalem? (22:4-5).
4. Name some of Jerusalem's sins. What sins do Christians commit today? (22:6-12).
5. What particular sin did the Israelites commit against God? (22:12).
6. What did God think of the lifestyle of His people? What is God's attitude about His people who do wrong today? (22:13-14).
7. What did God say He would do with the Israelites? Did He? (22:15-16).
8. God compared Israel to what metals or substances? (22:17-18).
9. What happened to God's people as He placed them in a "furnace?" (22:19-22).
10. Ezekiel wrote about the evil deeds of false prophets, princes, and lay people. What did they do? (22:23-29).
11. What did God look for? Is God still searching for people to "stand in the gap?" What does this mean? Do you know anyone who will stand in the family, church, business, work, national, and international "gap?" Is there such a need now? Why? (22:30).
12. What did God do to His sinful people? (22:31).

Ezekiel chapter 23

1. Two daughters of one mother committed adultery with what nation? (23:1-3).
2. What were the names of the daughters? They were symbolic names of what two cities? (23:4).
3. Aholah was the symbolic name of Samaria, the capital of the ten Northern Tribes. What symbolic name did Jerusalem receive? (23:4).

4. Aholah "played the harlot" with Assyria. In what way or how did Aholah (Samaria) become guilty? (23:5-7).

5. How was Aholah punished for her sins? (23:8-10).

6. Did Aholibah (Jerusalem) learn a great lesson about living right from the older sister? How do we know? (23:11).

7. What reaction did Jerusalem (Aholibah) have when she saw the Assyrian horseman and other attractive personalities from that country? Is sin appealing? (23:12-16).

8. Did Jerusalem's (Aholibah) relationship with Babylon please God? (23:17-21).

9. How did God punish Jerusalem (Aholibah) for her sins? (23:22-24).

10. What happened to the offspring of Jerusalem? (23:25-26).

11. What changed attitude did Jerusalem finally have toward Egypt? (23:27).

12. Does an ungodly world love and care for God's people who adopt the wicked ways of the world? (23:28-31).

13. How do sinful people react to godly people who emulate them? (23:32).

14. What are the consequences of those who "cast God behind their backs?" (23:33-35).

15. Do those who forsake God hurt themselves and others? (23:36).

16. What other damage is the "fall out" from those who forsake God? (23:37-39).

17. What did Israel do that attracted idolatrous people? (23:40-44).

18. What kind of judgment did God send to His people because of their spiritual lewdness? (23:45-49).

19. What lesson did God's people learn? Do you think we are "good learners?" (23:49).

Ezekiel chapter 24

1. What nation surrounded and conquered Jerusalem in 586 B.C.? (24:1-2).

2. What symbol showed coming destruction to God's people? Explain. (24:3-5).

3. The "boiling pot" had scum or pollution in it. The choice flock and bones referred to the corrupt princes and people. Why were they condemned? (24:6).

4. The symbol of taking flesh and bones out of the pot signified death. The words "let no lot fall upon it" meant that everyone was judged and would face death. What city was portrayed in this parable? (24:6-7).

5. Were the wicked people of Jerusalem going to have their sins covered? (24:8).

6. Describe the destruction that soon would come upon Jerusalem. (24:9-11).

7. What sins characterized God's people at that time? (24:12-13).

8. What is the attitude that God has toward people who refuse to repent? How do God's people show true repentance today? (24:14).

9. What personal loss did Ezekiel suffer? Did he love his wife? Why didn't he express grief? (24:15-18).

10. What lesson did the Israelites in exile (Babylon) learn from Ezekiel when news came about the destruction of Jerusalem? (24:19-26).

11. Seven years before the fall of Jerusalem, God limited Ezekiel's ministry to his house and a few public "pantomimes" or dramatic performances. What happened to this prophet when Babylon conquered their sacred city? (24:27).

12. What lesson did the Israelites learn? Do you think everyone has learned this lesson? Why or why not? (24:27).

Apr. 10

Ezekiel chapter 25

1. Who gave Ezekiel his messages? Ezekiel had prepared for the priesthood, had read the prophets before his time as well as Jeremiah during his lifetime, and stayed updated in his spiritual life. To receive a message from God also means that God touches the heart of those who have His Word in their hearts. Do you agree or disagree? Why? (25:1).

2. God told Ezekiel to prophesy against what nation? (25:2).

3. Locate the country of Ammon on a Bible map. Also identify the location of the seven nations that surrounded Israel. Most of those

were small countries. What was the origin of the Ammonites? (Genesis 19:33-38).

4. What did God tell Ezekiel to say about Ammon? (25:3).
5. God said the "men of the east" (Babylon) would conquer Ammon. What was the capital of Ammon across the Jordan River from Israel? (25:4-5).
6. What kind of punishment did Ammon suffer? (25: 6-7).
7. Review briefly the background story of Moab. (25:8; Genesis 19:33-38).
8. What nation did God use to punish Moab? (25: 9-11).
9. The Edomites descended from Esau. Who was this man? (Genesis 25).
10. What kind of punishment did God bring upon Edom? (25:12-14).
11. What kind of attitude did the Philistines have? (25:15).
12. The small nation of Philistia was located on the Mediterranean Sea coast. What punishment did this nation suffer? (25:16-17).

Ezekiel chapter 26
1. God told Ezekiel to speak against Tyre, a small country north of Philistia. What judgment did Tyre face? (26:1-6).
2. Describe the attack of King Nebuchadnezzar upon Tyre. (26:7-14).
3. How did other nations react to Tyre's destruction? (26:15-18).
4. What did God say He would do to Tyre? (26:19-21).

Ezekiel chapter 27
1. The people of Tyre became notable in what profession? (27:1-3).
2. What seemed to be Tyre's principal characteristic? What about people today? (27:4).
3. What countries furnished material and labor for Tyre? (27:5-25).
4. What response did the visiting workers have when Tyre's fell? (27:25-36).

Ezekiel chapter 28
1. Why did God tell Ezekiel to speak against the prince of Tyre? (28:1-2).

2. The prince of Tyre gained more knowledge than what prophet? (28:3).
3. What advantages came to the prince of Tyre because of his knowledge? What was his fallacy? (28:4-6).
4. What judgment did God bring against Tyre? (28:6-10).
5. What happened to the prince of Tyre? (28:11-19).
6. Sidon, a small nation north of Tyre, also came under God's judgment. What did Sidon learn from this judgment? (28:20-22).
7. What kind of judgment did Sidon face? (28:23).
8. How had the nations around Israel treated God's people? (28:24).
9. What promise did God make to Judah or Israel? (28:25).
10. What would eventually happen to God's people? (28:26).

Ezekiel chapter 29

1. Emphasis is given again to the source of Ezekiel's diatribe against Egypt. Where did the prophet get his messages? (29:1-2).
2. What boast did Pharaoh make? (29:3).
3. Explain the symbols of hooks, jaws, fish, scales, beasts, and fields that relate to the crocodile of Egypt. (29:4-5).
4. What help did Egypt give Judah when her king rebelled against Babylon? Does the "world" help Christians who turn away from God? (29:6-7).
5. Give a synopsis of God's judgment upon Egypt. (29:8-12).
6. How did God also promise to bless Egypt? (29:13-14).
7. What kind of future did Egypt have? (29:15-16).
8. What reward did Nebuchadnezzar get for conquering Tyre? (29:17-20).
9. What is the meaning of the prophesy in Ezekiel 29:21?

Ezekiel chapter 30

1. What was "the day of the Lord" like for Egypt? (30:1-3).
2. Name a few allies that suffered when judgment came to Egypt. (30:4-5).
3. How severe was "the day of the Lord" for those nations? (30:6-12).

4. What did God say would happen to the idols of Egypt? What do you think will happen to our "idols?" (30:13).
5. What other judgments are listed for Egypt? (30:14-19).
6. What "knockout blow" did God promise to Egypt's Pharaoh? (30:20-23).
7. What nation did God use to defeat Egypt? Describe the scene. (30:24-26).

Ezekiel chapter 31
1. What sin brought havoc to Egypt? How is this sin expressed in nations and individuals today? (31:1-2).
2. Describe the scenario of Egypt being compared to a great cedar tree. (31:3-10).
3. Describe Ezekiel's story on Egypt's demise. (31:10-17).
4. What future did Egypt and her Pharaoh have? (31:18).

Ezekiel chapter 32
1. What two creatures became a symbol of Egypt? Which became the principal symbol? In what ways did Pharaoh "muddy the water" of the Nile River? (32:1-2).
2. What did God do to Pharaoh? (32:3-8).
3. What kind of involvement did other nations have with Egypt? (32:9-10).
4. Describe the result of Babylon's attack upon Egypt. (32:11-16).
5. Describe the fall of Egypt. What other countries suffered a similar fate? (32:17-31).
6. Who brought about the destruction of the proud, evil nations? What is the final result of those who oppose God and go their own way? (32:32).

Ezekiel chapter 33
1. Chapter 33 is about a person who serves as a watchman for a city. Explain those duties. (33:1-6).
2. What did God call Ezekiel to do? Do you think he performed his duties well? Why or why not? What about today's "watchmen?" (33:7-9).
3. What is God's desire for His people? (33:10-11).

4. How should we interpret the Scripture in Ezekiel 33:12-14?
5. What is an indication of a person's repentance? (33:15-16).
6. Do you think God is fair in His judgments? Why or why not. (33:17-20).
7. Ezekiel was taken into Babylonian captivity in 597 B.C. Eleven years later Nebuchadnezzar destroyed Jerusalem. Ezekiel received the message about one year after Jerusalem was destroyed. What year was that? (33:21).
8. What happened to Ezekiel when he received news about Jerusalem? (33:22).
9. The people who lived in Jerusalem at the time the city fell did not inherit the land as they thought they would. Explain why not. 33:23-26).
10. What was going to happen to those who lived in Jerusalem? (33:27-29).
11. What did the people say about Ezekiel after hearing him? (33:30-32).
12. Regardless of the reaction of the people, what did they learn? (33:33).

Ezekiel chapter 34
1. God told Ezekiel to prophesy against what group? (34:1-2).
2. How did the greedy shepherds treat God's people? (34:3-5).
3. What happened to God's people who had greedy shepherds? (34:6).
4. What kind of reaction did God have towards selfish shepherds? (34:7-10).
5. What did God say He would do for His "sheep," or people (34:11).
6. Make a list of the ways God takes care of His people. (34:12-16).
7. What action did God say He would take with the good and mean sheep? (34:17-19).
8. How did the unruly sheep treat the good sheep? (34:20-22).
9. What did God say He would do with the selfish shepherds? (34:23-24).

10. What kind of an agreement or new covenant did God give His people? Explain the new covenant. What results would the new covenant produce? (34:25).

11. What spiritual blessings did God promise His people? What church hymn is based on Ezekiel 34:26?

12. What kinds of physical blessings are listed in God's new covenant? (34:27-28).

13. What is the meaning of the words, "A plant of renown?" (34:29; Isaiah 53:2).

14. Who is included in God's "flock?" (34:30-31). Read carefully and discuss: Matthew 3:9; Luke 1:55, 3:8; John 8:39; Acts 13:39; Romans 4:16; Galatians 3:7.

July 10

Ezekiel chapter 35

1. Mount Seir was south of the Dead Sea, the land of the Edomites. From whom did they descend? How did the Edomites relate to the Israelites? Discuss long-term envy and hatred. (35:1-3; Genesis 36:8; Numbers 20:14-22).

2. What happened to the descendants of Esau? Why? (35:3-5).

3. What happened to the valleys, mountains, and rivers of Edom? (35: 6-9).

4. The Edomites said they would possess Israel and Judah (Samaria and Judah). Why did they make such a boast? Did they achieve their dreams? (35:10-11).

5. What response did God make to the boasting of the Edomites? (35:12).

6. Does God know about the boasting of those who oppose Him? Idumea is another name for Edom or Mount Seir. (35:13. Mark 3:8).

7. What lessons should people learn when they turn from God? (35:14-15).

Ezekiel chapter 36

1. What is the meaning of the words, "the mountains of Israel?" Who did those people need to hear? Whose voice do we need to hear today? Are we hearing Him? (36:1).

2. What had heathen nations done against God's people? What does the world think about Christians today? (36:2-4).
3. Why did God become angry at heathen nations around Israel? (36:5).
4. How had the Hebrews suffered in the time of Ezekiel? What about today? (36:6).
5. What attitude and actions did the heathen have toward God? (36:7).
6. How did God say He would bless His people? How does God help His people today? (36:8-11).
7. What does God do to the enemies of His people? (36:12-15).
8. When Israel dwelt in their own land, how did they live? (36:16-20).
9. What did God say He would do for His holy name that had been profaned by His people? (36:21-23).
10. What did God promise to do for Israel? (36:24).
11. What kind of spiritual work did God say He would do for His people? Is He doing this kind of work in us today? (36:25-27).
12. What material as well as spiritual blessings did God promise His people? Does God always pour out blessings upon His people? Discuss. (36:28-30).
13. How did the Hebrews feel about their old "lifestyle?" Explain. (36:31).
14. Why did God bless His people? (36:32).
15. What was the outcome of the cleansing that God gave His people? (36:33-35).
16. What did pagan nations learn as God restored the Israelites? (36:36).
17. As a result of cleansing, would God's people learn to pray? What about us? (36:37).
18. When God blessed His people, what lesson did they learn? (36:38).

Ezekiel chapter 37
1. What spiritual experience did Ezekiel have? (37:1).
2. Describe the vision which Ezekiel saw "in the valley." (37:1-2).

3. What response to God's question did Ezekiel make? Do you think the prophet gave a good answer? How do you think you might have answered God? (37:3).

4. What did God tell Ezekiel to do? Elaborate. (37:4).

5. Who can give breath to bones and cause them to live? (37:5).

6. What did God do in addition to giving breath to the bones? (37:6).

7. What miracle took place in the valley of dry bones? (37:7-10).

8. How did God identify the valley of bones? Does this definitive word about "Israel" include all twelve tribes? Why or why not? What did God say? (37:11).

9. In what ways did the exiles in Babylon and elsewhere think of themselves? (37:11).

10. Did God's message of Ezekiel have meaning to God's people at that time? Describe what God said He would do for Israel. Do you think the words apply to a future work of God? (37:12-14; Romans 11:23-27).

11. What two nations did the two sticks that Ezekiel wrote upon represent? What happened to those sticks in Ezekiel's hands? (37:15-17).

12. What emphasis did God give about the symbols of the sticks? (3718-19).

13. Did God promise to take His people back to the mountains of Israel and unite them? Do you think this story has implications for God's people today? Why? (37:20-21).

14. Who has the authority to rule over God's people? (37:22).

15. What should be the lifestyle of God's people? Do you think these words are restricted to the ancient Israelites? Elaborate. (37:23).

16. What did God promise His people? Is cleansing taking place today? (37:23).

17. Do you think God referred to David or the Messiah in this passage? Why? (37:23).

18. Give an exhaustive interpretation of the last section of this chapter that relates to the land, David, the covenant of peace, and God's sanctuary. (37:25-28).

Ezekiel chapter 38

1. What's your interpretation of "Gog?" (38:1-2).
2. What is the meaning of Magog, Meschech, and Tubal? (38:2-3).
3. What did God say He would do with Gog and his allies? (38:4).
4. What nations are listed as Gog's coalition forces? (38:5-7).
5. What is the timeline of the prophecy about Gog and his troops? Did they come against God's people in Ezekiel's day? What about Gog's future? (38:8).
6. What plans did Gog formulate? Was that a one-time-only attack of God's people? Why or why not? (38:9-13).
7. What major surprise will happen in "the latter days" as evil forces attack God's people? (38:14-16; Revelation 20:7-10).
8. Before the time of Ezekiel who told something about Gog and his plans? (38:17).
9. Against whom did the Lord say Gog would come? What was God's response to the evil deeds of Gog? (38:18-19).
10. Is your interpretation of the fish, fowls, man, beast, and mountains that Ezekiel mentioned literal or symbolical? Why or why not? (38:20).
11. How will God's enemies suffer defeat? (38:21).
12. What action does God take against His enemies? (38:22).
13. What does God do for Himself in the midst of battles? Why? (38:23).
14. What lesson should people learn from God's dealing with everyone? (38:23).

Ezekiel chapter 39

1. What is the title given to Gog? (39:1).
2. Describe the battle scene between God and Gog. (39:2-6).
3. What does God say He will do about His holy name? (39:7).
4. What will God's people do with the weapons of their enemies? How do you interpret the disposal of those weapons that take months to burn or bury? (39:8-10).
5. What will eventually happen to Gog and his forces? (39:11; Revelation 20:7-10).
6. What is your interpretation of the "burial" of Gog? (39:12-15).

7. What is the name of the valley where Gog's evil forces will be buried? (39:16).

8. Describe the banquet for birds and beasts that Ezekiel wrote about in this chapter. Do you think this is literal or symbolical language? Why? (39:17-22).

9. What did the heathen learn about God's punishment of His people? (39:23-24).

10. What attitude did God say He would have toward those who repent? (39:25-27).

11. What spiritual blessings did (does) God give His people? (39:28-29; Joel 2:28-29).

Ezekiel Chapters 40-48

1. Ezekiel's vision of the temple came fourteen years after Jerusalem fell in 586 B.C. What year did the "visions of God" occur? (40:1).

2. Do you think that God carried Ezekiel to "the land of Israel" physically or symbolically? Why? (40:2).

3. Describe the heavenly visitor. What was the "man" doing? (40:3-5).

4. In the vision, Ezekiel observed the angelic being making detailed measurements. Do you regard those actions as symbolical or literal? Do the measurements show God's concern for the details of life? (40:6-26).

5. Does God want our attention to focus on buildings or upon Himself? Does the Bible identify Ezekiel's "visionary temple" with any historical moment? (41:1).

6. Do you think the description of the details of the temple measurements add to your spiritual life? Why or why not? (41:2-26).

7. The measurements and descriptive details of the temple continue in chapter 42. How many verses are in this chapter? Have you read the entire chapter? (Refer to major point 3 in the message about God's temple to help understand this part of the vision).

8. Who carried Ezekiel in vision to the eastern gate? (43:1).

9. Describe the vision of God's returning glory. (43:2).

10. How did Ezekiel respond to the vision? (43:3).

11. What do you think of Ezekiel's experience that he related? (43:4-6).

12. What promises did God give to the exiles? Are these promises limited to the ancient and future nation of Israel or to all the redeemed? (43:7-9).

13. What law did God give Ezekiel that His people are to observe? (43:10-12).

14. The temple measurements transcend the geographical limits of Jerusalem. Do you think the vision referred to an ideal temple or one that will be constructed in the future? Why or why not? Notice that no instructions are given to build that temple.

15. Do you discover any proof that Ezekiel's "visionary temple" was physical? (44:1-3).

16. What do you think of Ezekiel's continuing vision? (44:4).

17. Chapter 44 gives emphasis to God's holiness. Do you think we give enough emphasis to holiness today? Why or why not? (44:5-27).

18. What does God become for His people? How does this truth apply today? (44:28).

19. What instructions did God give for His people? (44:29-31).

20. What do you think about the emphasis on offerings, feasts, sacrifices, and other Old Testament rituals? Did those ceremonies hold meaning for the Babylonian exiles in Ezekiel's time? Has the death of Jesus fulfilled those "beggarly elements"? (45:1-46:24; John 19:30; Galatians 4:9; Hebrews 10:8-18).

21. Describe the river that Ezekiel saw flowing from the throne of God. (47:1-5).

22. What did Ezekiel's vision include that John described? (47:6-7; Revelation 21; 22).

23. What results come from the flow of God's river? What did Jesus say about a spiritual "river?" (47:8-12; John 7:37-39).

24. Does Ezekiel's vision change from the symbolical to the literal? Why or why not? Which is easier to understand? (47:13-48:34).

25. What is the name of God's city? What grand truth does this city teach? (48:35).

Limited Bibliograhy

—ɯ—

Alexander, Ralph, Everyman's Bible Commentary: Ezekiel, Moody Press, Chicago, 1976

Baxter, J. Sidlow, Explore the Book, Zondervan House, Grand Rapids, Mi. 1960.

Blackwood, Andrew W. Jr. Ezekiel's Prophecy of Hope. Baker Book House, Grand Rapids, Mi. 1965.

Block, Daniel, The Book of Ezekiel, (vs. 1 & 2). Eerdmans , Grand Rapids, Mi. 1998

Cooper, Lamar E, Sr. The New American Commentary: Ezekiel (v. 17). B&H Publishers, Nashville, Tn. 1994

Chapman, Colin, Whose Promised Land? Baker Books, Grand Rapids, Mi. 2002

Craige, Peter C. Ezekiel. The Westminster Press, Philadelphia, Pa. 1983.

Glaze, A.J. Jeremiah and Ezekiel. Baptist Spanish Publishers (Carib), El Paso, Tx. 1989.

Greenberg, Moshe. The Anchor Bible: Ezekiel. Doubleday & Company, Garden City, New York, 1983.

Halley, H. H. Halley's Bible Handbook. Zondervan Publishing Company, Grand Rapids, Mi. 1965

Huey, F.B., Jr. Layman's Bible Book Commentary (Ezekiel). V. 12. Broadman Press, Nashville, Tn. 1983.

Orr, James, General Editor. The International Standard Bible Encylopedia, Eerdmans Publishing Company. Grand Rapids, Mi. 1980

Spence, H.D.M. Exell, Plumptree, etc. The Pulpit Commentary (Ezekiel). Eerdmans Publishing Company, Grand Rapids, Mi. 1950.

Tate, Marvin E. From Promise To Exile. Smyth & Helwys. Macon, Georgia. 1999,

Taylor, John B. Ezekiel: InterVarsity Press, Downers Grove, Il. 1969.

Vawter & Hoppe, Ezekiel. Handsel Press, Edinburg, 1991. Eerdmans, 1994.

Wright, N.T. Jesus and the Victory of God. Fortress Press, Minneapolis, Mn. 1996.

About Preston A. Taylor

—ᨁ—

He grew up on a farm in Arkansas. Graduate of Ouachita Baptist University (literature and history). Southwestern Baptist Seminary (B.D., Th.M, M.Div.); Luther Rice Seminary (D.Min.). Additional studies at Baylor University, N.C. Baptist Hospital, and Moody Bible Institute. Naval Radio school, San Diego. Language school in Costa Rica. Nine years service with the Southern Baptist Convention's IMB in Argentina.

Books by Preston A. Taylor

The 13 Apostles (226 pp, 14 chs.) and *Jesus: King of Kings* (Revelation, 296 pp. 36 chs.) Tate Publishing (888-361-9473). *Abe's Books* give 30% discount via computer orders. Barnes and Noble, Amazon.com, Borders, Target, Religious bookstores.

102 Fascinating Bible Topics for Group Discussions. Xulon Press (866-381-2665). Topics like angels, evangelism, fasting, poverty, temptations, work, etc. *Abe's Books* gives almost 30% discount. Also order through Barnes & Noble, Amazon.com, etc.

Ezekiel: God's Prophet and His Puzzling Book ("Dry Bones Will Live Again). About 300 pages. 24 easy-to-read chapters. Xulon Press (866-381-2665). *Abe's Books* give almost 30% discount through computer orders. Barnes and Noble, Amazon.com, etc.

Ecclesiastes: Life Beneath the Blazing Sun (Solomon's Magnum Opus). 12 down-to-earth chapters. Nearly 200 pp. 866-361-2665.). *Abe's Books* give almost 30% discount through computer orders. Barnes and Noble, Amazon.com, etc.

Philippians: Joy in Jesus. Moody Press. 20 chapters. Out of print.

In Spanish

Exodo y Los 11 Mandamientos, 250 pp. Kregel's Portavoz@ portavoz.com
Unit Spanish House of Miami published four of this writer's books.

Spanish World Publishers has published eight books by Taylor. 800-755-5958; P.O. Box 4255, El Paso, Texas 79914. Epena@ CasaBautista.org

More comments on this book on Ezekiel:

—∿—

"Preston Taylor's work on Ezekiel is as fresh as the morning dew, as honest as a country preacher, as energetic as a new born Christian with an adventuresome missionary heart."
— Pastor Mike Barrera, United Baptist Church, Laredo, Texas

"With his incomparable clear and pleasant style, Preston Taylor leads us back to the depths of the Scriptures. This time he gives us this "tool" that every pastor should have and every Christian should look for. From now on, it will be much easier for any of us to teach and preach from the book of Ezekiel. Check it out!"
— Israel Rodriguez, pastor, Primera Iglesia Bautista, Piedras Negras, Coahuila, Mexico

"For me it was a pleasant surprise to discover such an easy-to-read and enjoyable book about Ezekiel. This OT prophet who had dramatic visions and surprising behavior has become a personal friend. He just steps right out of the book."
—Sarah Kinard, Sunday School teacher, First Baptist Church, El Dorado, Arkansas

"Ezekiel is an exciting book that you'll love! I gladly recommend it to my fellow pastors and members of churches everywhere who want to know the inside story on Ezekiel."
— Gary Lange, Pastor, Prince of Peace Lutheran Church, New Braunfels, Texas

"Preston has studied, prayed, researched, and creatively written on <u>Ezekiel.</u> He gives life and meaning to the prophet and his book for today's readers."

— Jesse Kidd, Brazil Missionary, retired. San Angelo, Texas

"Ezekiel's book came from Babylon (Iraq). In this book you'll see prophecy, visions of God's glory, and much more! This is a book for everyone. The questions on each chapter will keep you in God's book!"

— Dr. A. J. Glaze, retired rector del Seminario Bautista Internacional, Buenos Aires, Argentina, retired Professor of Missions, New Orleans Baptist Seminary, etc.

CPSIA information can be obtained
at www.ICGtesting.com
Printed in the USA
FFOW01n1304071014
7853FF